heritage
songster

320 FOLK AND FAMILIAR SONGS

heritage songster

WORDS • MUSIC • LEGENDS • CHORD SYMBOLS

GUITAR • UKULELE • BANJO • AUTOHARP • PIANO

LEON & LYNN
DALLIN

WM. C. BROWN COMPANY PUBLISHERS
Dubuque, Iowa

Music Series

Consulting Editor
Frederick W. Westphal, Ph.D.
Sacramento State College

Copyright © 1966 by
Wm. C. Brown Company Publishers

Library of Congress Catalog Card Number: 66-20669

ISBN 0–697–03452–6

Twelfth Printing, 1974.

Printed in the United States of America

For Judy

Acknowledgments

Sincere appreciation is expressed to the publishers, composers, authors, and collectors who have granted permission for the use of copyrighted materials. Copyright credits are given below individual songs. If any have been omitted, it is only because the song has become such an established part of our musical heritage that tracing it to its source was impossible. For these songs we are indebted to all who have sung and preserved them. Special thanks are due Frederick W. Westphal, Music Editor of Wm. C. Brown Company, and Lewis Roth, Editor-in-Chief of MCA MUSIC division of MCA, INC., for sympathetic editing and valuable suggestions.

Preface

These are the songs Americans sing. You will find your favorites in this book whatever your geographic or ethnic background. You will also find songs which are favorites in other parts of the country and with other groups.

The songs included in this collection were selected on the basis of a systematic analysis of approximately 15,000 songs contained in school music series, learned by children, remembered by adults, and sung by Americans of all ages. These 320 songs are the most widely known of the thousands in our vast and immensely varied musical heritage.

A common body of song literature known by all citizens is the cornerstone of a nation's music. These are the songs which, by widespread and enduring acceptance, have become a vital part of our culture. The *Heritage Songster* is dedicated to the preservation of these songs and to the people who sing them — the young and the young in heart.

Contents

heritage songster

Shenandoah
(ACROSS THE WIDE MISSOURI)

CHANTEY

Expressively

1. Oh, Shen-an-doah, I long to hear you, Way,— hey, you roll-ing riv-er! Oh, Shen-an-doah, I long to hear you, Way, hey, we're bound a-way, 'Cross the wide Mis-sour-i.

2. Oh, Shenandoah, I love your daughter,
Way, hey, you rolling river,
Oh, Shenandoah, I love your daughter,
Way, hey, we're bound away,
'Cross the wide Missouri.

3. Oh, Shenandoah, I love her truly,
Way, hey, you rolling river,
Oh, Shenandoah, I love her truly,
Way, hey, we're bound away,
'Cross the wide Missouri.

4. I long to see your fertile valley,
Way, hey, you rolling river,
I long to see your fertile valley,
Way, hey, we're bound away,
'Cross the wide Missouri.

5. Oh, Shenandoah, I'm bound to leave you,
Way, hey, you rolling river,
Oh, Shenandoah, I'm bound to leave you,
Way, hey, we're bound away,
'Cross the wide Missouri.

This capstan chantey is of American origin. Its subject is said to be the Valley of the Shenandoah (between the Blue Ridge and Allegheny mountains) and the great Indian chief after whom both the valley and river were named. American cavalrymen sang it, and it became a rowing song sung on Midwestern rivers. *Shenandoah* is typical of song stories of the period which told of actual happenings with color and accuracy.

1

Get Along Little Dogies

(WHOOPEE TI-YI-YO) (DOGIE SONG)

COWBOY

Persuasively

1. As I was a-walk-ing one morn-ing for pleas-ure, I spied a cow-punch-er a-rid-ing a-long. His hat was thrown back and his spurs were a-jin-gling, And as he ap-proached he was sing-ing this song:

Chorus

Whoo-pee ti-yi-yo,—— get a-long lit-tle do-gies, It's your mis-for-tune and none of my own. Whoo-pee ti-yi-yo,—— get a-long lit-tle do-gies, You know that Wy-o-ming will be your new home.

2. It's early in spring when we round up the dogies,
   And mark them and brand them and bob off their tails,
   We round up our horses and load the chuck wagon,
   And then herd the dogies right out on the trail.

Get Along Little Dogies

3. It's whooping and yelling and driving the dogies,
   Oh, how I wish you would only go on;
   It's whooping and punching, go on, little dogies,
   You know that Wyoming will be your new home.

4. Some cowboys go out on the trail just for pleasure,
   But that's where they do it most awfully wrong,
   For words couldn't tell all the trouble they give us,
   It takes all the time just to drive them along.

Cowboys sang this song on the long trail drives to pass the time and reassure the cattle between the plains and livestock loading points. Dogies (pronounced with a long "o") are yearlings, often deserted by their mothers. They are restless at night, and cause trouble with the herds. Cowboys sang endless verses to their songs. This not only soothed the dogies, but was a way of communicating their positions to the other riders on watch. *Get Along, Little Dogies* was included by the distinguished American composer, Aaron Copland, in his ballet suite *Billie The Kid* (1938).

Aura Lee

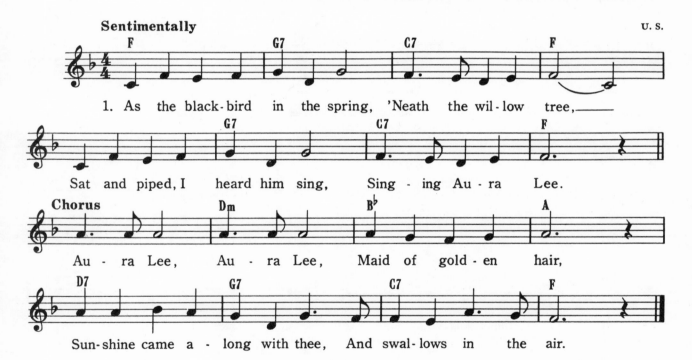

Sentimentally   U. S.

1. As the black-bird in the spring, 'Neath the wil-low tree,____

Sat and piped, I heard him sing, Sing - ing Au - ra Lee.

Chorus

Au - ra Lee, Au - ra Lee, Maid of gold - en hair,

Sun-shine came a - long with thee, And swal-lows in the air.

2. In her blush the rose was born,
   Music when she spoke,
   In her eyes the glow of morn
   Into splendor broke.

This old serenade has found favor on college campuses, and is widely used by barbershop quartet singers. Barbershop quartets are characterized by the close harmony of the male voices, especially in sentimental songs such as *Aura Lee*. There is a national organization, "The Society for the Preservation and Encouragement of Barber Shop Quartet Singing in America" (SPEBSQSA), which promotes such quartets throughout the country.

Wait for the Wagon

R. B. BUCKLEY

R. B. BUCKLEY

Buoyantly

1. Will you come with me, my Phyl - lis, to
It's ___ eve - ry Sun - day morn - ing when

yon blue moun - tain free? Where blos - soms smell the
I am by your side, We'll jump in - to the

sweet - est, come rove a - long with me.
wag - on, and all ___ take a ride.

Chorus

Wait for the wag - on, wait for the wag - on,

Wait for the wag - on, and we'll all take a ride.

2. Where the river runs like silver, and birds they sing so sweet,
   I have a cabin, Phyllis, and something good to eat.
   Come, listen to my story, it will relieve my heart,
   Now, jump into the wagon, and off we will start.

This song originally was credited to George Knauff in 1851 when it was published. Later, both the words and music were attributed to R. Bishop Buckley of the Buckley Serenaders, a popular mid-century minstrel group. The song was a great favorite of both Union and Confederate troops. Many parodies have been written to the melody of *Wait For the Wagon*.

Wayfaring Stranger

U. S.

Patiently

1. I'm just a poor way-far-ing strang-er, A trav-'ling

through this world of woe; But there's no sick-ness, toil nor

dan-ger in that bright world to which I

go. I'm go-ing there to see my fa-ther,* I'm go-ing

there no more to roam, I'm just a-go-ing o-ver

Jor-dan, I'm just a-go-ing o-ver home.

*2. mother   3. sister   4. brother

The United States was swept by a religious revival movement in the nineteenth century. Many great gospel hymns are the product of this period. This religious folk ballad is among the most famous, and reflects the hardships and the religious attitude of the people. It was sung widely at camp and revival meetings, and appeared in hymn books of the period.

Paper of Pins

Teasingly

BRITISH ISLES

(Boys) 1. I'll give to you a pa-per of pins, And that's the way true
(Girls) I'll not ac-cèpt your pa-per of pins, If that's the way your

love be-gins, If you will mar-ry me, me, me, If you will mar-ry me.
love be-gins, And I'll not mar-ry you, you, you, And I'll not mar-ry you.

2. (*Boys*)   I'll give to you a satin gown with silken tassles all around,
   If you will marry me, me, me, if you will marry me.

   (*Girls*)   I'll not accept your satin gown with silken tassles all around,
   And I'll not marry you, you, you, and I'll not marry you.

3. (*Boys*)   I'll give to you a dress of red all sewn around with golden thread, etc.

   (*Girls*)   I'll not accept your dress of red all sewn around with golden thread, etc.

4. (*Boys*)   I'll give to you my big black horse that's paced the meadow all across, etc.

   (*Girls*)   I'll not accept your big black horse that's paced the meadow all across, etc.

5. (*Boys*)   I'll give to you my hand and heart that you and I may never part, etc.

   (*Girls*)   I'll not accept your hand and heart that you and I may never part, etc.

6. (*Boys*)   I'll give to you a house and land, a William goat, a hired hand, etc.

   (*Girls*)   I'll not accept your house and land, your William goat, your hired hand, etc.

7. (*Boys*)   I'll give to you the key to my chest with gold whenever you request, etc.

   (*Girls*)   O, I'll accept the key to your chest with gold whenever I request, etc.

8. (*Boys*)   O, now I see that money is king and your love didn't mean a thing,
   So I won't marry you, you, you, so I won't marry you.

   (*Girls*)   An old maid, then, I'll have to be, another I won't wed, you see,
   So won't you marry me, me, me, so won't you marry me?

The origin of this old song is not clear. Some authorities believe it is based on an old mummer's dance and that it came from Scotland. Others claim the melody is based on an old English folk song, *Keys of Heaven*. Some think it is a version of another old English courting dialogue song, *Keys of Canterbury*. In America it found great popularity both as a singing and dancing song, and the pins mentioned in the words have significance. Pin money is a sum of money, in olden times often provided for in the marriage settlement, to be given by the husband to the wife for her separate use. She could spend it as she pleased, for the purchase of apparel, personal adornments, or any private expenditure. The earliest natural pins were thorns. Pins were imported to England from France until 1626 when John Tilsby manufactured them in Gloucester.

Get on Board

SPIRITUAL

With strong rhythm

Get on board, lit - tle chil - dren, Get on board, lit - tle

chil - dren, Get on, board lit - tle chil - dren, There's room for man-y a more.

1. The gos - pel train's a - com - ing, I hear it just at hand, I

hear the car wheels rum - bling And roll - ing through the land.

2. I hear the train a-coming, a-coming round the curve,
She loosened all her steam and brakes, she's straining every nerve.
3. The fare is cheap and all can go, the rich and poor are there,
No second class aboard this train, no difference in the fare.

The train described in this spiritual is the "gospel train," and its destination is the "promised land." It was a favorite gospel hymn in early America. Such spirituals made up the basic repertoire of the Fisk University Jubilee Singers, and comparable groups from other Negro institutions such as Tuskegee and Hampton, who made fund-raising tours singing their own songs. Since the schools derived their support largely from religious groups and home missionary movements, the emphasis was upon the religious songs of the Negro. References to Negro music date back to the eighteenth century. Thomas Jefferson wrote of the musical talents of the Negro in his *Notes on Virginia* (1784). The Negro race possesses great enthusiasm and instinctive talent for music, and this fact long has been recognized. Their reputation for choral singing is excellent, and many Negro choral societies now exist.

Down in the Valley

KENTUCKY

Plaintively

1. Down in the val - ley the val - ley so low, Hang your head

o - ver, hear the winds blow. Hear the winds blow, dear, hear the winds

blow, Hang your head o - ver, hear the winds blow.

2. Roses love sunshine, violets love dew,
   Angels in heaven know I love you,
   Know I love you, dear, know I love you,
   Angels in heaven know I love you.

3. Write me a letter containing three lines,
   Answer my question, "Will you be mine,
   Will you be mine, love, will you be mine?"
   Answer my question, "Will you be mine?"

4. If you don't love me, love whom you please,
   But hold me close, love, give my heart ease,
   Give my heart ease, love, give my heart ease,
   While there is time, love, give my heart ease.

5. Build me a castle forty feet high
   So I can see him as he goes by,
   As he goes by, love, as he goes by,
   So I can see him as he goes by.

This Southern mountain courting song seems to have originated in the United States. It dates from the pioneer days when young men did their courting in one-room cabins in front of the entire family. Lacking privacy, they told of their love in song rather than in words. Composer Kurt Weill (1900-1950) wrote a successful folk opera based on this song and bearing the same title. *Down In The Valley* is known in the Southern mountains as a "lonesome tune." Carl Sandburg commented that it is "full of wishes — and dances a little — and hopes a beloved dancing partner will come back."

The Twelve Days of Christmas

ENGLAND

Festively

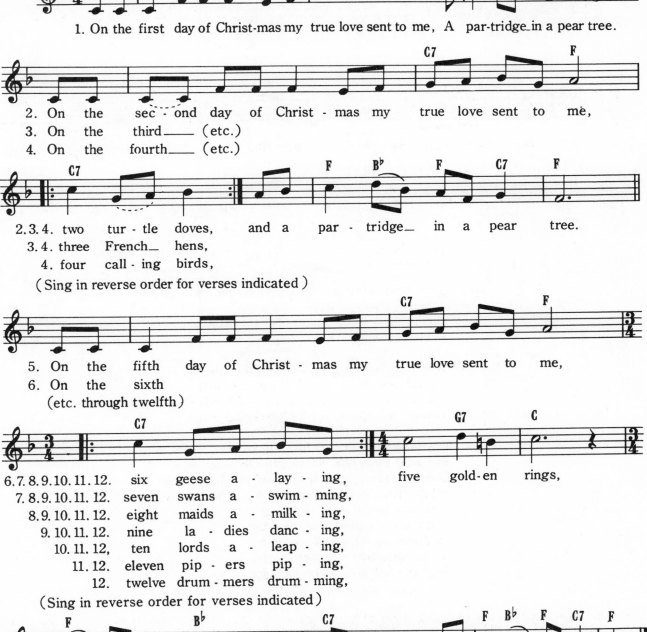

1. On the first day of Christ-mas my true love sent to me, A par-tridge in a pear tree.

2. On the sec-ond day of Christ-mas my true love sent to me,
3. On the third___ (etc.)
4. On the fourth___ (etc.)

2.3.4. two tur-tle doves, and a par-tridge___ in a pear tree.
3.4. three French___ hens,
4. four call-ing birds,

(Sing in reverse order for verses indicated)

5. On the fifth day of Christ-mas my true love sent to me,
6. On the sixth
(etc. through twelfth)

6.7.8.9.10.11.12. six geese a-lay-ing, five gold-en rings,
7.8.9.10.11.12. seven swans a-swim-ming,
8.9.10.11.12. eight maids a-milk-ing,
9.10.11.12. nine la-dies danc-ing,
10.11.12. ten lords a-leap-ing,
11.12. eleven pip-ers pip-ing,
12. twelve drum-mers drum-ming,

(Sing in reverse order for verses indicated)

four___ call-ing birds, three French hens, two___ tur-tle doves, and a par-tridge in a pear tree.

The Twelve Days of Christmas

The twelve days of Christmas are those between Christmas day and Epiphany, a Christian feast day which falls on January 6. The night of January 6, or the Twelfth Night, is the traditional end of the Christmas season, and the night the Three Kings visited the Christ Child and brought their gifts of gold, frankincense, and myrrh. The celebration of Epiphany also includes the playing of games of forfeit. At one time, the test of true love was judged by the number and variety of gifts, and how difficult each gift was to obtain.

Greensleeves
(WHAT CHILD IS THIS)

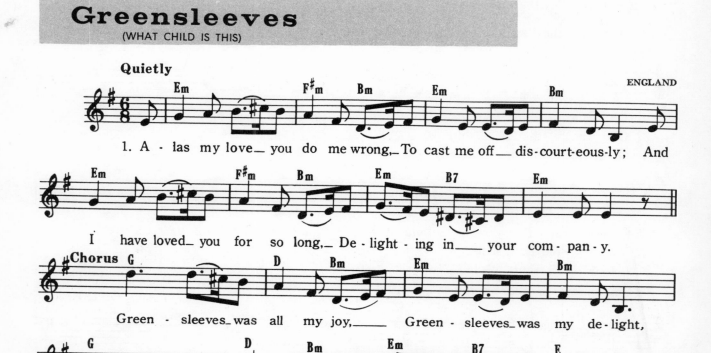

Quietly

ENGLAND

1. A - las my love__ you do me wrong,__To cast me off__ dis-court-eous-ly; And I have loved__ you for so long,__ De - light - ing in__ your com - pan - y.

Chorus

Green - sleeves__was all my joy,____ Green - sleeves__was my de - light,

Green - sleeves was my heart of gold,__ And who but my lad - y Green - sleeves.

2. I long have waited at your hand
   To do your bidding as your slave,
   And waged, have I, both life and land
   Your love and affection for to have.

3. If you intend thus to disdain
   It does the more enrapture me,
   And even so, I will remain
   Your lover in captivity.

4. Alas, my love, that yours should be
   A heart of faithless vanity,
   So here I meditate alone
   Upon your insincerity.

5. Ah, Greensleeves, now farewell, adieu,
   To God I pray to prosper thee,
   For I remain thy lover true,
   Come once again and be with me.

Greensleeves

WHAT CHILD IS THIS

1. What Child is this, who, laid to rest
   On Mary's lap is sleeping?
   Whom angel's greet with anthems sweet
   While shepherds watch are keeping?
   This, this is Christ the King
   Whom shepherds guard and angels sing;
   Haste, haste to bring Him laud,
   The Babe, the Son of Mary!

2. Why lies He in such mean estate
   Where ox and ass are feeding?
   Good Christian, fear, for sinners here
   The silent word is pleading;
   Nails, spear shall pierce Him through,
   The cross be borne for me, for you;
   Hail, hail, the word made flesh,
   The Babe, the Son of Mary!

3. So bring Him incense, gold and myrrh,
   Come peasant, king, to own Him;
   The King of Kings salvation brings,
   Let loving hearts enthrone Him;
   Raise, raise the song on high,
   The Virgin sings her lullaby;
   Joy, joy, for Christ is born,
   The Babe, the Son of Mary!

This tune first appeared in print in England in 1580 when it was entered in the register of the Stationer's Company as "a new Northern Dittye." Evidence indicates that it predates this entry. Shakespeare mentioned it twice in *The Merry Wives of Windsor*, and Pepys alluded to it under the name of *The Blacksmith*, by which it also was known. The Cavaliers sang political verses to it during the Civil War in England during the seventeenth century. The English organist and composer Sir John Stainer adapted the melody as a setting for the text *What Child Is This* by the noted hymn writer William Chatterton Dix. The love ballad and the hymn sung to this lovely old folk melody are equally popular in America.

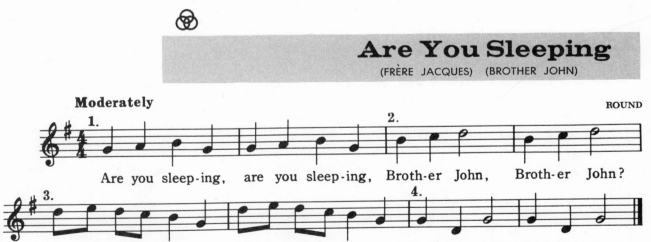

Are you sleep-ing, are you sleep-ing, Broth-er John, Broth-er John?

Morn-ing bells are ring-ing, morn-ing bells are ring-ing, Ding, ding, dong, ding, ding, dong.

Frère Jacques, Frère Jacques, dormez-vous, dormez-vous?
Sonnez les matines, Sonnez les matines, din, dan, don, din, dan, don.

Children find this French round delightful because it is easy to sing, and it provides an excellent initial experience for singing in the original language.

Cielito Lindo
(BEAUTIFUL HEAVEN)

Quick waltz

MEXICO

1. From Si - er - - - ra Mo - re - na, Cie - li - to

Lin - do, comes_____ soft - ly steal - ing,_____

Laugh - ing eyes,_____ black and ro - guish, Cie - li - to

Lin - do, beau - - ty re - veal - ing._____

Chorus

Ay, ay, ay, ay !_____

Sing, ban - ish sor - row !_____ To

pass the hours_____ light - ly sing - ing, Cie - li - to

Cielito Lindo

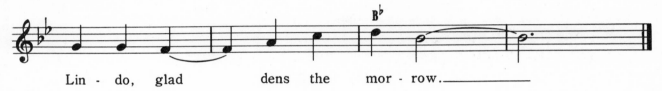

Lin - do, glad dens the mor - row._____

2. In the air brightly flashing,
   Cielito Lindo, flies Cupid's feather,
   My heart it is striking,
   Cielito Lindo, wounding forever.

1. De la Sierra Morena, Cielito Lindo, vienen bajando;
   Un parde ojitos negros, Cielito Lindo, de contrabando.

Chorus: ¡Ay, ay, ay, ay! Canta y no llores,
   Porque cantando se alegran, Cielito Lindo los corazones.

2. Una flecha en aire, Cielito Lindo, lanzo Cupido.
   Y como fué jugando, Cielito Lindo, yo fui el herido.

As the Spanish missionary priests established missions throughout the western United States, the Spanish people followed and built towns around these missions. Guitars accompanied their lilting songs, and these soon were absorbed into our own culture. *Cielito Lindo* was one such song, and it enjoyed great popularity in California in pioneer times.

Good Night

ROUND

Calmly

Good night to you all, and sweet be thy sleep; May

an - gels a - round you their si - lent watch keep, Good

night, good night, good night, good night.

Aloha Oe
(FAREWELL TO THEE)

QUEEN LILIUOKALANI   QUEEN LILIUOKALANI

With feeling

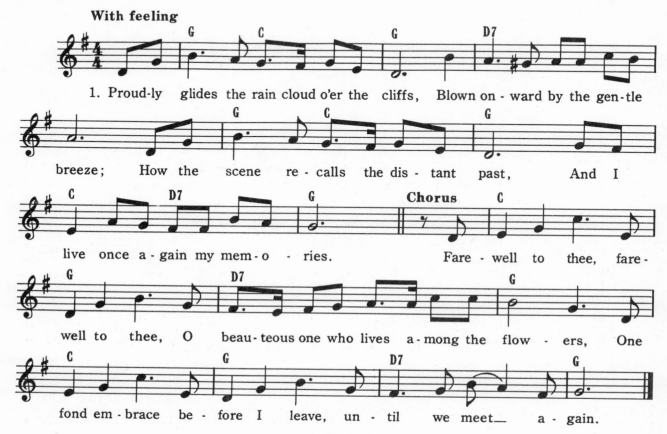

1. Proud-ly glides the rain cloud o'er the cliffs, Blown on-ward by the gen-tle
breeze; How the scene re-calls the dis-tant past, And I
live once a-gain my mem-o-ries.

Chorus Fare-well to thee, fare-well to thee, O beau-teous one who lives a-mong the flow-ers, One
fond em-brace be-fore I leave, un-til we meet__ a-gain.

2. Thoughts of you will fill the lonely hours,
   I'll see you standing on the shore
   Of this lovely island of my dreams
   Till the day I return to you once more.

1. Haaheo eka ua ina pali Ke nihi ae la i kanahele
   E uhai ana paha i ka liko Pua ahihilehua o uka.
   Aloha oe, aloha oe, E ke ona ona noho i ka lipo;
   One fond embrace a hoi ae au, Until we meet again.

2. O ka halia aloha kai hiki mai Ke hone ae nei i kuu manawa,
   O oe no ka'u ipo aloha A loko e hana nei.
   Aloha oe, aloha oe, E ke ona ona noho i ka lipo;
   One fond embrace a hoi ae au, Until we meet again.

This song of hail and farewell was written by the last reigning Hawaiian Island queen, Liliuokalani. After a rule of two years, she was dethroned in 1893 for refusing to establish a constitution. The native words were adapted to a melody of uncertain origin, but one which may have been written much earlier by Charles C. Converse. *Aloha Oe* often is sung at Hawaiian festivals and gatherings. To many, it has come to be a symbol of farewell.

Nelly Bly

STEPHEN C. FOSTER   STEPHEN C. FOSTER

With abandon

1. Nel - ly Bly, Nel - ly Bly, bring the broom a - long, We'll sweep the kitch - en clean, my dear, and have a lit - tle song.

Poke the wood my la - dy love, and make the fire___ burn, And while I take the ban - jo down, just give the mush a turn.

Chorus

Heigh! Nel - ly, Ho! Nel - ly, lis - ten, love, to me, I'll sing for you, play for you a dul - cet mel - o - dy.

2. Nelly Bly has a voice like the turtle dove,
   I hear it in the meadow and I hear it in the grove,
   Nelly Bly, she has a heart, warm as a cup of tea,
   And bigger than the sweet potato down in Tennessee.

Many of the songs written by Stephen Foster were marked by sentiment and nostalgia. Foster was by nature sensitive and somewhat a dreamer. He was not an astute business man, and people often took advantage of him financially. Much of his personal life was marred by tragedy. However, *Nelly Bly*, published in 1849, is marked by gaiety and good humor.

Bow Belinda

Crisply

U. S.

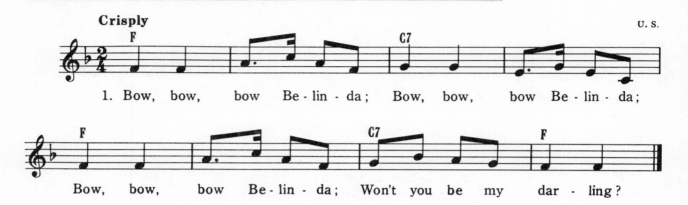

1. Bow, bow, bow Be-lin-da; Bow, bow, bow Be-lin-da;

Bow, bow, bow Be-lin-da; Won't you be my dar-ling?

2. Right hand around, Belinda, etc.
3. Left hand around, Belinda, etc.
4. Both hands around, Belinda, etc.
5. Shake your foot, Belinda, etc.
6. Join right hands, Belinda, etc.
7. Join left hands, Belinda, etc.
8. Promenade, Belinda, etc.
9. Circle, all, Belinda, etc.

In this American singing game song, the actions are fitted to the words. The game begins with boys and girls in separate lines facing each other. Verses can be made up to fit the music and direct the action as the dance progresses.

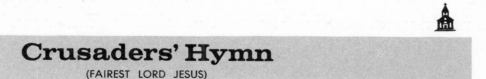

Crusaders' Hymn
(FAIREST LORD JESUS)

With devotion

GERMANY

1. Fair are the mea-dows, Fair-er still the wood-lands,

Robed in the bloom-ing___ garb of spring;

Crusaders' Hymn

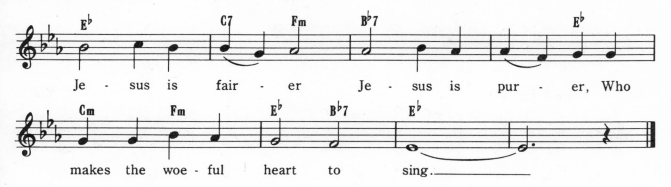

Je - sus is fair - er Je - sus is pur - er, Who

makes the woe - ful heart to sing.———

2. Fair is the sunshine, fairer the moonlight,
   And the twinkling starry host;
   Jesus shines brighter, Jesus shines purer
   Than all the angels heaven can boast.
3. Beautiful Saviour, Lord of the nations,
   Son of God and son of man;
   Glory and honor, praise, adoration,
   Now and forever more be Thine.

Legend has it that this old hymn was a twelfth century air sung during the Crusades by German pilgrims on their way to Jerusalem. However, evidence does not support this theory. The words can be traced only to 1677. The melody is thought to be a Silesian melody first published in 1842 in Leipzig. Whatever its origin, the *Crusader's Hymn* is widely known and frequently sung in community and religious services.

A-Hunting We Will Go

Briskly

ENGLAND

Oh, a - hunt - ing we will go, a -

hunt - ing we will go. We'll catch a lit - tle fox and

put him in a box and nev - er let him go.

This is an old English folk and game song. The action is fitted to the words, and added verses may be made up to provide for further dramatization.

He Shall Feed His Flock

THE BIBLE   G. F. HANDEL

Tranquilly

He ___ shall feed His flock like a shep - - herd, and

He ___ shall ___ gath - er the lambs ___ with ___ His arm,

with ___ His arm; He ___ shall feed His flock like a

shep - - herd, and He ___ shall ___ gath - er the

lambs ___ with ___ His arm, with ___ His arm;

And car - ry ___ them in His

bos - - om, and gen - - tly lead ___ those that

are ___ with young, ___ and gen - - tly lead ___ and

gen - - tly lead ___ those that are ___ with young. ___

He Shall Feed His Flock

He Shall Feed His Flock is an aria from the oratorio *The Messiah* by George Frideric Handel (1685-1759). Handel was born in Halle in Saxony. His father was a barber who also served as valet and surgeon to the Prince of Saxe-Magdeburg. The father wanted his son to be a lawyer, but in spite of strenuous parental opposition, Handel taught himself to play the harpsichord. When he was seven years of age, his father took him on a visit at the court of Saxe-Weissenfels where he gained access to the chapel organ. The Duke heard him, and insisted that such a talented boy receive a good musical education. He became a composer of great stature, and has been called "the father of the oratorio." *The Messiah* was first performed in Dublin April 13, 1742. In America, it was performed in part in New York (1770), and in its entirety in Boston in 1801. *He Shall Feed His Flock* is one of the best known and best loved arias of the oratorio. The work frequently is performed at the Christmas season since it tells of the promise, coming, suffering, death, and resurrection of the Messiah. Handel completed writing the oratorio in less than four weeks. The performance time is approximately three hours.

All Glory, Laud and Honor

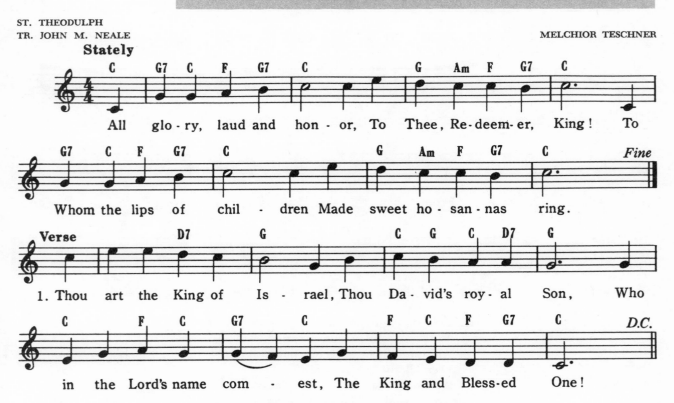

ST. THEODULPH
TR. JOHN M. NEALE

MELCHIOR TESCHNER

All glo-ry, laud and hon-or, To Thee, Re-deem-er, King! To Whom the lips of chil-dren Made sweet ho-san-nas ring.

Verse

1. Thou art the King of Is-rael, Thou Da-vid's roy-al Son, Who in the Lord's name com - est, The King and Bless-ed One!

2. The company of angels are praising Thee on high,
   And mortal men and all things created make reply.

3. The people of the Hebrews with palms before Thee went;
   Our praise and prayers and anthems before Thee we present.

4. To Thee before Thy passion they sang their hymns of praise;
   To Thee, now high exalted, our melody we raise.

5. Thou didst accept their praises; accept the praise we bring,
   Who in all good delightest, Thou good and gracious King.

St. Theodulph, Bishop of Orleans, wrote the words to this hymn in 820 A.D. while he was a captive in a cloister at Anjou. The melody was written in 1619 by Melchior Teschner. *All Glory, Laud and Honor* is often performed at Easter.

It Came Upon the Midnight Clear

EDMUND H. SEARS

RICHARD S. WILLIS

Gently

1. It came up-on— the mid-night clear, That glo-ri-ous song— of old,——————— From an-gels bend-ing· near the earth, To touch their harps— of gold;——————— "Peace on the earth,— good will to men, From hea-ven's all-gra-cious King;"——————— The world in sol-emn still-ness lay, To hear the an-gels sing.——————

2. Still through the cloven skies they come
   With peaceful wings unfurled,
   And still their heavenly music floats
   O'er all the weary world;
   Above its sad and lowly plains
   They bend on hovering wing;
   And ever o'er its Babel sounds
   The blessed angels sing.

3. O ye, beneath life's crushing load
   Whose forms are bending low,
   Who toil along the·climbing way
   With painful steps and slow
   Look now! for glad and golden hours
   Come swiftly on the wing;
   O rest beside the weary road
   And hear the angels sing.

20

It Came Upon the Midnight Clear

4. For lo! the days are hastening on,
By prophet bards foretold,
When with the ever-circling years
Comes round the age of gold;
When peace shall over all the earth
Its ancient splendors fling;
And the whole world give back the song
Which now the angels sing.

Edmund Sears sat in his study one evening in Wayland, Massachusetts, looking out the window at the lovely countryside. War clouds, caused by the slavery issue, were gathering over the country, and Sears thought of the peace the Saviour taught. It was Christmas time, and as the words of a poem came to him, he wrote them down. He sent the poem to Dr. Morrison, an editor friend in Boston who published the *Christian Register*. Dr. Morrison recited the poem from his own pulpit, and urged Sears to have it set to music. Sears gave it to another friend, Richard S. Willis, a noted Boston musician and composer, who wrote the musical setting for *It Came Upon The Midnight Clear*.

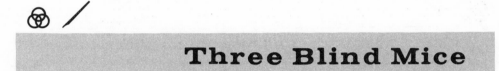

Three Blind Mice

MOTHER GOOSE RHYME   ROUND

Zestfully

1. Three blind mice, ____ three blind mice, ____

2. See how they run, ____ see how they run, ____ They

3. all run af - ter the farm - er's wife, who cut off their tails with a carv - ing knife. Did you

4. ev - er see such a sight in your life as three blind mice. ____

Rounds have been popular song forms since the thirteenth century. This round has been well-known in England since the days of Queen Elizabeth. In the United States it has been widely sung at social gatherings and in schools.

Praise to the Lord

JOACHIM NEANDER
TR. CATHERINE WINKWORTH

GERMANY

Gatefully

1. Praise to the Lord, the Al - might - y, the King of cre - a - tion.
   O my soul, praise Him, for He is thy health and sal - va - tion.

All ye who hear Now to His tem - ple draw near, Join - ing in glad ad - o - ra - tion.

2. Praise to the Lord, who o'er all things so wondrously reigneth,
   Shieldeth thee gently from harm, or when fainting sustaineth.
   Hast thou not seen how thy heart's wishes have been granted in what He
       ordaineth.

3. Praise to the Lord, who doth prosper thy work and defend thee,
   Surely His goodness and mercy shall daily attend thee.
   Ponder anew what the Almighty can do, if with His love He befriend thee.

4. Praise to the Lord, O let all that is in me adore Him,
   All that hath life and breath, come now with praises before Him.
   Let the "Amen" sound from His people again, gladly for aye we adore Him.

Joachim Neander (1650-1680) was an excellent musician and one of Germany's finest hymnists. His hymns were published only after his early death. Nineteen of them were set to his own chorale tunes. His great love of nature and God is evident in *Praise To The Lord*. J. Julian, in his *A Dictionary of Hymnology*, describes it as "a magnificent hymn of praise to God, perhaps the finest production of its author, and of the first rank in its class."

Hark! The Herald Angels Sing

CHARLES WESLEY   FELIX MENDELSSOHN

Sustained

1. Hark! the her-ald an-gels sing,— "Glo-ry to the new-born King!
Peace on earth and mer-cy mild,— God and sin-ners rec-on-ciled."
Joy-ful, all ye na-tions, rise,— Join the tri-umph of the skies,—
with th'an-gel-ic host pro-claim, "Christ is— born in Beth-le-hem."
Hark! the her-ald an-gels sing, "Glo-ry— to the new-born King!"

2. Christ, by highest heaven adored; Christ, the everlasting Lord;
   Late in time behold Him come, Offspring of the favored one.
   Veiled in flesh, the Godhead see; hail th'incarnate Deity.
   Pleased, as man with men to dwell, Jesus, our Immanuel!
   Hark! the herald angels sing, "Glory to the newborn King!"

3. Hail! the heaven-born Prince of Peace! Hail! the Son of Righteousness!
   Light and life to all He brings, risen with healing in His wings.
   Mild He lays His glory by, born that man no more may die;
   Born to raise the sons of earth, born to give them second birth.
   Hark! the herald angels sing, "Glory to the newborn King!"

When Charles Wesley, author of this famous carol, was a youth in England, a wealthy man wanted to adopt him and make him heir to a vast fortune. The boy was fond of his friend, but he loved his family more. Poor though they were, he couldn't imagine life without his eighteen brothers and sisters, his mother, and his father, the Reverend Samuel Wesley. In 1735 Charles and his brother, John, visited America briefly to help General James Oglethorpe manage the Georgia colony. Back in England, they enrolled in Oxford University where they excelled in music. Charles wrote nearly 7,000 hymns during his life, and is considered one of the great hymn writers. *Hark! The Herald Angels Sing* is one of the most popular in English speaking countries. Charles helped his brother, John, found the Methodist Church. More than a century after the original words were written, Dr. William Haymen Cummings, organist at Waltham Abbey in England, adapted them to a festival song composed by Felix Mendelssohn. It is this union of the words and music of two great masters, Wesley and Mendelssohn, that we sing today.

Bendemeer's Stream

THOMAS MOORE

IRELAND

With longing

1. There's a bow-er of ros-es by Ben-de-meer's stream, And the night-in-gale sings round it all the day long.
In the time of my child-hood 'twas like a sweet dream, To ___ sit in the ros-es and hear the bird's song.
That bower and its mu-sic I ne'er shall for-get, But oft when a-lone in the bloom of the year, I think, "Is the night-in-gale sing-ing there yet? Are the ros-es still bright by the calm Ben-de-meer?"

2. No, the roses soon withered that hung o'er the wave,
But some blossoms were gathered while freshly they shone,
And the dew was distilled from their flowers that gave
All the fragrance of summer when summer is gone.
Thus memory draws from delight e'er it dies
An essence that breathes of it many a year;
Thus bright to my soul, as 'twas then to my eyes,
Is that bower on the banks of the calm Bendemeer.

Thomas Moore (1779-1852), Dublin-born Irish poet and balladeer, was noted for setting poems to Irish melodies. Moore was esteemed in the British Isles as a poet, and was compared favorably with Scott and Byron. In

Bendemeer's Stream

addition to *Bendemeer's Stream*, his other well-known songs include *Believe Me If All Those Endearing Young Charms, The Harp That Once Through Tara's Halls, The Last Rose of Summer,* and *The Vesper Hymn.* Moore was an ardent Irish nationalist who is remembered as a defender of Irish freedom and as the author of imperishable songs.

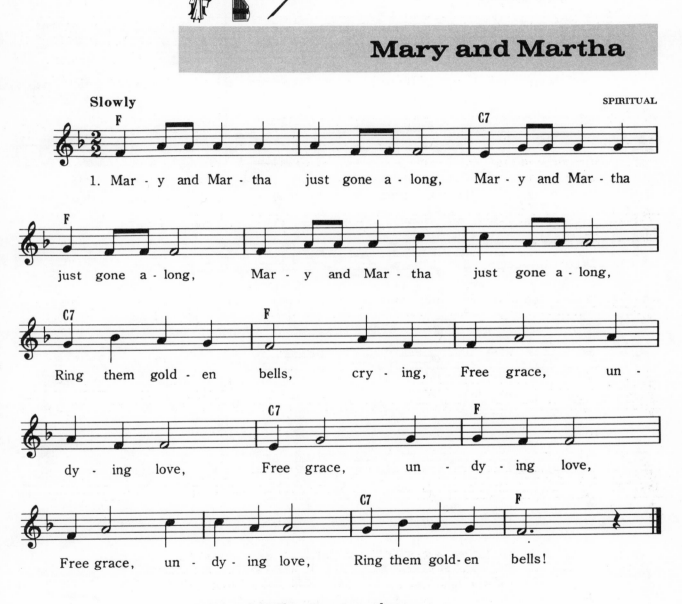

Mary and Martha

Slowly

SPIRITUAL

1. Mar - y and Mar - tha just gone a - long, Mar - y and Mar - tha just gone a - long, Mar - y and Mar - tha just gone a - long, Ring them gold - en bells, cry - ing, Free grace, un - dy - ing love, Free grace, un - dy - ing love, Free grace, un - dy - ing love, Ring them gold - en bells!

2. Sister and brother, just gone along,
   Sister and brother, just gone along,
   Sister and brother, just gone along,
   Ring them golden bells, crying,
   'Way over Jordan, Lord, 'way over Jordan, Lord,
   'Way over Jordan, Lord, to ring them golden bells!

This was one of the spirituals used by the Fisk University singers on fund raising tours.

Battle Hymn of the Republic

JULIA WARD HOWE

WILLIAM STEFFE

With fervor

1. Mine eyes have seen the glo-ry of the com-ing of the Lord; .He is

tram-pling out the vin-tage where the grapes of wrath are stored; He hath

loosed the fate-ful light-ning of His ter-ri-ble swift sword; His

truth is march-ing on. **Chorus** Glo-ry, glo-ry hal-le-

lu-jah! Glo-ry, glo-ry hal-le-

lu-jah! Glo-ry, glo-ry hal-le-

lu-jah! His truth is march-ing on.

Battle Hymn of the Republic

2. I have seen Him in the watch-fires of a hundred circling camps,
   They have builded Him an altar in the evening dews and damps;
   I can read His righteous sentence by the dim and flaring lamps,
   His day is marching on.

3. He has sounded forth the trumpet that shall never call retreat,
   He is sifting out the hearts of men before His judgment seat,
   O, be swift, my soul, to answer Him! Be jubilant, my feet,
   Our God is marching on.

4. I have read a fiery gospel, writ in burnished rows of steel:
   "As ye deal with my condemners, so with you my grace shall deal;
   Let the Hero, born of woman, crush the serpent with His heel,
   Since God is marching on."

5. In the beauty of the lilies Christ was born across the sea,
   With a glory in His bosom that transfigures you and me;
   As He died to make men holy, let us die to make men free,
   While God is marching on.

6. He is coming like the glory of the morning on the wave,
   He is wisdom to the mighty, He is honor to the brave,
   So the world shall be His footstool, and the soul of wrong His slave,
   Our God is marching on!

Julia Ward Howe (1819-1910) visited a Union Army Camp near Washington, D. C. The men were singing *John Brown's Body*. A chorus of this song had been written by Thomas Brigham Bishop and published in Cincinnati in 1861. After hearing it sung by the soldiers, Mrs. Howe wrote a poem which was published without credit in the *Atlantic Monthly* magazine in February, 1862. For this publication she received five dollars and was elected the only woman member of the American Academy of Arts and Letters. The poem and the tune filled a great need during a national crisis, and *The Battle Hymn Of The Republic* became the marching song of the Union Army.

Row, Row, Row Your Boat

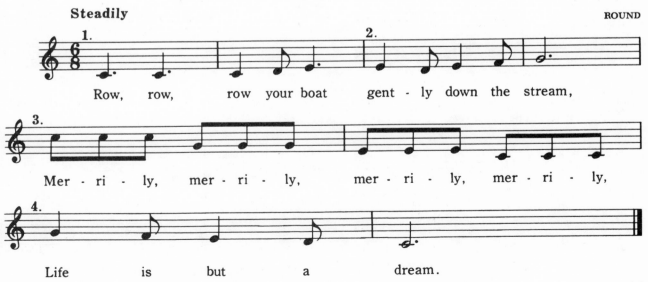

All Night, All Day

SPIRITUAL

With conviction

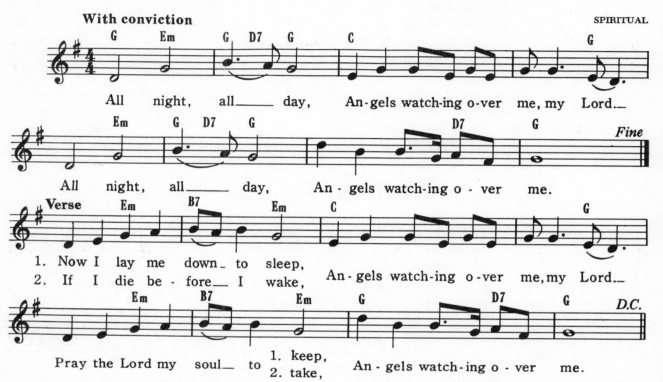

All night, all____ day, An-gels watch-ing o-ver me, my Lord.____

All night, all____ day, An-gels watch-ing o-ver me.

Verse

1. Now I lay me down___ to sleep,
2. If I die be-fore___ I wake,

An-gels watch-ing o-ver me, my Lord.____

Pray the Lord my soul___ to 1. keep, 2. take, An-gels watch-ing o-ver me.

This is one of the lasting and lovely spirituals which helps to form the great heritage of American folk music. The famous Bohemian composer, Anton Dvořák, came to the United States in 1892 to direct the National Conservatory of Music in New York. He greatly admired the American Negro spirituals. He wrote, "In the Negro melodies of America I discover all that is needed for a great and noble school of music. They are pathetic, tender, passionate, melancholy, solemn, religious, bold, and merry."

Drill, Ye Tarriers

THOMAS CASEY   THOMAS CASEY

With zeal

1. Eve - ry morn - ing at sev - en o' - clock There's

twen - ty tar - ri - ers a - work - ing at the rock, And the

Drill, Ye Tarriers

boss comes a - long and he says, "Keep still, And

come down heav - y on the cast iron drill."

Chorus

So drill, ye tar - ri - ers drill, And drill, ye tar - ri - ers

drill! Oh, it's work all day for sug - ar in your "tay,"

Down be - yond the rail - way, And drill, ye tar - ri - ers drill!

(After the last chorus — Repeat ad. lib. getting softer) (Loud)

And drill, and blast, and fire!

2. Our new foreman is Dan McCann,
   I'll tell you true, he's a real mean man;
   Last week a premature blast went off,
   And a mile in the air went Big Jim Goff.

3. Next time pay day came around
   Jim Goff was short one buck, he found,
   "What for?" says he, then this reply,
   "You're docked for the time you were up in the sky."

Much of the unskilled labor in America in the eighties was done by Irish immigrants. This was especially true on the railroads. These workmen were called "tarriers." The work was hard and rough. Mountains were blasted, and steam drills were used to remove the displaced rock. Thomas Casey was himself a tarrier before turning from the labor gangs to the entertainment world. He drew heavily on his experiences with the rock drilling crews to write this song which was an immediate hit. *Drill, Ye Tarriers* was included in a musical, *A Brass Monkey*, by Charley Hoyt.

The Marines' Hymn

Brisk march

U. S. MILITARY

1. From the Halls of Mon-te-zu-ma To the
shores of Trip-o-li; _____ We _____ fight our
coun-try's bat - tles In the air, on land and
sea; _____ First to fight for right and free - dom And to
keep our hon-or clean; _____ We are proud to claim the
ti - tle Of U - nit - ed States Ma - rine. _____

2. Our Flag's unfurled to every breeze from dawn to setting sun;
   We have fought in every clime and place where we could take a gun;
   In the snow of far off Northern lands and in sunny tropic scenes;
   You will find us always on the job The United States Marines.

3. Here's health to you and to our Corps which we are proud to serve;
   In many a strife we've fought for life and never lost our nerve;
   If the Army and the Navy ever look on Heaven's scenes;
   They will find the streets are guarded by United States Marines.

The Marines' Hymn has been sung around the world for more than a century. The United States Marine Corps was established in 1775. The *Hymn* was written in 1847 during the Mexican War by a Marine Corps poet who set the original lyrics to music from an old French opera. Some of the words refer to the Mexican War (Montezuma had been the Aztec emperor of Mexico). The Treaty of Guadalupe Hidalgo (February, 1848) ended the war. By its terms, Mexico recognized the United States' annexation of Texas and California, and ceded the territories of New Mexico and Utah for $15 million.

Barbara Allen

Sadly   D   Bm   SCOTLAND

1. In Scar - let town where I was born, There

D   A   G

was a fair maid dwell-in', Made ev -'ry youth cry——

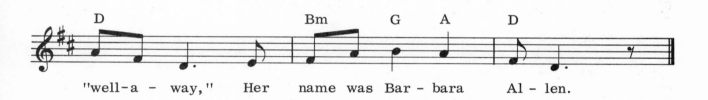

D   Bm   G   A   D

"well-a - way," Her name was Bar - bara Al - len.

2. All in the merry month of May
When green buds they were swellin',
Young Jimmy Grove on his deathbed lay
For love of Barbara Allen.

3. He sent his man unto her then,
To the place where she was dwellin',
To bring her to poor Jimmy Grove,
The lovely Barbara Allen.

4. And death was printed on his face,
And o'er his heart was stealin',
Before she came to comfort him,
The willful Barbara Allen.

5. So slowly, slowly she came up,
And slowly she came nigh him,
And all she said, when there she came,
"Young man, I think you're dying."

6. He said, "I am a dying man,
One kiss from you will cure me."
"One kiss from me you will never get,"
Said cruel Barbara Allen.

7. As she was walking o'er the fields,
She heard the death bells knellin'
And every peal did again reveal
How cruel Barbara Allen.

8. When he was dead and in his grave,
Her heart was struck with sorrow,
"Oh, mother, mother make my bed,
For I shall die tomorrow."

9. And on her deathbed as she lay,
She begged a place beside him,
And sore repented of that day
That she did e'er deny him.

10. "Farewell," she said, "ye virgins all,
And shun the fault I fell in,
Henceforth take warning by the fall
of heartless Barbara Allen."

11. Then she was buried on the moor,
And he was laid beside her,
Above his grave red roses grew,
Above hers, a green briar.

Samuel Pepys found "perfect pleasure in a new Scottish song of Barbary Allen" in 1665, and noted this in his *Diary.* This song of unrequited love came to America with the pilgrims, and its charm persists. Hundreds of versions of the song exist, and everyone knows his favorite.

Away in a Manger

CARL MÜLLER

Peacefully

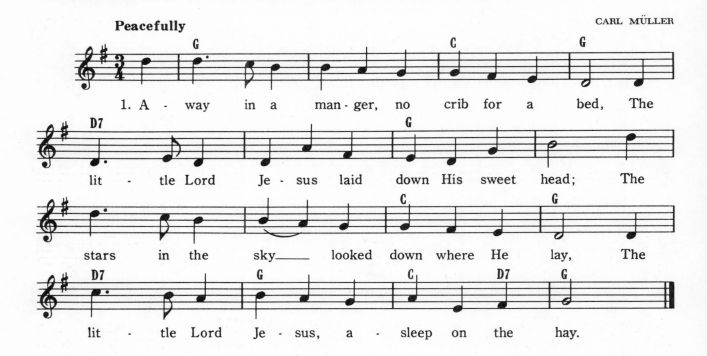

1. A - way in a man - ger, no crib for a bed, The lit - tle Lord Je - sus laid down His sweet head; The stars in the sky____ looked down where He lay, The lit - tle Lord Je - sus, a - sleep on the hay.

2. The cattle are lowing,
   The poor Baby wakes,
   But little Lord Jesus
   No crying He makes;
   I love Thee, Lord Jesus!
   Look down from the sky
   And stay by my cradle
   Till morning is nigh.

3. Be near me, Lord Jesus,
   I ask Thee to stay
   Close by me forever
   And love me, I pray;
   Bless all the dear children
   In Thy tender care,
   And take me to heaven
   To live with Thee there.

A son was born in 1182 to a rich merchant and his wife in the Italian town of Assisi. The devoted parents named the baby Francis. Because he was frail, they gave him everything a child could desire. When he was just out of his teens, he realized suddenly that wealth does not mean happiness, and that a life spent pursuing pleasure is empty. He decided to devote his life to serving others, and cast aside all his material comforts. His fame spread, and crowds flocked to hear him preach. He wanted to make the meaning of Christmas live, and so he dramatized it by re-creating the manger scene in his church at Graecia. Today we know this man as St. Francis of Assisi. The author of these words is unknown. Once attributed to Martin Luther, there now is conclusive evidence he did not write them. The text first appeared in print as a poem in 1885, unsigned. Countless tunes have been used with the words of this carol.

TR. STUART PAUL

CREOLE SONG

Rhythmically

1. If ev-er with-in your heart, ay, ay, ay, No home you can find for my love, If ev-er with-in your heart, ay, ay, ay, No home you can find for my love; As 'twere a child de-ceive him; But for an hour re-ceive him; De-ceive as you would a child, ay, ay, ay, And nev-er let my love know.

2. My love, like a bird awing, ay, ay, ay,
   Would fly from the frown on your brow,
   My love, like a bird awing, ay, ay, ay,
   Would fly from the frown on your brow.
   So smile, and then receive him,
   And though your smile deceive him,
   If ever within your heart, ay, ay, ay,
   No home you can find for my love.

1. Si alguna vez en tu pecho ay, ay ay,
   mi cariño no lo abrigas,
   Si alguna vez en tu pecho ay, ay, ay,
   mi cariño no lo abrigas,
   Engáñalo como a un niño
   pero nunca se lo digas,
   Engáñalo como a un niño ay, ay, ay,
   pero nunca se lo digas.

The Boll Weevil

SOUTHERN U. S.

Rousing rhythm

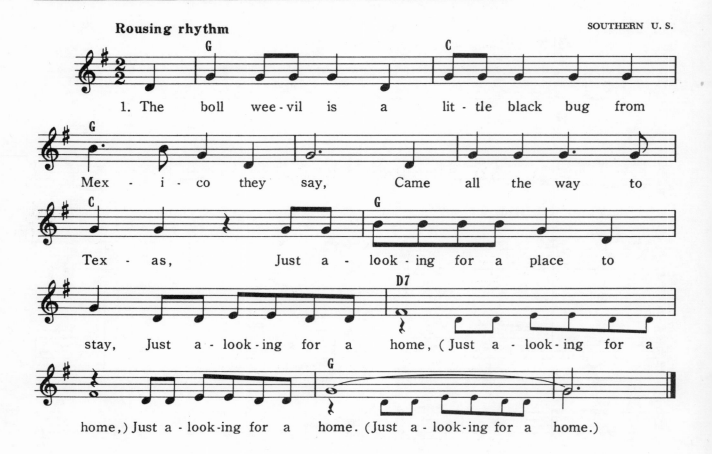

1. The boll wee-vil is a lit-tle black bug from Mex-i-co they say, Came all the way to Tex-as, Just a-look-ing for a place to stay, Just a-look-ing for a home, (Just a-look-ing for a home,) Just a-look-ing for a home. (Just a-look-ing for a home.)

2. The first time I saw the boll weevil he was sitting on the square,
   The next time I saw that boll weevil he had all his family there,
   Just a-looking for a home, etc.

3. The farmer took the boll weevil and stuck him in hot sand,
   The weevil told the farmer, "I am going to stand it like a man
   'Cause it's going to be my home," etc.

4. The farmer then took the boll weevil and stuck him on a cake of ice,
   The weevil told the farmer, "This is mighty cool and nice,
   And it's going to be my home," etc.

5. The merchant got half the cotton, and the boll weevil took the rest,
   He only left the farmer just a single old ragged vest,
   He had found himself a home, etc.

This song about the boll weevil is said to have been sung by a Negro plantation worker who recognized the fact that the little black cotton-borer was "a-looking for a home," and told the story in song. This destructive pest came from Mexico. The boll weevil is only about one-eighth of an inch long, but of some 20,000 species, it is responsible for the most extensive crop loss. After crossing the Rio Grande into Texas in the 1890's, the boll weevil invaded every cotton-growing state.

Old Dan Tucker

DAN EMMETT

DAN EMMETT

With wry humor

1. I came to town the oth-er night, I heard the noise and saw the fight. The watch-man, he was run-ning 'round, said "Old Dan Tuck-er's come to town."

Chorus

Get out the way, old Dan Tuck-er, Get out the way, old Dan Tuck-er,

Get out the way, old Dan Tuck-er, You're too late to come to sup-per.

2. Old Dan Tucker was a fine old man, he washed his face in the frying pan,
   He combed his hair with a wagon wheel, and died with a toothache in his heel.
3. Now, Old Dan Tucker and I fell out, and what do you think it was all about?
   He borrowed my old setting hen and didn't bring her back again.
4. Old Dan began in early life to play the banjo and win a wife,
   But every time a date he'd keep he'd play himself right fast asleep.
5. Now, Old Dan Tucker he came to town to swing the ladies all around,
   Swing them right and swing them left then to the one he liked the best.
6. And when Old Dan had passed away they missed the music he used to play,
   They took him on his final ride and buried his banjo by his side.

Dan Emmett not only helped create the prototype of the minstrel show but was one of the medium's principal composers. His minstrels presented *Old Dan Tucker* to the American people in 1843, and it became immensely popular in a very short time. It was adopted by New York farmers in their revolt against feudal conditions, and a short time later by the abolitionists to promote the abolition of slavery. In each case, the words were changed to suit the cause. Emmett was well known for this song, and others such as *The Blue Tail Fly* and *Dixie*. He was born in Mt. Vernon, Ohio, October 29, 1815, and died there June 28, 1904. As a boy he worked in a print shop, but he hated the job so much that he ran away from home and joined the army. His father promptly removed him from the service since he was under age. Young Emmet ran away again, this time with a circus, and he spent the rest of his life in show business. He helped organize the Virginia Minstrels who opened at the Chatam Square Theatre in New York in 1843. He later went to New York and joined Bryant's Minstrels. He made a tour of the South when he was in his 80's, and they lionized him again as their "son." Despite his northern birthplace, he belonged to the south because he gave them *Dixie*. He died in poverty and relative obscurity in his home town at the age of 89. Some of the best-loved songs of the pre-Civil War period were born in the minstrel acts, and Dan Emmett was one of the foremost figures of this overwhelmingly popular entertainment media.

Sailing

GODFREY MARKS   GODFREY MARKS

Rollicking rhythm

1. Heave ho!_____ my lads,_____ the wind blows free,_____ A pleas - ant gale_____ is on our lee;_____ And soon_____ a - cross_____ the o - cean clear,_____ Our gal - - lant bark_____ shall brave - - ly_____ steer;_____ But ere we part_____ from Eng - land's shores to - night,_____ A song we'll sing_____ for home and beau - ty bright._____ Then here's to the sail - or, and here's to the hearts_ so

Sailing

true, Who will think of him up - on the wa - ter blue!_____

Chorus

Sail - ing, sail - ing, o - ver the bound - ing main,_____ For

man - y a storm - y wind shall blow ere Jack comes home a - gain;

Sail - ing, sail - ing, o - ver the bound - ing main,_____ For

man - y a storm - y wind shall blow ere Jack comes home a - gain._____

2. The sailor's life is bold and free, his home is on the rolling sea;
   And never heart more true or brave than his who launches on the wave;
   Afar he speeds in distant climes to roam, with joyous song he rides the
      sparkling foam,
   Then here's to the sailor, and here's to the hearts so true
   Who will think of him upon the water blue.

3. The tide is flowing with the gale, heave ho! my lads, set every sail,
   The harbor bar we soon shall clear, farewell, once more to home most dear,
   For when the tempest rages loud and long, that home shall be our guiding
      star and song,
   Then here's to the sailor, and here's to the hearts so true
   Who will think of him upon the water blue.

Many folk songs survived in the sea life of sailing ship days. For amusement the sailor sang about his life on the sea and the things he missed ashore. Many of his songs were working songs, rhythmically fitted to work aboard the ship. Chanteymen with strong voices were hired to sing the work songs, and the crew joined in with a periodical refrain. This turned the work into a sort of game, and unanimity in pulling the ropes or pushing the capstan was attained. The words to these songs often were extemporized, and in addition to the stories they told, some also were used to inform the captain about good and bad aspects of the voyage. When passengers were aboard, often the captain imposed a sort of censorship, since the refrains could be heard over the entire ship.

I've Been Working on the Railroad

(DINAH)

Well measured rhythm

U. S.

I've been work-ing on the rail - road all the live-long day; I've been work-ing on the rail - road to pass the time a - way. Don't you hear the whis-tle blow-ing? Rise up so ear-ly in the morn. Don't you hear the cap-tain shout-ing, "Di - nah, blow your horn!" Di - nah won't you blow, Di - nah won't you blow, Di - nah won't you blow your horn?_____ Di - nah won't you blow

I've Been Working on the Railroad

Countless miles of railroad track have been laid to the rhythm of this familiar work song. Singing made the time pass more quickly and pleasantly, and reduced fatigue. The first railroad in the United States was the Baltimore & Ohio (1828), which changed from horses to steam in 1830. The improvement of the steam engine made railroads practical. By 1850 there were about 9,000 miles of railroad, and by the time the Civil war broke out in 1861 there were about 30,000 miles. After the war, railroads stretched from coast to coast and began a rapid spread throughout the country. The origin of *I've Been Working On The Railroad* is unknown. In the South it was entitled *I've been Working On The Levee*. Under its present name it has become popular as a campfire song, college song, and as a barbershop quartet selection. The last line of the song includes the phrase "Dinah, blow your horn!" *Dinah* is another well-known song, and somehow the suggestion of the second title brought the two together. Now, they frequently are sung as one song.

All Through the Night

Serenely

1. Sleep, my child and peace at-tend thee, All through the night;

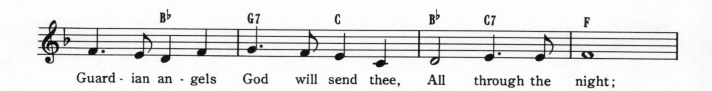

Guard-ian an-gels God will send thee, All through the night;

Soft the drow-sy hours are creep-ing, Hill and vale in slum-ber steep-ing;

I my lov-ing vig-il keep-ing, All through the night.

2. While the moon her watch is keeping
   All through the night;
   While the weary world is sleeping
   All through the night;
   O'er thy spirit gently stealing,
   Visions of delight revealing,
   Breathes a pure and holy feeling
   All through the night.

1. Holl amrantaur sêr ddywedant, Ar hyd y nos,
   "Dyma'r ffordd i fro gogoniant," Ar hyd y nos.
   Golen arall yw tywyllwch, I arddaug os gwir brydferthwch,
   Teulu'r nef oedd mewn tawelwch, Ar hyd y nos.

This lullaby is sung to a very old folk melody which was known in Wales as *Ar Hyd y Nos*, and in England as *Poor Mary Ann*, with words by novelist Amelia Opie. Settlers from the British Isles brought it with them to America where it found lasting favor.

Twinkle, Twinkle Little Star

FRANCE

1. Twin - kle, twin - kle lit - tle star, How I won - der what you are, Up a - bove the world so high, Like a dia - mond in the sky.

When the ev - 'ning sun is set, And the grass with dew is wet, Then I see your lit - tle light, Twin - kle, twin - kle all the night.

2. When the blazing sun has set
   And the grass with dew is wet,
   Then I see your lovely light,
   Twinkle, twinkle all the night.

3. As your bright and shining spark
   Lights the heavens in the dark,
   How I wonder what you are,
   Twinkle, twinkle little star.

This old French nursery rhyme has delighted children the world over for years as they dramatized the familiar words.

41

The Glendy Burk

STEPHEN C. FOSTER

STEPHEN C. FOSTER

Steadily

1. The Glen - dy Burk is a might - y fast boat, With a
   I can't stay here for they work to hard, I'm

   might - y fast cap - tain, too; He sits up there on the
   bound to leave this town; I'll take my duds and

1. hur - ri - cane roof, And he keeps an eye on the crew.

2. tote 'em on my back, When the Glen - dy Burk comes down.

Chorus

Ho! for Lou' - si - an - a! I'm bound to leave this town, I'll

take my duds and tote 'em on my back, When the Glen - dy Burk comes down.

2. The Glendy Burk has a funny old crew, and they sing the boatman's song,
   They burn the pitch and the pine knot, too, just to shove the boat along;
   The smoke goes up and the engine roars and the wheel goes round and round,
   Then fare you well, for I'll take a little ride when the Glendy Burk comes down.

River boats with huge stern paddles carried cargo down the Mississippi River in early America. The widely varied merchandise was sold on the open market in New Orleans. First arrivals in the spring commanded the highest prices, so time was money. Races between river boats were common. Captains paced their decks, shouted commands to their crews, and urged their stokers to feed the blazing furnaces. There was a river-boat named the *Glenn D. Burk* which may have inspired this song. This song is another lasting one by Stephen Foster, in whose honor the United States Post Office issued a one cent stamp bearing his picture in 1940.

America the Beautiful

KATHARINE LEE BATES

SAMUEL A. WARD

With dignity

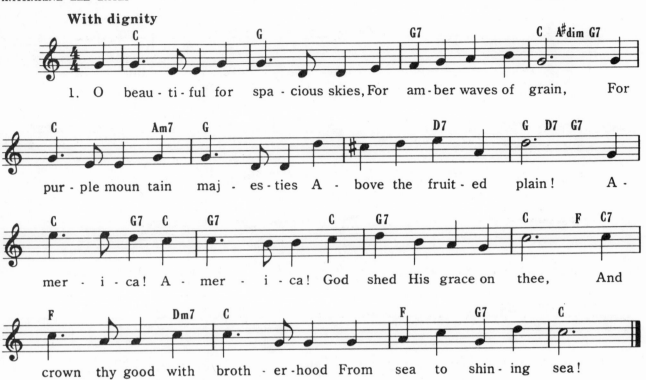

1. O beau-ti-ful for spa-cious skies, For am-ber waves of grain, For pur-ple moun tain maj-es-ties A - bove the fruit-ed plain! A - mer - i - ca! A - mer - i - ca! God shed His grace on thee, And crown thy good with broth - er -hood From sea to shin-ing sea!

2. O beautiful for Pilgrim feet,
Whose stern impassioned stress
A thoroughfare for freedom beat
Across the wilderness.
America! America! God mend thine every flaw,
Confirm thy soul in self-control,
Thy liberty in law.

3. O beautiful for heroes proved
In liberating strife,
Who more than self their country loved,
And mercy more than life.
America! America! May God thy gold refine
Till all success be nobleness
And every gain divine.

4. O beautiful for patriot dream
That sees beyond the years,
Thine alabaster cities gleam
Undimmed by human tears.
America! America! God shed His grace on thee,
And crown thy good with brotherhood
From sea to shining sea.

In 1893, Katherine Lee Bates, professor of English at Wellesley College, climbed Pike's Peak. As she viewed the vast expanse of the country she loved, she was inspired to write the words of *America The Beautiful*. The song was first printed on July 4, 1895, and was sung to an old hymn tune written by Samuel A. Ward. Since that time, approximately sixty melodies have been written to the words by a number of composers. In 1904 Miss Bates rewrote the words to make them "less literary and ornate." This patriotic hymn is known around the world.

Billy Boy

Lightheartedly

ENGLAND

1. Oh,— where have you been Bil - ly Boy, Bil - ly Boy, Oh— where have you been, charm-ing Bil - ly?— I have been to see my wife, she's the joy— of my life, She's a young thing and can-not leave her moth - er.—

2. Did she bid you to come in, Billy Boy, Billy Boy,
Did she bid you to come in, charming Billy?
Yes, she bade me to come in, there's a dimple in her chin,
She's a young thing and cannot leave her mother.

3. Can she make a cherry pie, Billy Boy, Billy Boy,
Can she make a cherry pie, charming Billy?
She can make a cherry pie, quick's a cat can wink her eye,
She's a young thing and cannot leave her mother.

4. How old is she, Billy Boy, Billy Boy,
How old is she, charming Billy?
She's three times six, four times seven, twenty-eight and eleven,
She's a young thing and cannot leave her mother.

This is an example of a question-answer song, a type which abounds in folk song literature, including that of primitive societies. This song came from England to New England and found great favor in the southern mountain country. The words exist in many versions, and additional verses can be improvised describing various household chores. A common practice in singing question-answer songs is for the group to ask the question and a soloist to provide the answer.

Pat-a-pan

TR. JANET TOBITT

FRENCH CAROL

Gladly

Em B7 Em

1. Wil - lie, take your lit - tle drum; Rob-in, bring your fife, and

B7 Em

come; Play - ing on the fife and drum, Tu - re - lu - re -

Am B7

lu, pat - a - pat - a - pan, We'll make mu - sic loud and

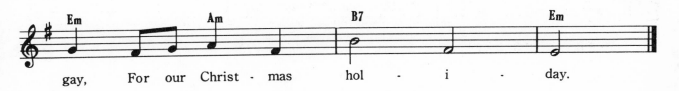

Em Am B7 Em

gay, For our Christ - mas hol - i - day.

2. Shepherds glad, in ancient days,
   Gave the King of Kings their praise;
   Playing on the fife and drum,
   Tu-re-lu-re-lu, pat-a-pat-a-pan,
   They made music loud and gay,
   On the Holy Child's birthday.

3. Christian men, rejoice as one,
   Leave your work and join our fun;
   Playing on the fife and drum,
   Tu-re-lu-re-lu, pat-a-pat-a-pan,
   We'll make music loud and gay,
   For our Christmas holiday.

In olden times, carols used to be circle or ring dances. They were not only played on instruments, but sung and danced as well. Many were joyful in character, and *Pat-a-pan* emphasizes the gaiety of Christmas.

Cindy

Sprightly

APPALACHIA

1. I wish I had a nick-el, I wish I had a dime, I wish I had a pret-ty girl to love me all the time.

Chorus

Get a-long home, Cin-dy, Cin-dy, Get a-long home, Cin-dy, Cin-dy, Get a-long home, Cin-dy, Cin-dy, I'll mar-ry you some day.

2. You ought to see my Cindy,
   She lives a-way down south,
   And she's so sweet the honey bees,
   Swarm around her mouth.

3. The first time I saw Cindy,
   She was standing in the door.
   Her shoes and stockings in her hand,
   Her feet all over the floor.

4. She took me to the parlor,
   She cooled me with her fan,
   She said I was the prettiest thing,
   In the shape of mortal man.

5. I wish I were an apple,
   A-hanging on a tree,
   And every time my Cindy passed,
   She'd take a bite of me.

6. I wish I had a needle,
   As fine as I could sew,
   I'd sew that gal to my coat tail,
   And down the road I'd go.

This is a typical Appalachian courting song. Such songs, named after favored ladies, were common in the southern mountain regions. *Cindy* was a popular square dance and party song.

Angels We Have Heard on High

With exaltation

CAROL

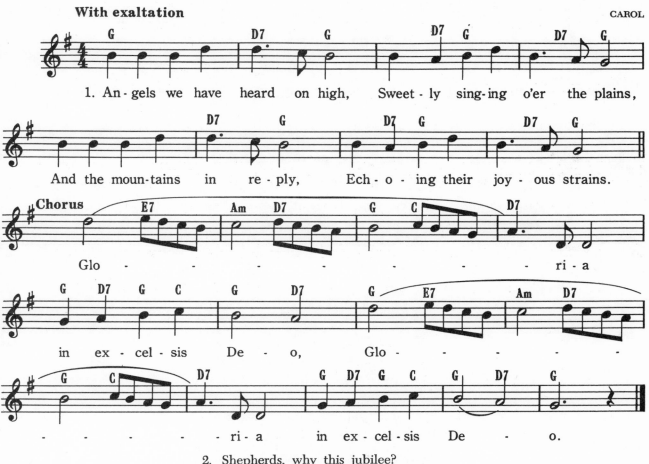

1. An - gels we have heard on high, Sweet - ly sing-ing o'er the plains,

And the moun-tains in re - ply, Ech - o - ing their joy - ous strains.

Chorus

Glo - - - - - - - ri - a

in ex - cel - sis De - o, Glo - - - - -

- - - - - ri - a in ex - cel - sis De - o.

2. Shepherds, why this jubilee?
   Why your joyous strains prolong?
   What the gladsome tidings be
   Which inspire your heavenly song?

3. Come to Bethlehem and see
   Him whose birth the angels sing;
   Come, adore on bended knee
   Christ, the Lord, the newborn King.

Many legends are associated with the phrase *gloria in excelsis Deo* (glory to God in the highest) which the angels supposedly sang to the shepherds on the night of the nativity. The date and place of origin of *Angels We Have Heard on High* is unknown. Some believe that St. Telesphorus, Bishop of Rome from 125 to 136, decreed that it be sung in all churches on Christmas Eve; others date the origin in the third century; still others in the eighteenth century. It sometimes is called the Westminster Carol because it is performed in England's Westminster Abbey at Christmas time. Some believe it originated in France, and others attribute it to French descendents in Quebec. Regardless of origin, it remains a favorite of people throughout the world at the Christmas season.

Humpty Dumpty

MOTHER GOOSE RHYME

J. W. ELLIOTT

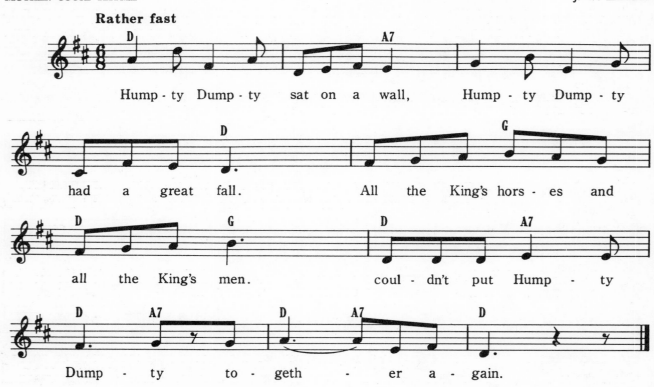

Hump - ty Dump - ty sat on a wall, Hump - ty Dump - ty

had a great fall. All the King's hors - es and

all the King's men. coul - dn't put Hump - ty

Dump - ty to - geth - er a - gain.

The Caisson Song

EDMUND L. GRUBER

EDMUND L. GRUBER

1. O - ver hill, o - ver dale, we have hit the dust - y

trail And those cais - sons go roll - ing a - long._____ In and

48

quarter
rest

The Caisson Song

out hear them shout "Count-er march and right a-bout" And those

cais-sons go roll-ing a-long.

Chorus

Then it's Hi! Hi! Hee! in the Field Ar-til-ler-y,

Sound off your num-bers loud and strong. Where

e'er you go you will al-ways know that those

cais-sons are roll-ing a-long, Keep them roll-ing, And those

cais-sons go roll-ing a-long.

2. Through the storm, through the night,
   Up to where the doughboys fight,
   And our Caissons go rolling along.
   At zero we'll be there,
   Answering every call and flare,
   While our Caissons go rolling along.

This is the official song of the United States Field Artillery. At one time the composer of the stirring march tune was in dispute. John Philip Sousa claimed to have written *The Field Artillery March*, subtitled *The Caisson Song*, for a special benefit concert at the New York Hippodrome during a Liberty Bond drive. It later was established that Sousa's instrumental version came out in 1918, and that *The Caisson Song* as we know it today was written by Lieutenant (Later Brigadier General) Edmund L. Gruber in 1908 while he was on a tour of duty in the Philippines. *The Caisson Song* was published in 1921 with proper credit to Gruber.

Blow the Winds Southerly
ROUND

Smoothly
ENGLAND

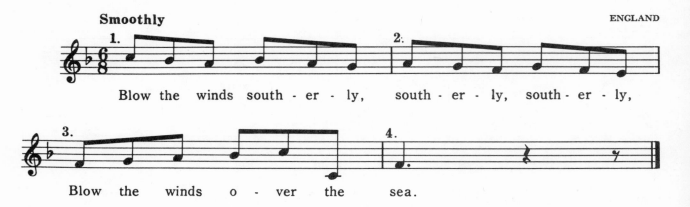

Blow the winds south - er - ly, south - er - ly, south - er - ly,

Blow the winds o - ver the sea.

Rounds were highly popular in England during the seventeenth and eighteenth centuries, and were sung on convivial occasions. The form goes back to the medieval *rota* (wheel), of which the most famous example is *Sumer Is Icumen In*.

I Saw Three Ships

Festively
ENGLAND

1. I saw three ships come sail - ing in On Christ - mas Day, on Christ - mas Day, I

saw three ships come sail - ing in On Christ - mas Day in the morn - ing.

2. And what was in those ships all three?
3. The Virgin Mary and Christ were there
4. Pray whither sailed those ships all three?
5. O they sailed into Bethlehem

6. And all the bells on earth shall ring
7. And all the angels in heaven shall sing
8. And all the souls on earth shall sing
9. Then let us all rejoice amain

Experts believe that this legendary carol is at least 500 years old, and possibly much older. It was among the first carols published in England where it still is a favorite. Songs reflecting distinctive features of their land of origin are common. Countries bordering on or surrounded by water often have songs about sailing and the sea. In this carol the cargo is precious, and the three ships often are associated with the three Wise Men and the three traditional gifts.

50

Joy to the World

ISAAC WATTS

LOWELL MASON

Joyously

1. Joy to the world! the Lord is come; Let earth re - ceive her King; _____ Let ev - 'ry _____ heart _____ pre - pare _____ Him _____ room, _____ And heav'n and na - ture _____ sing, And _____ heav'n and na - ture _____ sing, And _____ heav'n _____ and heav'n _____ and na - ture sing.

2. Joy to the world! the Savior reigns; let men their songs employ;
While fields and floods, rocks, hills and plains,
Repeat the sounding joy, repeat the sounding joy,
Repeat, repeat the sounding joy.

3. He rules the world with truth and grace, and makes the nations prove
The glories of His righteousness,
And wonders of His love, and wonders of His love,
And wonders, and wonders of His love.

The words of *Joy to the World* come from Isaac Watts' *The Psalms of David in the Language of the New Testament* published in 1719. The musical setting was provided by Lowell Mason more than a century later. The melody has been widely attributed, probably erroneously, to Handel.

Jennie Jenkins

With animation

U. S.

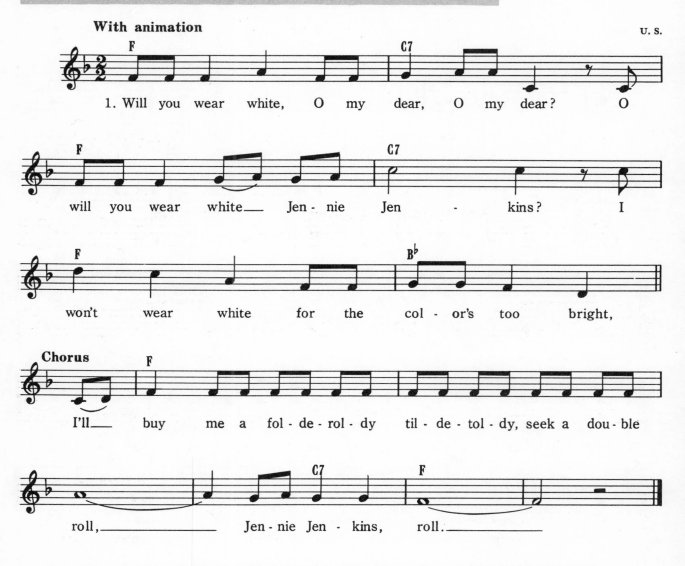

1. Will you wear white, O my dear, O my dear? O will you wear white Jen-nie Jen - kins? I won't wear white for the col - or's too bright,

Chorus
I'll buy me a fol-de-rol-dy til-de-tol-dy, seek a dou-ble roll, Jen-nie Jen-kins, roll.

2. Will you wear red, O my dear, O my dear? Oh, will you wear red, Jennie Jenkins?
   I won't wear red, it's the color of my head; etc.
3. Will you wear blue, O my dear, O my dear? Oh, will you wear blue, Jennie Jenkins?
   I will wear blue, if your love is true; etc.
4. Will you wear green, O my dear, O my dear? Oh, will you wear green, Jennie Jenkins?
   I won't wear green, it's a shame to be seen, etc.
5. Will you wear purple, O my dear, O my dear? Oh, will you wear purple, Jennie Jenkins?
   I won't wear purple, it's the color of a turtle; etc.
6. Will you wear black, O my dear, O my dear? Oh, will you wear black, Jennie Jenkins?
   I won't wear black, it's the color of my back, etc.
7. What will you wear, O my dear, O my dear? Oh, what will you wear, Jennie Jenkins?
   I have nothing to wear, I can't go anywhere, etc.

Jennie Jenkins

Dialogue and conversation songs like *Jennie Jenkins* were popular in early America. In this song the nonsense syllables traditionally are sung as rapidly as possible. Colors are associated with similar meanings in this folk song and in an old jingle:

Married in white, it will turn out all right.
Married in red, you'll come out ahead.
Married in blue, you'll always be true.
Married in green, ashamed to be seen.
Married in black, you'll wish yourself back.
Married in yellow, catch another fellow.

Reveille

U. S. ARMY BUGLE CALL

Lively

I can't get 'em up, I can't get 'em up, I can't get 'em up in the morn - ing, I can't get 'em up I can't get 'em up, I can't get 'em up at all.

Fine

The corp - 'rals worse than pri - vates, The ser - geants worse than corp - 'rals, Lieu - ten - ants worse than ser - geants, And cap - tains worst of all.

D.C.

Reveille (rev-ah-lee) is sounded at the time set for members of the Armed Forces to arise for the first assembly of the day. Various sets of words have been sung to this famous bugle call.

Baa, Baa, Black Sheep

MOTHER GOOSE RHYME

FRANCE

Lightly

Baa, baa, black sheep have you an-y wool?

"Yes, sir, yes, sir, three bags full.

One for my mas-ter and one for my dame, And

one for the lit-tle boy who lives in the lane;"

Baa, baa, black sheep have you an-y wool?

"Yes, sir, yes, sir, three bags full."

This is another version of the melody used for *Twinkle, Twinkle Little Star*. Several famous composers, including Mozart (1756-1791) and Dohnanyi (1877-1960), have used it in their compositions. The origin of this nursery rhyme is not established.

54

Pony Song

GERMANY

Unpretentiously

Hop, hop, hop, Go and nev-er stop.

Where its smooth and where its ston-y, Go a-long my lit-tle po-ny.

Go and nev-er stop, Hop, hop, hop, hop, hop.

Pawpaw Patch

SOUTHERN U. S.

Playfully

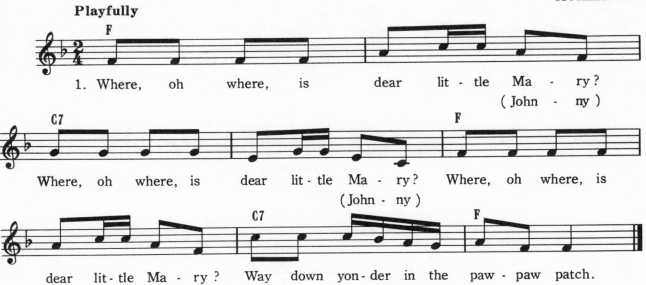

1. Where, oh where, is dear lit-tle Ma-ry?
(John - ny)

Where, oh where, is dear lit-tle Ma-ry? Where, oh where, is
(John - ny)

dear lit-tle Ma-ry? Way down yon-der in the paw-paw patch.

2. Come on, boys (girls), let's go and find her (him), etc.
3. Picking pawpaws, filling her (his) pockets, etc.

In this singing game the names of boys and girls reluctant to join in group activities are sung as a means of encouraging participation. It also is popular as a square dance tune. A pawpaw is an oblong, yellow fruit which grows on tropical trees in central and southern United States, Hawaii, and the Philippines.

All Creatures of Our God and King

ST. FRANCIS OF ASSISI

TR. W. H. DRAPER

GERMANY

2. Thou rushing wind that art so strong,
Ye clouds that sail in heaven along,
O praise Him! Alleluia!
Thou rising morn, in praise rejoice,
Ye lights of evening, find a voice,
O praise Him, O praise Him!
Alleluia! Alleluia! Alleluia!

3. Thou flowing water, pure and clear,
Make music for thy Lord to hear,
Alleluia! Alleluia!
Thou fire so masterful and bright
That givest man both warmth and light,
O praise Him, O praise Him!
Alleluia! Alleluia! Alleluia!

All Creatures of Our God and King

> 4. Dear Mother Earth, who day by day
> Unfoldest blessings on our way,
> O praise Him, Alleluia!
> The flowers and fruits that in thee grow,
> Let them His glory also show,
> O praise Him, O praise Him!
> Alleluia! Alleluia! Alleluia!

St. Francis was born in the small Italian hill town of Assisi in 1182. He was the son of a wealthy cloth merchant and was indulged by his parents in every possible way. He was the leader of a mischievous group of young men who were noted for their escapades. After a serious illness Francis decided that his life was a shallow one and turned to religion. He gave himself to a life of rigorous proverty in 1208 and founded the Franciscans, or Gray Friars as they are sometimes called. He took the life of Jesus as his ideal and preached for years. When he knew he did not have long to live, he visited Sister Clara, a dear friend who had also forsaken wealth and station and taken vows of poverty. During St. Francis' visit at St. Damian Convent he wrote *The Canticle of the Sun*. It was translated by the Rev. William H. Draper in 1910, and these words are the ones we sing today to the melody of a German Chorale.

Mary's Lullaby

DAVID STEVENS

POLAND

Soothingly

> 1. Ma-ry___ sang soft-ly that night by the___ man-ger:
> "Sleep, sleep,___ my Babe, I will guard Thee from dan-ger.
> An-gels, bright___ an-gels,___ their___ night watch are keep-ing."
> Ma-ry___ sang soft-ly while Je-sus lay sleep-ing.

> 2. Mary sang sweetly as shepherds were kneeling:
> "Sleep, while in heaven the joy bells are pealing.
> Sleep, Thou, till dawn o'er the mountain comes peeping."
> Mary sang softly while Jesus lay sleeping.

Annie Laurie

WILLIAM DOUGLAS

LADY JOHN SCOTT

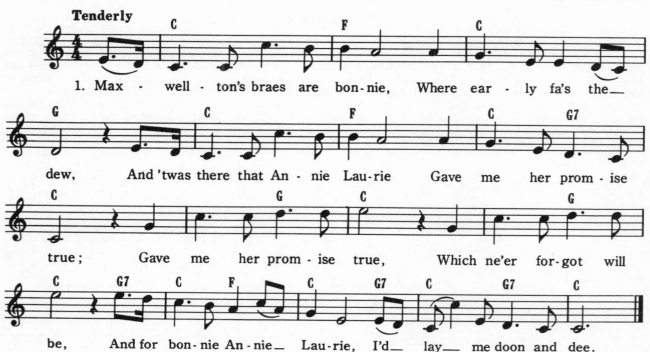

1. Max - well - ton's braes are bon-nie, Where ear-ly fa's the dew, And 'twas there that An - nie Lau-rie Gave me her prom-ise true; Gave me her prom-ise true, Which ne'er for-got will be, And for bon-nie An-nie Lau-rie, I'd lay me doon and dee.

2. Her brow is like the snowdrift,
   Her throat is like the swan,
   Her face, it is the fairest
   That e'er the sun shone on;
   That e'er the sun shone on,
   And dark blue is her e'e,
   And for bonnie Annie Laurie
   I'd lay me doon and dee.

3. Like dew on th' gowan lying
   Is th' fa' o her fairy feet,
   And like winds in summer sighing,
   Her voice is low and sweet;
   Her voice is low and sweet,
   And she's a' the world to me,
   And for bonnie Annie Laurie
   I'd lay me doon and dee.

This version of *Annie Laurie* was first published in 1838. The heroine was the daughter of Sir Robert Laurie, first Baronet of Maxwelltown, who lived on the Nith River in southern Scotland. The first two verses were written by William Douglas in 1685 in tribute to Annie and to express his love for her. Annie married another despite this devotion. The music was written by Lady John Scott, who may also have written the third verse. This Scottish dialect song was very popular with British troups during the Crimean war.

The Girl I Left Behind Me

BRITISH ISLES

With vitality

1. I'm__ lone-some since I crossed the hill and o'er the moor__ and__ val-ley, Such__ heav-y thoughts my heart do fill since part-ing with my__ Sal-ly I__ seek no more the fine and gay, for each does but re-mind me, How__ swift the hours did pass a-way with the girl I left be-hind me.

2. Oh, I never shall forget the night, the stars were twinkling bright above me,
   And they gently shed their silvery light when first she vowed to love me.
   But now I'm off for Brighton Camp, and may good favor find me,
   And send me safely back again to the girl I left behind me.

3. My thoughts her beauty shall retain if sleeping or if waking,
   Until I see my love again, for her my heart is aching.
   Whenever I return that way, if she should not decline me,
   I have vowed I evermore will stay with the girl I left behind me.

4. The bee shall honey taste no more, the dove become a ranger,
   And the ocean's waves shall cease to roar before to me she's a stranger.
   The vows we made when last we met shall never cease to bind me,
   And my heart will ever more be true to the girl I left behind me.

The origin of this melody is uncertain. It was known in the eighteenth century as *Brighton Camp*. Some authorities date the music around 1758, and the words about 1770. Both were printed in Ireland in 1791. The song has enjoyed wide appeal, and the verses which have been sung to it are many. It probably is one of the finest fife and drum tunes ever known. Both British and American fifers and drummers play it regularly. It also is a favorite parade and march tune, square-dance melody, and stage song. It is the traditional leave-taking song of the British army.

Auld Lang Syne

ROBERT BURNS   SCOTLAND

With nostalgia

1. Should auld ac-quaint-ance be for-got, And nev-er brought to mind? Should auld ac-quaint-ance be for-got, And days of auld lang syne?

Chorus

For auld lang syne, my dear, For auld lang syne; We'll take a cup of kind-ness yet for auld lang syne.

2. We twa ha'e ran aboot the braes,
   And pu'd the gowans fine,
   We're wander'd mony a weary foot
   Sin auld lang syne.

3. We twa ha'e sported i' the burn
   Frae mornin' sun till dine,
   But seas between us braid ha'e roared
   Sin auld lang syne.

4. And here's a hand, my trusty friend,
   And gie's a hand of thine;
   We'll take a cup of kindness yet
   For auld lang syne.

This ancient Scottish folk song has come to be both a traditional song of parting and a salute to the new year. Popular at social gatherings, it came to the colonies with settlers from the British Isles in the seventeenth century. In Scotland it is sung on the birthday of their famous poet, Robert Burns (January 25, 1759), who revived it. He sent a copy of the original song to the British Museum in 1791 with the note, "The following song, an old song of olden times and which has never been in print, nor even in manuscript until I took it down from an old man's singing, is enough to recommend any air." A version of the tune we now use was included by William Shield in the overture of his opera, *Rosina*, at Covent Garden in 1783. Some scholars believe he wrote it.

Wondrous Love

SOUTHERN U. S.

Plaintively

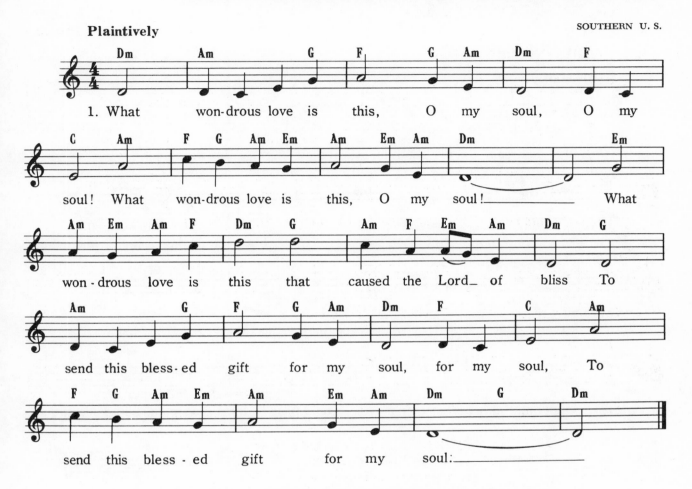

1. What won-drous love is this, O my soul, O my soul! What won-drous love is this, O my soul!_____ What won-drous love is this that caused the Lord of bliss To send this bless-ed gift for my soul, for my soul, To send this bless-ed gift for my soul:_____

2. When I was sinking down, sinking down, sinking down,
   When I was sinking down, sinking down;
   When I was sinking down beneath God's righteous frown,
   Christ laid aside His crown for my soul, for my soul,
   Christ laid aside His crown for my soul.

3. And when from death I'm free, I'll sing on, I'll sing on,
   And when from death I'm free, I'll sing on;
   And when from death I'm free, I'll sing and joyful be,
   And through eternity I'll sing on, I'll sing on,
   And through eternity I'll sing on.

The back country and the frontier experienced an extended period of religious revival starting in 1800. Virtually all denominations participated. The great revival movement swept through the West, and pioneer people attended camp meetings and revival services by the tens of thousands. *Wondrous Love* was born of this climate and reflects the tenor of the period. The melody is based on a scale (Dorian) which is now less usual but which is much older than present-day major and minor. The tonal center of the melody is D, but there are no sharps or flats in the key signature. The harmonization is based on the same scale as the melody to preserve its quaint flavor.

Jeanie With the Light Brown Hair

STEPHEN C. FOSTER

STEPHEN C. FOSTER

Dreamily

1. I dream of Jean-ie with the light brown hair,
Borne, like a va-por, on the sum-mer air; I see her trip-ping where the
bright streams play, Hap-py as the dais - sies that dance on her way.
Man-y were the wild notes her mer-ry voice would pour, Man-y were the blithe birds that
war - bled them o'er: Oh!___ I dream of Jean - ie with the
light brown hair, Float-ing, like a va-por, on the soft sum-mer air.

2. I long for Jeanie with the day dawn smile,
   Radiant in gladness, warm with winning guile;
   I hear her melodies, like joys gone by,
   Sighing with my heart o'er the fond hopes that die.
   Moaning like the night wind, and sobbing like the rain,
   Wailing for a lost love that comes not again;
   I long for Jeanie and my heart hangs low,
   Never more I'll find her where the bright waters flow.

Jeanie With the Light Brown Hair

> 3. I sigh for Jeanie, but her light form strayed
> Far from the fond hearts 'round her native glade;
> Her smiles have vanished and her sweet songs flown,
> Flitting like the dreams that have cheered us and gone.
> Now, the nodding wild flowers lay withered on the shore,
> And her gentle fingers will pluck them no more;
> I long for Jeanie with the light brown hair,
> Floating like a vapor, on the soft summer air.

Stephen Foster (1826-1864) wrote this song in 1854 as a tribute to his wife, Jane McDowell, whom he called Jean or Jeanie. It was dedicated to her and advertised as a song "embellished with a beautiful vignette." It scored another hit for Foster, who was the best-loved popular song writer in the nation at that time. Seven years later the Civil War broke out, and Foster dropped to virtual obscurity. Born in Pennsylvania, he was a northerner who wrote songs about the South, all complimentary and some sentimental in character. He became estranged from both factions. He died in a New York hospital, alone and destitute, four months before the war ended. It was years before his songs regained their rightful place in the musical heritage of America. In 1937, a Stephen Foster memorial was dedicated on the campus of the University of Pittsburgh.

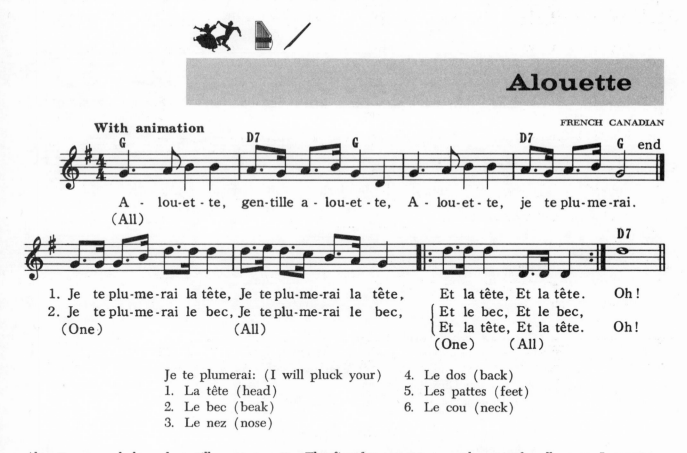

Alouette

FRENCH CANADIAN

With animation

A - lou-et - te, gen-tille a - lou-et - te, A - lou-et - te, je te plu-me-rai.
(All)

1. Je te plu-me-rai la tête, Je te plu-me-rai la tête,   Et la tête, Et la tête.   Oh!
2. Je te plu-me-rai le bec, Je te plu-me-rai le bec,   { Et le bec, Et le bec,
   (One)   (All)   { Et la tête, Et la tête.   Oh!
                                                           (One)   (All)

Je te plumerai: (I will pluck your)   4. Le dos (back)
1. La tête (head)   5. Les pattes (feet)
2. Le bec (beak)   6. Le cou (neck)
3. Le nez (nose)

Alouette means lark, and *gentille* means pretty. The first four measures are the same for all verses. In measures five and six a different part of the body is named in each verse. In the repeated measure the words of all previous verses are sung in reverse order before proceeding to the next measure. After the last verse the first four measures are sung again to end the song. To make this an action song, point to the parts of the body as they are named.

The words to this Canadian voyageur song are adapted to an old French melody. It originally was a canoe paddling song. The lark is commonplace in France and the British Isles, and is a favorite cage bird there. It also flourishes in British Columbia and on Vancouver Island. Its famous stirring song, often sung in flight, is familiar to Canadians.

63

Fum, Fum, Fum

Placidly

CATALONIA

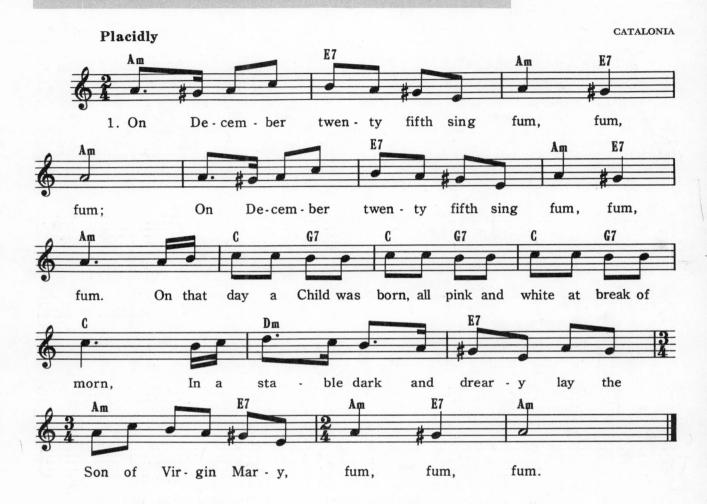

1. On De-cem-ber twen-ty fifth sing fum, fum, fum; On De-cem-ber twen-ty fifth sing fum, fum, fum. On that day a Child was born, all pink and white at break of morn, In a sta-ble dark and drear-y lay the Son of Vir-gin Mar-y, fum, fum, fum.

2. Christmas is a day of feasting, fum, fum, fum,
Christmas is a day of feasting, fum, fum, fum.
In hot lands and in cold, for young and old, for young and old,
We tell the Christmas story,
Ever singing of its glory, fum, fum, fum.

1. Veinticinco de dicembre, fum, fum, fum.
Veinticinco de dicembre, fum, fum, fum.
Nacido ha por nuestro amor, el Niño Dios, el Niño Dios;
Hoy de la Virgen Maria en esta noche tan fria,
Fum, fum, fum.

This lovely folk carol is written in the minor mode, and comes from the old province of Catalonia in the northeastern part of Spain. In olden times, children are said to have marched to the rhythm of this carol during the Christmas season as they spread good will around the countryside. Fum is pronounced "foom."

64

Sumer Is Icumen In
ROUND

Merrily

ENGLAND

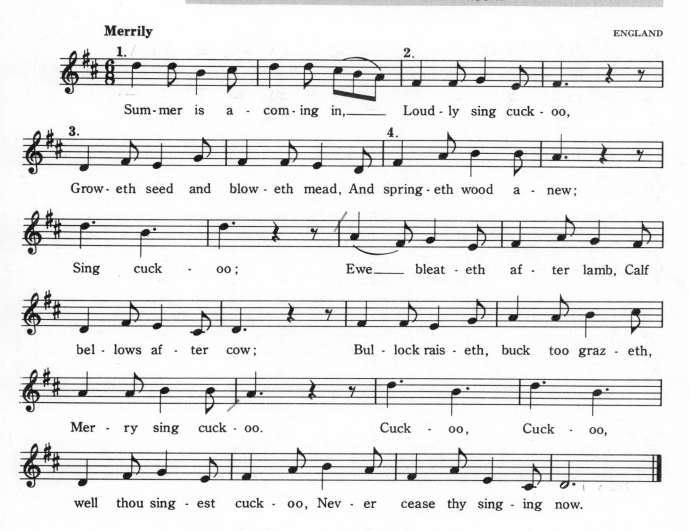

Sum-mer is a - com-ing in,____ Loud-ly sing cuck-oo,

Grow-eth seed and blow-eth mead, And spring-eth wood a - new;

Sing cuck - oo; Ewe____ bleat-eth af - ter lamb, Calf

bel - lows af - ter cow; Bul - lock rais - eth, buck too graz - eth,

Mer - ry sing cuck - oo. Cuck - oo, Cuck - oo,

well thou sing - est cuck - oo, Nev - er cease thy sing - ing now.

Sumer is icumen in, lhude sing cucu,
Groweth sed and bloweth med, and springth the woode nu;
Sing cucu;
Awe bleteth after lomb, louth after calve cu;
Bulloc sterteth, bucke verteth, murie sing cucu.
Cucu, cucu wel singes thu cucu,
Ne swik thu naver nu.

This is one of the monuments in the history of music. The original manuscript is preserved in the British Museum. The manuscript is in the hand of John of Fornsete, monk of Reading Abbey, and may have been written by him. Some scholars date the manuscript as early as 1226, others as late as 1310. It is the earliest example of the form which has been preserved, but the complexity and perfection of the round suggests an extended development. Since rounds can be learned by rote and sung from memory, it is possible that similar rounds existed during the period but were either lost or never written down. The manuscript copy of *Sumer Is Icumen In* has a Latin text inscribed below the Middle English, but the way the words fit leaves little doubt that the melody and the English poem of spring were conceived to go together.

Old MacDonald Had a Farm

Not dragging

U. S.

The introduction is sung only once. The first verse (without repeat) and refrain follow in order. After the second verse, the section of the first verse between the repeat signs is repeated before the refrain. Additional verses may be added at will using the names and sounds of various farm animals, for example:

3. Turkey — gobble, gobble

4. Pig — oink, oink

After each new verse, the parts of all previous verses between the repeat signs are sung in reverse order before going on to the refrain. Following the last verse and all repeated sections, the refrain is sung louder and slower for the final time.

The Wraggle Taggle Gypsies

Not too slowly

BRITISH ISLES

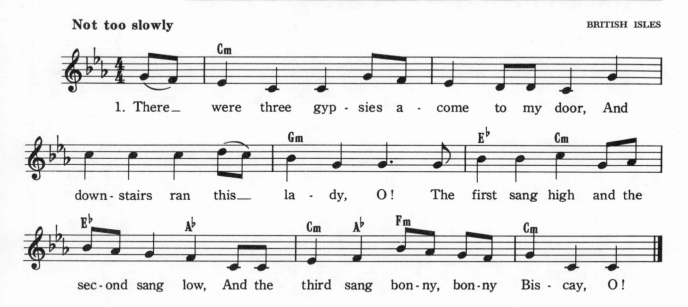

1. There were three gyp-sies a-come to my door, And down-stairs ran this la-dy, O! The first sang high and the sec-ond sang low, And the third sang bon-ny, bon-ny Bis-cay, O!

2. Then she pulled off her silk finished gown, and put on hose of leather, O!
   The ragged ragged rags about our door, she's gone with the wraggle taggle gypsies, O!

3. It was late last night when my lord came home, inquiring for his lady, O!
   The servants said, on every hand, she's gone with the wraggle taggle gypsies, O!

4. O saddle for me my milk-white steed, and go fetch me my pony, O!
   That I may ride and seek my bride who is gone with the wraggle taggle gypsies, O!

5. O he rode high and he rode low, he rode through woods and copses too,
   Until he came to an open field, and there he espied his lady, O!

6. What makes you leave your house and land? What makes you leave your money, O!
   What makes you leave your wedded lord to join with the wraggle taggle gypsies, O!

7. What care I for my house and land? What care I for my money, O!
   What care I for my new wedded lord? I'm off with the wraggle taggle gypsies, O!

8. Last night you slept on a goose-feather bed, with the sheet turned down so bravely, O!
   Tonight you'll sleep in a cold open field along with the wraggle taggle gypsies, O!

9. What care I for a goose-feather bed with the sheet turned down so bravely, O!
   Tonight I shall sleep in a cold open field along with the wraggle taggle gypsies, O!

Gypsies are a wandering nation of uncertain origin, but believed to have come from India. The main body of their language, though mixed with many borrowed words, has close affinity with some of the Indian languages. In appearance they generally are similar with olive or yellow-brown skin, black hair and eyes, and very white teeth. They rarely settle anywhere permanently, often live in tents, support themselves telling fortunes or working in wood and iron, making domestic items. Their talent for music is outstanding, and many of their melodies are lovely. They first appeared in Germany and Italy about the beginning of the fifteenth century, and in England about the beginning of the sixteenth century. In Scotland they were more favorably received, and frequently intermarried with the natives. The town of Yetholm, in Roxburghshire, became a sort of headquarters for the entire race, and was inhabited almost entirely by gypsies. Gypsies were banished from Scotland in 1624. *The Wraggle Taggle Gypsies* is a ballad which probably relates an actual love of a noble lady for a roving gypsy and her decision to follow him rather than spend the rest of her life with her noble bridegroom in his uneventful castle.

Columbia, the Gem of the Ocean

With pride

U. S.

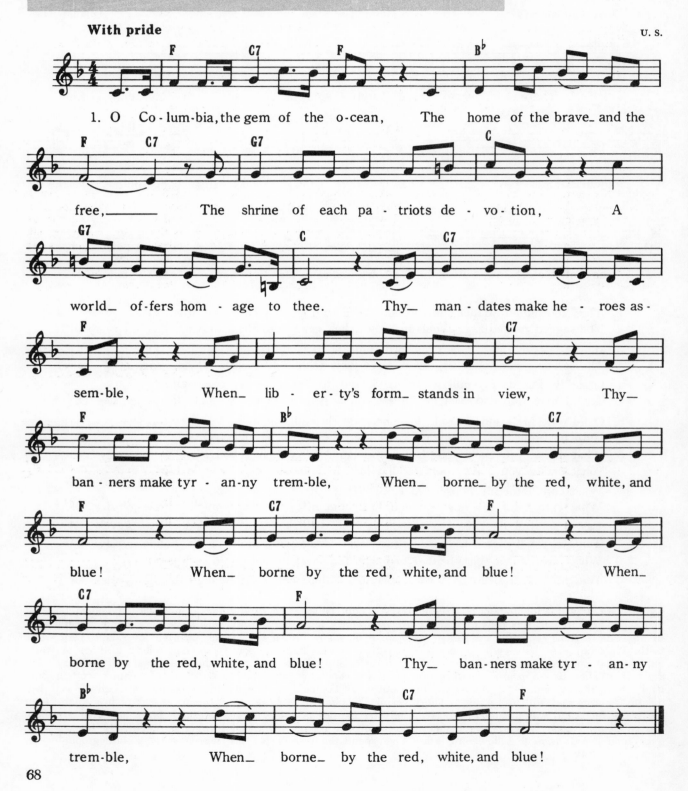

1. O Co·lum·bia, the gem of the o·cean, The home of the brave_ and the

free,_____ The shrine of each pa·triots de·vo·tion, A

world_ of·fers hom·age to thee. Thy_ man·dates make he·roes as·

sem·ble, When_ lib·er·ty's form_ stands in view, Thy_

ban·ners make tyr·an·ny trem·ble, When_ borne_ by the red, white, and

blue! When_ borne by the red, white, and blue! When_

borne by the red, white, and blue! Thy_ ban·ners make tyr·an·ny

trem·ble, When_ borne_ by the red, white, and blue!

68

Columbia, the Gem of the Ocean

2. When war winged its wide desolation,
   And threatened the land to deform,
   The ark then of freedom's foundation,
   Columbia rode safe through the storm
   With her garlands of victory around her,
   When so proudly she bore her brave crew
   With her flag proudly floating before her,
   The boast of the red, white, and blue!
   The boast of the red, white, and blue!
   The boast of the red, white, and blue!
   With her flag proudly floating before her,
   The boast of the red, white, and blue!

3. The Star-Spangled Banner bring hither,
   O'er Columbia's true sons let it wave;
   May the wreaths they have won never wither
   Nor its stars cease to shine on the brave;
   May thy service, united ne'er sever,
   But hold to their colors so true;
   The army and navy forever,
   Three cheers for the red, white, and blue!
   Three cheers for the red, white, and blue!
   Three cheers for the red, white, and blue!
   The army and navy forever,
   Three cheers for the red, white, and blue!

The origin of this song is uncertain, and it has been claimed both in the United States and in Great Britain. According to some authorities, Irish journalist Stephen Joseph Meany wrote the words in 1842 for a theatrical benefit and set them to a tune of the period composed by Thomas E. Williams. This English version was entitled *Britannia, The Pride of the Ocean.* Evidence seems to indicate, however, that the song was written in America in 1843 by actor Thomas a'Becket during the period he was appearing at the Chestnut Street Theatre in Philadelphia. In a letter written to Rear Admiral George Henry Preble December 16, 1876, a'Becket stated that in the fall of 1843 singer David T. Shaw had requested him to write a song to be presented at a benefit performance. He complied with his friend's request and wrote *Columbia, the Gem of the Ocean* which Shaw sang in the Chestnut Street Theatre in 1843. Soon after, the song was published naming Shaw as the writer, composer, and singer. The dismayed a'Becket took his original pencil manuscript to the publisher, and subsequent printings carried the credit "written and composed by T. a'Becket and sung by David T. Shaw." According to a'Becket, the song later was introduced in England by singer T. Williams of Cheapside and after achieving great popularity, was published there without authorization under the title *Britannia, The Pride of the Ocean.*

Barnyard Song

KENTUCKY MOUNTAINS

1. I had a bird, and the bird pleased me, I fed my bird by yon-der tree;
2. I had a hen, and the hen pleased me, I fed my hen by yon-der tree;

(2.) Hen goes chim-my chuck, chim-my chuck, Bird goes fid-dle-ee - fee.

3. Duck: quack, quack
4. Goose: swishy, swashy
5. Sheep: baa, baa

6. Pig: griffy, gruffy
7. Cow: moo, moo
8. Horse: neigh, neigh
   etc.

Omit the three-four measure in the first verse and sing it only once in the second. After the second verse sing the animal names and sounds of all the previous verses in reverse order before going on to "Bird goes fiddle-ee-fee."

Bring a Torch, Jeannette, Isabella

Joyfully

FRANCE

1. Bring a torch,— Jean - nette, Is - a - bel - la, Bring a torch— and quick - ly run. Christ is born,— good folk of the vil - lage, Christ— is born and Ma - ry's call - ing, Ah! ah! beau - ti - ful is the Moth - er, Ah! ah! beau - ti - ful is Her Son.

2. Quiet all nor waken Jesus, quiet all and whisper low,
   Silence all, and gather around Him, talk and noise might waken Jesus,
   Hush, hush, quietly now He slumbers, hush, hush, quietly now He sleeps.

3. Come and see within the stable, come and see the Holy One,
   Come and see the lovely Jesus, white His brow, His cheeks are rosy,
   Hush, hush, quietly now He slumbers, hush, hush, quietly now He sleeps.

1. Un flambeau, Jeannette, Isabella, Un flambeau, Courons au berceau.
   C'est Jésus, bonnes gens du hameau, Le Christ est né, Marie appelle.
   Ah! Ah! Ah! que la Mère est belle!
   Ah! Ah! Ah! que l'Enfant est beau.

In Europe, torches or candles are widely used and figure importantly in the celebration of Christmas. Torches and candles were used in the Jewish Hanukkah or Festival Of Lights. This carol from Provence, France, is a lovely example of an old torch song.

America

SAMUEL FRANCIS SMITH

HENRY CAREY

Expressively

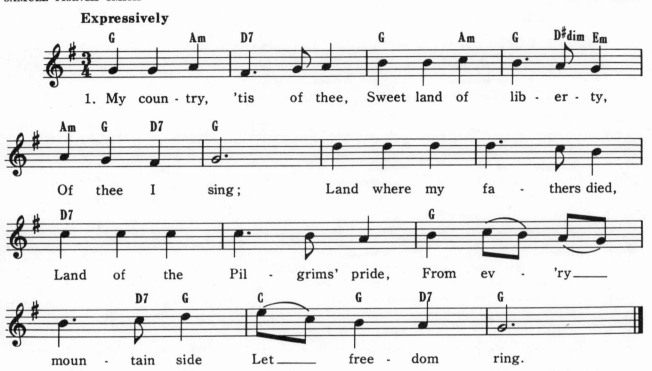

1. My coun - try, 'tis of thee, Sweet land of lib - er - ty,
Of thee I sing; Land where my fa - thers died,
Land of the Pil - grims' pride, From ev - 'ry____
moun - tain side Let____ free - dom ring.

2. My native country, thee, land of the noble free,
   Thy name I love.
   I love thy rocks and rills, thy woods and templed hills,
   My heart with rapture thrills
   Like that above.

3. Let music swell the breeze, and ring from all the trees
   Sweet freedom's song.
   Let mortal tongues awake, let all that breathe partake,
   Let rocks their silence break,
   The sound prolong.

4. Our fathers' God, to Thee, Author of liberty,
   To Thee we sing.
   Long may our land be bright with freedom's holy light,
   Protect us by Thy might,
   Great God, our King!

The origins of this melody are unknown. The present version is attributed to Henry Carey, an Englishman who first sang it in 1740 at a dinner party being held in celebration of a naval victory. Carey claimed to have written both the words and music to this song he called *God Save Great George, Our King*. The words to *America* were written by the Rev. Samuel Francis Smith, clergyman and a language professor at Colby College. They first were sung in 1831 at a children's Fourth of July celebration in Boston's Park Street Church. This song was very popular during the Civil War.

Camptown Races
(DO-DA-DAY)   (SACRAMENTO)

STEPHEN C. FOSTER   STEPHEN C. FOSTER

With humor

1. The Camp-town la-dies sing this song, do-da, do-da! The
Camp-town race track five miles long, Oh, do-da-day. Oh,
see those hor-ses round the bend, do-da, do-da!
Guess that race will nev-er end, Oh, do-da-day.

Chorus

Going to run all night, going to run all day, I'll
bet my mon-ey on the bob-tail nag, Some-bod-y bet on the bay.

2. The long tail filly and the big black horse, do-da, do-da,
   They flew the track, and both cut across, Oh, do-da day.
   The blind horse sticking in a big mud hole, do-da, do-da,
   Couldn't touch bottom with a ten-foot pole, Oh, do-da day.
3. See them fly on a ten-mile heat, do-da, do-da,
   Around the track, and then repeat, Oh, do-da day.
   I win my money on the bob-tail nag, do-da, do-da,
   I keep my money in an old towbag, Oh, do-da day.
4. Old muley cow came on the track, do-da, do-da,
   The bob-tail threw her over his back, Oh, do-da day.
   Then flew along like a railroad car, do-da, do-da,
   Like running a race with a shooting star, Oh, do-da day.

Camptown Races

SACRAMENTO

1. As I was walking on the quay, Hoo-dah to my hoo-dah,
   A pretty girl I chanced to see, Hoo-dah hoo-dah day.
   Her hair was brown, her eyes were blue, Hoo-dah to my hoo-dah,
   Her lips were red and sweet to view, Hoo-dah hoo-dah day.

Chorus: Blow, boys, blow for Californio.
           There's plenty of gold, so I've been told,
           On the banks of the Sacramento.

2. I tipped my hat and said "How do?" Hoo-dah to my hoo-dah,
   She bowed and said, "Quite well, thank you." Hoo-dah hoo-dah day.
   I asked her then to come with me, Hoo-dah to my hoo-dah,
   Down to the dock my ship to see, Hoo-dah hoo-dah day.

3. She promptly answered "Oh, dear, no." Hoo-dah to my hoo-dah,
   "I thank you, but I cannot go." Hoo-dah hoo-dah day.
   "I have a sweetheart young and true," Hoo-dah to my hoo-dah,
   "And I can't give my love to you." Hoo-dah hoo-dah day.

4. I said "Farewell" and strode away, Hoo-dah to my hoo-dah,
   Although with her I longed to stay, Hoo-dah hoo-dah day.
   And as I bade this girl adieu, Hoo-dah to my hoo-dah,
   I said that girls like her were few, Hoo-dah hoo-dah day.

In 1850 Stephen Foster (1826-1864) wrote a minstrel show hit that was the top song of the year, *The Camptown Races*. It originally was published under the title *Gwine To Run All Night*. Foster was largely a self-taught musician since he was unable to obtain formal music training. He enrolled in Jefferson College in 1841, but his attendance there was brief. The twentieth century has brought an increasing interest in the enduring and loved music of Foster and in his life. Various shrines and memorials have been erected in his memory. For the songs he contributed to America, he is more famous than his father who twice was mayor of Allegheny City, or than his brother who figured prominently in the building of the Pennsylvania Railroad. Many verses to *The Camptown Races* have been improvised to fit desired situations. Some authorities believe that the words to *Sacramento* may have been adapted to the Foster melody by American sailing men shipping out to California in the gold rush days. However, there is no proof of which song came first. In some versions of *Sacramento* the nonsense syllables vary, and "do-da day" is used. With a minimum of adaptation, both songs may be sung to the Stephen Foster melody.

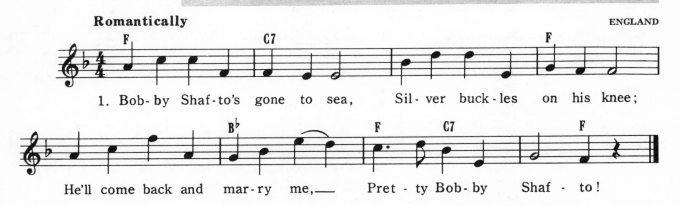

Bobby Shafto

Romantically

ENGLAND

1. Bob-by Shaf-to's gone to sea, Sil-ver buck-les on his knee;
   He'll come back and mar-ry me,— Pret-ty Bob-by Shaf-to!

2. Bobby Shafto's fine and fair,   He's my love for ever more,
   Combing out his yellow hair;   Pretty Bobby Shafto!

The Skaters' Waltz

CHRISTINE TURNER CURTIS

EMIL WALDTEUFEL

Waltz tempo

Skat - ers, a - way! _____ Glide,

glide and sway, _____ Dart - ing and

fly - ing like gulls at play. _____ On your

sil - ver - y skates you go swirl - ing, swirl - ing,

O - ver the ice mad - ly whirl - ing, whirl - ing,

Scarves in the breez - es un - furl - ing, furl - ing.

Clink, ting - a - ling, a - ling, ting - a - ling, a - ling, ling _____ On your

sil - ver - y blades you go swirl - ing swirl - ing,

The Skaters' Waltz

From *On Wings of Song* of *The World of Music* series, copyright 1945, 1949 by Ginn and Company. Used by permission.

The waltz is a dance in moderate triple time which developed from the Ländler, an Austrian peasant dance, about the middle of the eighteenth century. The introduction of the waltz marked an epoch in social dancing, because partners for the first time danced in the embracing position. The reactions to this innovation ranged from wild enthusiasm to violent protest, much like the reactions to early jazz and the dancing of the "roaring twenties." In the 1760's waltzing achieved great popularity in spite of, or perhaps because of, being banned. The poet Goethe learned the dance during his student days, and knowing it became a requirement for the social elite on the continent. By 1791 the dance had reached England, and Lord Byron was deploring its indecorum. Within a few decades, however, it was accepted in royal circles and danced by Queen Victoria. Its popularity remains undiminished to this day. Emil Waldteufel (1837-1915) was a master composer of the waltz. He was born in Strasbourg but lived most of his life in Paris. In 1865 he was appointed chamber musician to the Empress Eugénie and director of court balls. Of the hundreds of dance pieces he composed, 268 were published during his lifetime, and his popularity for a time rivaled that of the waltz king, Johann Strauss, Jr.

At the Gate of Heaven
(A LA PUERTO DEL CIELO)

TR. A. D. ZANZIG

SPAIN

Simply

1. At the gate of heav'n lit-tle shoes they are sell-ing

For the lit-tle bare-foot-ed an-gels there dwell-ing.

Chorus

Slum-ber, my ba-by, slum-ber my ba-by,

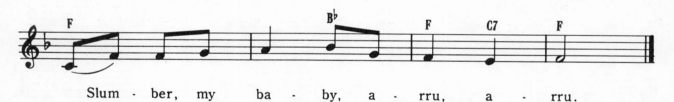

Slum-ber, my ba-by, a-rru, a-rru.

2. God will bless the children so peacefully sleeping,
   God will help the mothers whose love they are keeping.

1. A la puerto del cielo Venden zapatos,
   Para los angelitos que endan descalzos,
   Duermete, niño, duermete, niño,
   Duermete, niño, arru, arru.

2. A los niños que duermen Dios los bendice,
   A las madres que velan Dios las asiste,
   Duermete, niño, duermete, niño,
   Duermete, niño, arru, arru.

This beautiful Basque folk lullaby came to New Mexico from the Pyrenees Mountains of Spain.

76

O Tannenbaum
(O CHRISTMAS TREE)

GERMANY

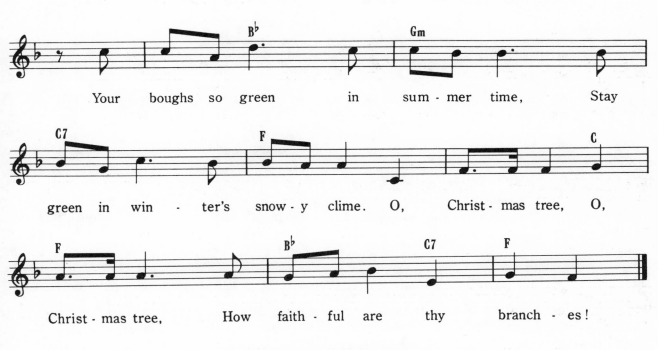

Firmly

O, Christ-mas tree, O, Christ-mas tree, How faith-ful are thy branch-es!

Your boughs so green in sum-mer time, Stay

green in win-ter's snow-y clime. O, Christ-mas tree, O,

Christ-mas tree, How faith-ful are thy branch-es!

O, Tannenbaum, O, Tannenbaum,
Wie treu sind deine Blätter!
O, Tannenbaum, O, Tannenbaum,
Wie treu sind deine Blätter!

Du Grünst nicht nur zur Sommerzeit,
Nein auch im Winter, wenn es schneit.
O, Tannenbaum, O, Tannenbaum,
Wie treu sind deine Blätter!

Some authorities believe this may be one of the oldest of the tunes familiar today, and date it back to the twelfth century as a drinking song. By 1824 it was being sung in Germany to the words of a Christmas carol, *O Tannenbaum*. Greens have been used to symbolize Christmas in many countries for centuries. Holly was considered sacred, as was mistletoe — which surely grew from heaven since it had no roots in the ground. Laurel represented happiness, good luck, and success. These greens decorated public places as well as private homes. The Christmas tree, of course, was the most famous green of all. During the Civil War the tune of *O Tannenbaum* was used for one of the best known of the Confederate songs, *Maryland, My Maryland*.

When I was a Lad

WILLIAM S. GILBERT

ARTHUR S. SULLIVAN

Nimbly

1. When I was a lad I served a term As

of - fice boy to an at - tor - ney's firm; I

cleaned the win - dows and I swept the floor, And I

pol - ished up the han - dle of the big front door. He
(Group)

pol - ished up the han - dle of the big front door. I
(Solo)

pol - ished up the han - dle so care - ful - lee That

When I Was a Lad

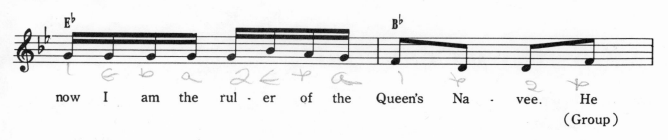

now I am the rul - er of the Queen's Na - vee. He
(Group)

pol - ished up the han - dle so care - ful - lee That

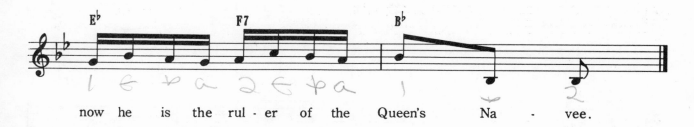

now he is the rul - er of the Queen's Na - vee.

2. (*solo*)   As office boy I made such a mark
That they gave me the post of a junior clerk;
I served the writs with a smile so bland,
And I copied all the letters in a big round hand;

    (*group*)   He copied all the letters in a big round hand;

    (*solo*)   I copied all the letters in a hand so free
That now I am the ruler of the Queen's Navee.

    (*group*)   He copied all the letters in a hand so free
That now he is the ruler of the Queen's Navee.

3. (*solo*)   Now, landsmen all, whoever you may be,
If you want to rise to the top of the tree,
If your soul isn't fettered to an office stool
Be careful to be guided by this golden rule:

    (*group*)   Be careful to be guided by this golden rule:

    (*solo*)   Stick close to your desks, and never go to sea,
And you all may be rulers of the Queen's Navee.

    (*group*)   Stick close to your desks, and never go to sea,
And you all may be rulers of the Queen's Navee.

This song is from *H.M.S. Pinafore,* an opera in two acts by Arthur Seymour Sullivan (1842-1900), London-born composer, organist and conductor. The libretto was written by William Schwenk Gilbert (1836-1911), English humorous poet and librettist. *Pinafore* was first performed in London May 25, 1878. Sullivan was a composer of the first rank, but he is remembered chiefly for his comic operas. *Pinafore* was an immediate success, had 700 consecutive performances in London, and enjoyed an enormous vogue in "pirated" productions throughout the United States. Sullivan received the degree of Music Doctor (hon. causa) from Cambridge and from Oxford. He was awarded many honors and was knighted by the Queen of England in 1883. His songs were highly popular in their day. Among these is the familiar one used currently, *The Lost Chord.*

Down in a Coal Mine

J. B. GEOGHEGAN

Jauntily

1. I am a jo-vial col-lier lad, and blithe as blithe can be,_____ For

let the times be good or bad, they're all the same to me;_____ 'Tis

lit-tle of the world I know and care less for its ways,_____ For

where the Dog Star nev-er glows I wear_ a-way my days._____

Chorus

Down in_ a coal mine, un-der-neath_ the ground,_____

Where a gleam_ of sun-shine nev-er can be found;_____

Dig-ging dusk-y dia-monds all_ the sea-son round,_____

Down in a Coal Mine

Down in__ a coal mine un - der - neath the ground.__

2. My hands are horny, hard and black with working in the vein,
   And, like the clothes upon my back, my speech is rough and plain;
   And, if I stumble with my tongue I've one excuse to say,
   It's not the collier's heart that's wrong, it's the head that goes astray.

3. Then, cheer up, lads, and make you much of every joy you can,
   And let your mirth be always such as best becomes a man,
   However fortune turns about we'll still be jovial souls,
   What would this country be without the lads who look for coals?

This song, one of the best known mining songs in our country, was published in 1872. It was written for the stage by J. B. Geoghegan. Popular performer J. W. Rowley sang it widely, and did much to promote its popularity. It found great favor among the early anthracite coal miners, many of whom were Irish immigrants. It also has been widely sung on college campuses.

Bingo

Humorously

SCOTLAND

There was a farm - er had a dog, And Bin - go was his name - O. B - I - N - G - O, B - I - N - G - O, B - I - N - G - O, And Bin - go was his name - O.

Sing the song through as written. Then repeat it and clap instead of singing the letter "B" in B-I-N-G-O. On the next repetition substitute clapping for the letters "B" and "I." On each subsequent repetition clap in place of an additional letter. When clapping has replaced all of the letters, end the song by singing very loudly, "And Bingo was his name-O." This song was first published in 1780, and is of Scotch derivation.

Lone Star Trail

U. S. COWBOY

1. I start-ed on the trail on June twen-ty-third, I've been punch-ing Tex-as cat-tle on the Lone Star Trail;

Chorus

Sing-ing ki-yi yip-pi yap-pi yay, yap-pi yay! Sing-ing ki-yi yip-pi yap-pi yay._____

2. I'm up in the morning long before daylight,
   And before I'm sleeping the moon is shining bright, etc.

3. My feet are in the stirrups and my rope is at my side,
   And I never yet have seen the horse that I can't ride, etc.

4. Oh, it's bacon and beans about every day,
   And I'd just about as soon be eating prairie hay, etc.

5. Now my seat is in the saddle, and my hand is on my rope,
   And my eye is on the dogies, I'm a good cow poke, etc.

6. With my knees in the saddle and my seat in the sky,
   I'll continue punching cattle in the sweet by and by, etc.

This lighthearted trail song was very popular with cowboys as they drove cattle across the plains to market points. As with many such songs, verses without number were made up to the melody of *Lone Star Trail*.

Streets of Laredo
(COWBOY'S LAMENT)

COWBOY

Woefully

1. As I____ walked out in the streets of La - re - do, As
I____ walked out in La - re - do one day, I
spied a young cow - boy all wrapped in white lin - en, All
wrapped in white lin - en as cold as the clay.

2. "I see by your outfit that you are a cowboy,"
These words he did say as I boldly stepped by;
"Come, sit down beside me and hear my sad story,
I'm shot in the breast and I'm going to die."

3. "Now once in the saddle I used to go dashing,
Yes, once in the saddle I used to be gay,
I'd dress myself up and go down to the card-house,
I got myself shot and I'm dying today."

4. "Get six husky cowboys to carry my coffin,
Get ten lovely maidens to sing me a song,
And beat the drum slowly and play the fife lowly,
For I'm a young cowboy who knows he was wrong."

5. "Oh, please go and bring me a cup of cold water
To cool my parched lips, they are burning," he said,
Before I could get it, his soul had departed
And gone to its Maker, the cowboy was dead.

6. We beat the drum slowly and played the fife lowly
And wept in our grief as we bore him along,
For we loved the cowboy, so brave and so handsome,
We loved that young cowboy although he'd done wrong.

This melody is similar to an old and popular Irish folk air from which it probably was adapted by sentimental cowboys to fit their own experiences and locale.

Home on the Range

Peacefully

COWBOY

1. Oh, give me a home where the buf-fa-lo roam, Where the
deer and the an-te-lope play;____ Where sel-dom is heard a dis-
cour-ag-ing word, And the skies are not cloud-y all day.____

Chorus
Home, home on the range,____ Where the deer and the an-te-lope
play;____ Where sel-dom is heard a dis-
cour-ag-ing word, And the skies are not cloud-y all day.____

2. How often at night when the heavens are bright
   From the light of the glittering stars
   Have I stood there, amazed, and asked as I gazed
   If their glory exceeds that of ours.

3. Where the air is so pure and the zephyrs so free,
   And the breezes so balmy and light,
   Oh, I would not exchange my home on the range
   For the glittering cities so bright.

4. Oh, give me the land where the bright diamond sand
   Flows leisurely down with the stream,
   Where the graceful, white swan glides slowly along
   Like a maid in a heavenly dream.

This is one of the most enduring home songs of the west. Neither the author of the words nor the composer of the music is known, but they must have shared the love and pride early settlers of the west felt for their new homes.

Short'nin' Bread

SOUTHERN U. S.

Lively

1. Three lit-tle ba-bies ly-in' in bed,

Two were sick and the oth-er 'most dead. Sent for the doc-tor and the

doc-tor said, "Give those ba-bies some short-'nin' bread."

Chorus

Mam-my's lit-tle ba-by loves short-'nin', short-'nin',

Mam-my's lit-tle ba-by loves short-'nin' bread. Mam-my's lit-tle ba-by loves

short-'nin', short-'nin', Mam-my's lit-tle ba by loves short-'nin' bread.

2. Put on the skillet, put on the lid,
   Mammy's goin' to make a little short'nin' bread,
   That isn't all she's goin' to do,
   Mammy's goin' to make a little coffee, too.

3. Go in the kitchen, lift up the lid,
   Fill my pockets with short'nin' bread;
   Stole the skillet, stole the lid,
   Stole the gal makin' short'nin' bread.

4. Caught with the skillet, caught with the lid,
   Caught with the gal makin' short'nin' bread.
   Paid six dollars for the skillet, six dollars for the lid,
   Spent six months in jail eatin' short'nin' bread.

This Negro folk song was popular on the plantations. It often was sung to pantomime, and verses were made up as the song progressed.

The First Noel

With joy

CAROL

1. The first Noel the angel did say, Was to certain poor shepherds in fields as they lay, In fields where they lay Keeping their sheep On a cold winter's night that was so deep. Noel, Noel, Noel, Noel, Born is the King of Israel.

2. They looked up and saw a star
Shining in the east beyond them far,
And to the earth it gave great light,
And so it continued both day and night;
Noel, Noel, Noel, Noel,
Born is the King of Israel!

3. And by the light of that same star
Three Wise Men came from a country afar,
To seek for a king was their intent,
And to follow the star where'er it went;
Noel, Noel, Noel, Noel,
Born is the King of Israel!

4. This star drew nigh to the northwest,
O'er Bethlehem it took its rest,
And there it did both stop and stay
Right over the place where Jesus lay;
Noel, Noel, Noel, Noel,
Born is the King of Israel!

5. Then entered in those Wise Men three
Full reverently upon their knee
And offered there, in His presence,
Their gold, and myrrh, and frankincense;
Noel, Noel, Noel, Noel,
Born is the King of Israel!

6. Then let us all with one accord
Sing praises to our Heavenly Lord
That hath made heaven and earth of naught,
And with His blood mankind hath bought;
Noel, Noel, Noel, Noel,
Born is the King of Israel!

The First Noel

No one really knows the origin of this popular folk carol. Both the English and French claim it. It first appeared in print in England in 1833 in a collection of William Sandys, but it may have been much older than that. Traditionally, the verses were said to have been sung by the shepherds and the refrain by the angelic hosts. The word "Noel" means Christmas. French in origin, it undoubtedly found its way into the English language during the Norman Conquest of England in 1066, and remained as part of the English language.

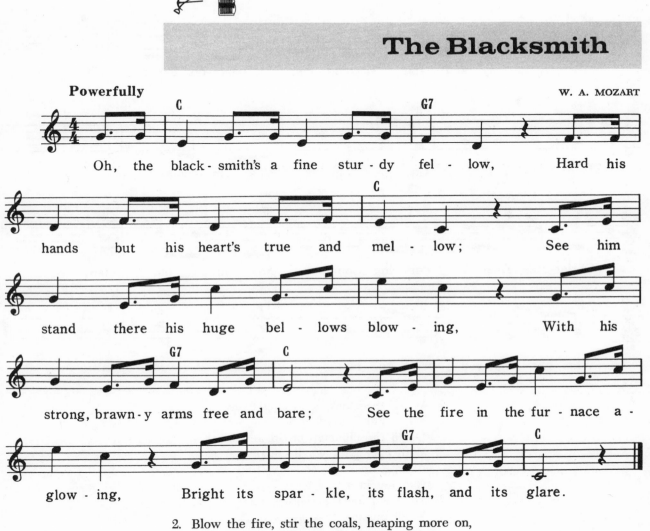

The Blacksmith

Powerfully

W. A. MOZART

Oh, the black-smith's a fine stur-dy fel-low, Hard his hands but his heart's true and mel-low; See him stand there his huge bel-lows blow-ing, With his strong, brawn-y arms free and bare; See the fire in the fur-nace a-glow-ing, Bright its spar-kle, its flash, and its glare.

2. Blow the fire, stir the coals, heaping more on,
   Till the iron is aglow, let it roar on!
   As the smith high his hammer keeps swinging
   Fiery sparks fall in showers all around;
   And the sledge on the anvil keeps ringing,
   Giving out with its loud clanging sound.

The melody to which these words are sung is an aria from Mozart's opera, *The Marriage of Figaro*. Wolfgang Amadeus Mozart (1756-1791) was a child prodigy. He was born in Salzburg, Germany and started concert tours of Europe when he was six years old. He is recognized as one of the world's great musical geniuses. *The Marriage of Figaro* was first performed in Vienna in 1786. At that time, it was considered revolutionary. It portrayed a group of servants who mocked their aristocratic master, deprived him of what he assumed were his rights, and had him pleading for mercy before the opera ended. This was of particular significance since it happened when the French Revolution stormclouds were gathering. It was an instant hit, and it remains a favorite of opera audiences today.

Jolly Old Saint Nicholas

Brightly

CAROL

1. Jol-ly old Saint Ni-cho-las, Lean your ear this way;
Don't you tell a sin-gle soul What I'm going to say;
Christ-mas Eve is com-ing soon, Now, you dear old man,
Whis-per what you'll bring to me, Tell me if you can.

2. When the clock is striking twelve,
When I'm fast asleep,
Down the chimney broad and black
With your pack you'll creep;
All the stockings you will find
Hanging in a row,
Mine will be the shortest one,
You'll be sure to know.

3. Johnny wants a pair of skates;
Susy wants a dolly;
Nellie wants a story book,
She thinks dolls are folly;
As for me, my little brain
Isn't very bright;
Choose for me, Dear Santa Claus,
What you think is right.

According to an old legend, St. Nicholas was Bishop of Myra in the fourth century, and a favorite Saint both in the Roman and Greek churches. He was noted for his great kindness to children, and because of this he was designated patron saint of children. There were many tales of his great goodness to the poor and the gifts he took when he visited them. This custom he started is carried on in the exchange of Christmas gifts.

Hot Cross Buns

Moderately

ENGLAND

1. Hot cross buns, hot cross buns,

One a pen-ny, two a pen-ny, hot cross buns.

2. If you have no daughters, feed them to your sons,
   One a penny, two a penny, hot cross buns.

In olden times, English streets resounded to the cries of hawkers advertising their wares. The words of *Hot Cross Buns* are sung to an old English folk melody.

Follow On

Rapidly

CANON

Come a-long, Sing a-long, Fol-low me;

It is eas-y as you see. Eve-ry day,

In this way Just re-peat Till the tune's com-plete.

In a canon two or more voices sing the same melody starting at different times. This practice dates back at least several centuries. In *Follow On* the second voice, the follower, enters after one measure and echoes the notes of the first voice, the leader, throughout. The way the two parts fit together, one is usually resting while the other is singing.

Under the Spreading Chestnut Tree

ENGLAND

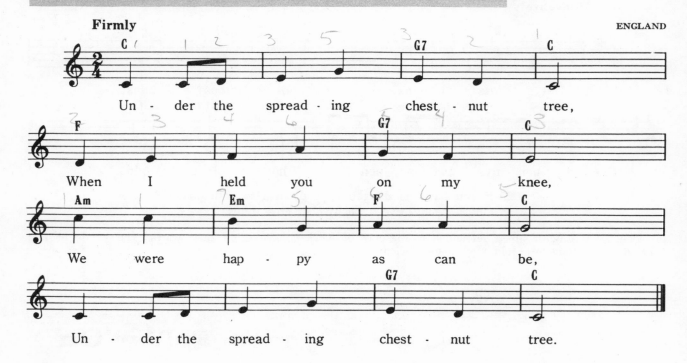

Firmly

Un - der the spread - ing chest - nut tree,

When I held you on my knee,

We were hap - py as can be,

Un - der the spread - ing chest - nut tree.

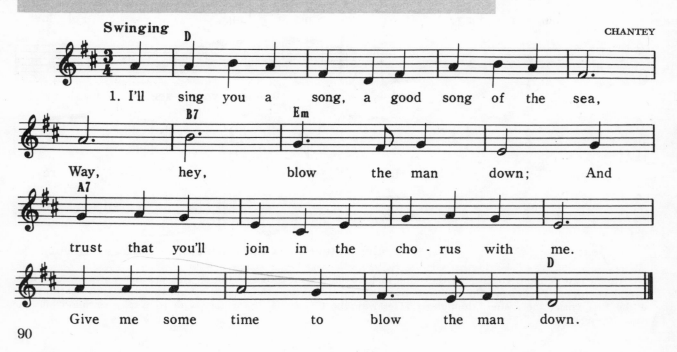

Blow the Man Down

CHANTEY

Swinging

1. I'll sing you a song, a good song of the sea,

Way, hey, blow the man down; And

trust that you'll join in the cho - rus with me.

Give me some time to blow the man down.

Blow the Man Down

2. On board the Black Baller I served in my prime,
   And in the Black Baller I wasted my time.

3. Tinkers and tailors and sailors and all
   Shipped as good seamen aboard the Black Ball.

4. With "larboard" and "starboard" we jumped to the call,
   The skipper's commands we obeyed, one and all.

This British sea chantey was adopted by the sailors of American clipper ships. Their earliest version was about the first and most famous line of American packet ships. The Blackball Line, which was started in 1818 and ran between New York and Liverpool. Speed was critical, so crews were driven hard, and discipline was administered without mercy. This line flew crimson flags with a black ball in the center. In *Blow The Man Down*, the melody of which has remained virtually unchanged, the word "blow" means "knock." Sailors often were knocked unconscious and shanghaied aboard ships which could not hire a full crew.

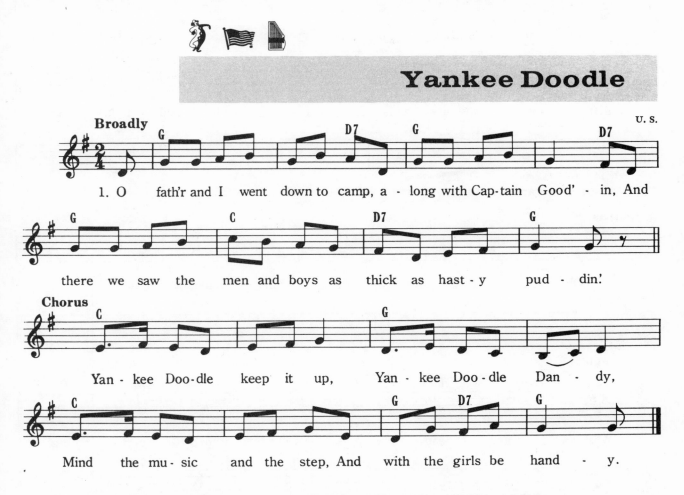

Yankee Doodle

U. S.

Broadly

1. O fath'r and I went down to camp, a-long with Cap-tain Good'-in, And there we saw the men and boys as thick as hast-y pud-din'!

Chorus

Yan-kee Doo-dle keep it up, Yan-kee Doo-dle Dan-dy, Mind the mu-sic and the step, And with the girls be hand-y.

2. And there was Captain Washington upon a slapping stallion,
   A-giving orders to his men; I guess there were a million.

3. And there I saw a swamping gun, large as a log of maple,
   Upon a mighty little cart; a load for father's cattle.

This song, a parody meant to mock the Continental Army, was presented to the colonists in 1775 by a British army surgeon who passed it off as popular English martial music. The joke backfired. The song delighted the colonists, as it has Americans ever since, and they sang it throughout the war and on to victory. The origin of both the words and music is confused. A version of the tune first appeared in print about 1778 in a Glasgow publication, *Aird's Selection of Scottish, English, Irish and Foreign Airs*. The first American publication to include it seems to have been the *Federal Overture* in 1795.

We Three Kings of Orient Are

JOHN H. HOPKINS

JOHN H. HOPKINS

Melchior: Born a babe on Bethlehem's plain,
Gold I bring to crown Him again;
King forever, ceasing never
Over us all to reign.

Caspar: Frankincense to offer have I;
Incense owns a Deity nigh,
Prayer and praising all men raising,
Worship Him, God on high.

Balthasar: Myrrh is mine; its bitter perfume
Breathes a life of gathering gloom;
Sorrowing, sighing, bleeding, dying,
Sealed in the stone-cold tomb.

All: Glorious now, behold Him arise,
King and God and Sacrifice;
Heaven sings "Hallelujah!"
"Hallelujah!" earth replies.

We Three Kings of Orient Are

This quaint modern carol is one of the few based on the story of the Wise Men as told in St. Matthew. Just more than a century old, its folk style and modal flavor have persuaded many editors that it is an old, traditional Christmas song. Both the words and music were written in 1857 by Dr. John Henry Hopkins Jr., and the carol achieved immediate success at home and abroad. The carol lends itself to the popular old custom of dramatizing the Nativity. It is the story of King Melchior of Nubia, small of stature and bearer of gold, symbol of royalty for the Babe; King Caspar of Chaldea, medium of build, whose gift was frankincense in honor of the Babe's divinity, and King Balthazar, tall, black-skinned ruler of Tarshish, who bore myrrh which foretold the suffering the Babe would endure.

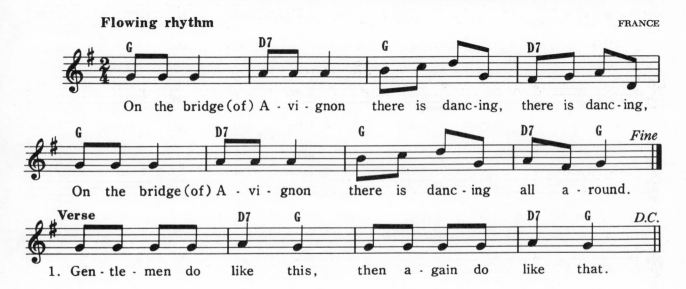

The dancers improvise the gestures and movements to this French singing game.

Many years ago a young French shepherd by the name of Benezet told the Bishop of Avignon that God's voice had directed him to build a bridge across the Rhone River to join the towns of Avignon and Villeneuve in the southeast of France. The Bishop asked the people of both towns to help with the project. They did, giving money, materials, and labor until the Bridge of Avignon was completed. Avignon has a large and ancient cathedral on a rock overlooking the town. The manufacture of silk and raising of silk worms are the principal employments in the district. The great Italian poet and writer Petrarch lived in Avignon for several years where he made the acquaintance of Laura, whose tomb is in the Franciscan church. Avignon was formally united to the French Republic in 1791.

Finlandia

GRACE S. DAWSON   JEAN SIBELIUS

Solemnly

1. Dear land of mine, my home, my na-tive coun-try,___ Now green be-fore me spread thy fields of grain!___ How blue thy lakes with heav-en's bless-ing on them,___ While free-dom's light makes beau-ti-ful the plain!___ Strong be thy sons to cher-ish and de-fend thee,___ That ev-'ry foe shall threat-en___ in vain.___

2. Through storm and stress thy heroes shall not fail thee,
   Though perils press them hard on every hand;
   God grant them strength and courage when the need be,
   Clear eyes to see, and hearts to understand.
   God lead thee on through nobleness to triumph,
   God make thee great, my own native land.

Words from *Singing Teen-agers* of *Our Singing World* series, © Copyright, 1954, 1961, by Ginn and Company. Used by permission. Melody from *Finlandia*, Copyright by Breitkopf and Haertel. Used by permission of Associated Music Publishers, Inc., agents for the United States.

Jean Sibelius (1865-1957) was the son of an army surgeon. He also was Finland's most important and esteemed composer. The Finnish government rewarded his genius by granting him a yearly allowance which enabled him to devote most of his time to composing. He drew inspiration from his native countryside, and loved his

Finlandia

country very much. His music is strongly nationalistic in character. His works have been performed with great acclaim throughout the world. In 1913 Sibelius accepted a commission to do a new orchestral work to be performed in the United States at the twenty-eighth annual Norwalk Festival (Connecticut). He wrote a symphonic poem, *Oceanides,* and conducted it at the Festival in 1914. The program also included another of his works, a tone poem, *Finlandia.* This successful program established his prestige in the United States, and Yale University conferred upon him the honorary degree of Music Doctor. The melody of the song *Finlandia* is one of the principal themes of the tone poem. The work had been written when Finland was oppressed by Russia, and its effect on the Finns was inflammatory. Its performance was banned by the Russians since it served as such a rallying song for the Finns. After Finland won her independence, *Finlandia* became a musical symbol of freedom.

We Wish You a Merry Christmas

ENGLAND

Sparkling

1. We wish you a merry Christ-mas, We wish you a merry Christ-mas, We wish you a mer-ry Christ-mas, and a hap-py New Year.

Chorus

Good ti-dings to you and to all your kin, Good ti-dings for Christ-mas and all the New Year.

2. Please bring us some figgy pudding, please bring us some figgy pudding,
   Please bring us some figgy pudding, please bring it right here.

3. We won't leave until we get some, we won't leave until we get some,
   We won't leave until we get some, please bring it right here.

Swing Low, Sweet Chariot

With dedication   SPIRITUAL

Swing low, sweet char - i - ot,___ Com-ing for to car-ry me home,

Swing low, sweet char - i - ot,___ Com-ing for to car-ry me home

Verse

1. I looked o - ver Jor - dan and what did I see,___

Com-ing for to car - ry me home, A band___ of an - gels

com - ing af - ter me,___ Com-ing for to car - ry me home:

2. If you get there before I do, coming for to carry me home,
   Tell all my friends I'll be there, too, coming for to carry me home.

3. The brightest day I ever saw, coming for to carry me home,
   When Jesus washed my sins away, coming for to carry me home.

4. I'm sometimes up and sometimes down, coming for to carry me home,
   But still my soul feels heavenward bound, coming for to carry me home.

The beliefs expressed in *Swing Low, Sweet Chariot* are typical of those found in the many spirituals which originated with the American Negroes. Home represents the promised land, and the River Jordan is symbolic of an obstacle which has to be overcome or crossed to get there. The words "Coming for to carry me home" may be sung by the entire group and the alternating phrases by a soloist for varied effect. There is an ancient legend of a wise and good king in Africa who was taken to heaven in a golden chariot before the eyes of his amazed people. This song may have come from Africa to southern plantations.

This Is My Father's World

MALTBIE D. BABCOCK
With conviction

ADAPTED
FRANKLIN L. SHEPPARD

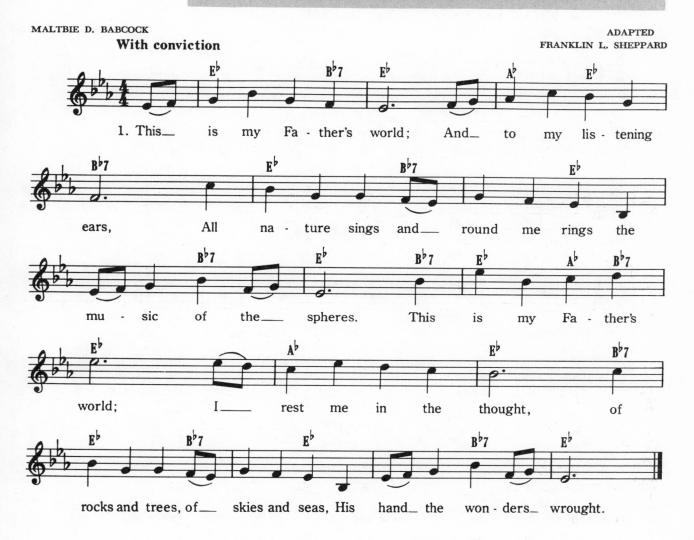

2. This is my Father's world, the birds their carols raise,
   The morning light, the lily white declare their Maker's praise;
   This is my Father's world, He shines in all that's fair,
   In the rustling grass I hear Him pass, He speaks to me everywhere.

3. This is my Father's world, O let me ne'er forget
   That though the wrong seems oft so strong God is the Ruler yet;
   This is my Father's world, why should my heart be sad?
   The Lord is King, let the heavens ring; God reigns, let the earth be glad.

The Rev. Maltbie Davenport Babcock (1858-1901) was born in Syracuse, New York, and was graduated from Syracuse University. He had great love both for his fellow man and for nature. About the latter, he often remarked, "This is my Father's world." He wrote a sixteen-verse poem which was adapted to an old English air. Today we sing it as *This Is My Father's World.*

Orchestra Song

ROUND

With spirit

1. The vi - o - lin's ring - ing like love - ly___ sing - ing, The

2. The clar - i - net, the clar - i - net makes doo - dle, doo - dle, doo - dle, doo - dle det, The

3. The trum - pet is sound - ing ta ta ta ta ta ta ta ta ta ta ta ta ta, The

4. The horn, the horn a - wakes me at morn, The

5. The drum's play - ing two tones and al - ways the same tones, Five

vi - o - lin's ring - ing like love - ly___ song.

clar - i - net the clar - i - net makes doo - dle, doo - dle, doo - dle det.

trum - pet is sound - ing ta ta ta ta ta ta ta ta ta.

horn, the horn a - wakes me at morn.

one, one five, five, five, five, five one.

98

Orchestra Song

The *Orchestra Song* can be performed in a variety of ways. As a round, the first group sings the top line (violin) alone and then moves down to the second line (clarinet) as the second group enters on the top line. As a line is completed, each group moves down to the next lower line and a new group enters on line 1. After singing line 5 (drum) the group may drop out or return to line 1 and repeat the process. The five parts may be sung in any order and in any combination. See how many different combinations of the five parts you can devise. The motions of playing the various instruments can be mimed as their sounds are imitated.

The Orchestra

Moderately fast

U. S.

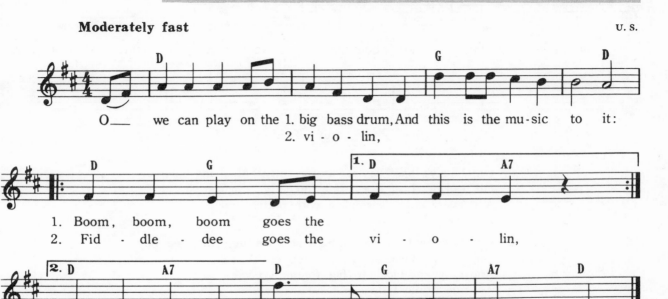

O— we can play on the 1. big bass drum, And this is the mu-sic to it:
2. vi - o - lin,

1. Boom, boom, boom goes the
2. Fid - dle - dee goes the vi - o - lin,

big bass drum, And that's the way we do it.

3. Tootle-too goes the slide trombone, etc.

4. Oo-oo-oo goes the saxophone, etc.

5. Pah-pah-pah goes the alto horn, etc.

6. Zoom-zoom-zoom goes the double bass, etc.

7. Ring-ring-ring goes the tambourine, etc.

8. Bang-bang-bang goes the timpani, etc.

9. Tee-tee-tée goes the piccolo, etc.

In the first verse skip the first ending and go directly to the second ending. In the following verses, repeat the sounds and names of the instruments in the preceding verses in reverse order. Many more instruments can be named and appropriate imitations made by the singers.

Lukey's Boat

With spirit

CANADA

1. Oh, Lu-key's boat is paint-ed green, A - ha, me boys! Oh, Lu-key's boat is paint-ed green, The fin-est boat you've ev-er seen, A - ha me rid-dle I day.

2. Oh, Lukey's boat has a fine forecutty, Aha, me boys!
Oh, Lukey's boat has a fine forecutty,
And every seam is chinked with putty,
Aha me riddle I day.

3. Oh, Lukey's boat has a high stopped jib, Aha, me boys!
Oh, Lukey's boat has a high stopped jib,
And a patent block to her foremast head,
Aha me riddle I day.

4. Oh, Lukey's boat has cotton sails, Aha, me boys!
Oh, Lukey's boat has cotton sails,
And planks put on with galvanized nails,
Aha me riddle I day.

5. Oh, Lukey's rolling out his grub, Aha, me boys!
Oh, Lukey's rolling out his grub,
A barrel, a bag, and a ten-pound tub,
Aha me riddle I day.

6. Oh, Lukey he sailed down the shore, Aha, me boys!
Oh, Lukey he sailed down the shore
To catch some fish from Labrador,
Aha me riddle I day.

From *Folk Songs of Canada* by Edith Fulton Fowke and Richard Johnston, published by Waterloo Music Company Limited, Waterloo, Ontario, Canada. Used by permission.

Canadian fishermen have high regard for boats, and the aim of every fisherman and his family is to acquire a boat of their own. The jib is a triangular sail projecting ahead of the foremast, and the patent block is a pulley which hoists the jib. Canadian fishermen sing this song. It is excellent for dramatization.

Buffalo Gals
(THREE LITTLE GIRLS)

Animated

COOL WHITE

1. As I was walk-ing down the street, down the street, down the street, A

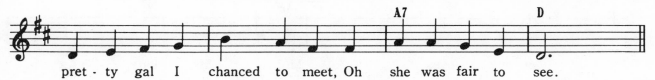

pret-ty gal I chanced to meet, Oh she was fair to see.

Chorus

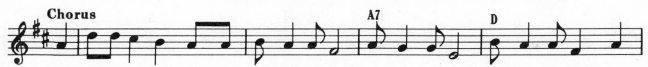

Oh, Buf-fa-lo Gals won't you come out to-night, come out to-night, come out to-night? Oh,

Buf-fa-lo Gals won't you come out to-night, and dance by the light of the moon?

2. I asked her if she'd stop and talk, stop and talk, stop and talk,
   Her feet took up the whole sidewalk, and left no room for me.

3. I asked her if she'd be my wife, be my wife, be my wife,
   Then I'd be happy all my life, if she'd marry me.

This song was written for the Virginia Serenaders in 1844 by John Hodges under the pen name, Cool White. The melody was known originally as *Lubly Fan*. Another song, *Three Little Girls*, is sung to an approximation of this melody. The words to this American singing game are given below.

THREE LITTLE GIRLS

1. Three little girls went sliding on the ice,
   Sliding on the ice, sliding on the ice,
   Three little girls went sliding on the ice,
   Early in the month of May.
   Swing them all about, and bring them in, bring them in, bring them in,
   Swing them all about and bring them in, so early in the month of May.

2. The ice was thin, and they all fell in,
   All fell in, all fell in,
   The ice was thin, and they all fell in,
   Early in the month of May.
   Swing them all about, and bring them in, bring them in, bring them in,
   Swing them all about, and bring them in, so early in the month of May.

Cockles and Mussels

With feeling

IRELAND

1. In Dub-lin's fair cit-y, Where girls are so pret-ty, I first set my eyes on sweet Mol-ly Ma-lone, As she wheeled her wheel-bar-row, Through streets broad and nar-row, Cry-ing cock-les and mus-sels, a-live, a-live oh!

Chorus

A-live, a-live oh!__ A-live, a-live oh!__ Cry-ing cock-les and mus-sels a-live, a-live oh!

2. She was a fish monger and sure 'twas no wonder
   Since so were her father and mother before;
   They each wheeled a barrow through streets broad and narrow,
   Crying cockles and mussels, alive, alive oh!

3. She died of a fever, and no one could save her,
   And that was the end of dear Molly Malone.
   But her ghost wheels the barrow through streets broad and narrow,
   Crying cockles and mussels, alive, alive oh!

The echoing cry of a pretty street vendor calling out the varieties of shell fish she has for sale in Dublin streets is the inspiration for this song. Street selling was commonplace in Ireland. The melody is an old Irish folk song.

102

Mary Had a Little Lamb

SARA J. HALE

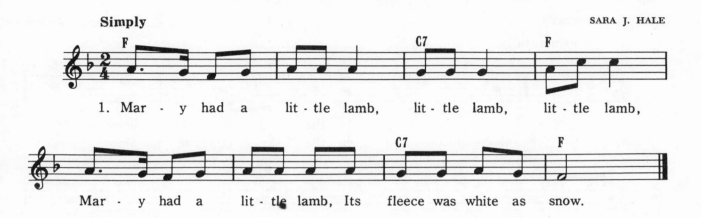

Simply

1. Mar - y had a lit - tle lamb, lit - tle lamb, lit - tle lamb,

Mar - y had a lit - tle lamb, Its fleece was white as snow.

2. Everywhere that Mary went the lamb was sure to go.
3. It followed her to school one day which was against the rule.
4. It made the children shout and play to see the lamb in school.
5. And so the teacher turned it out but home it would not go.
6. It waited there till school was out for it loved Mary so.

Little Tom Tinker

ROUND

Quickly

1. Lit - tle Tom Tin - ker got burned with a clink - er and

2. he be - gan to cry, 3. "Ma,

Ma, 4. what a poor fel - low am I."

My Old Kentucky Home

STEPHEN C. FOSTER   STEPHEN C. FOSTER

Sentimentally

1. The sun shines bright in the old Ken-tuck-y home, 'Tis
young folks roll on the lit-tle cab-in floor, All

sum - mer, the peo - ple are gay, The
mer - ry, and hap - py and bright; By'n

corn - top's ripe and the mead - ow's in the bloom, While the
by hard times come a - knock - ing at the door, Then my

1. birds make mu - sic all the day; The

2. old Ken - tuck - y home, good - night!

Chorus
Weep no more my la - dy, O weep no more to -

day! We will sing one song for the

My Old Kentucky Home

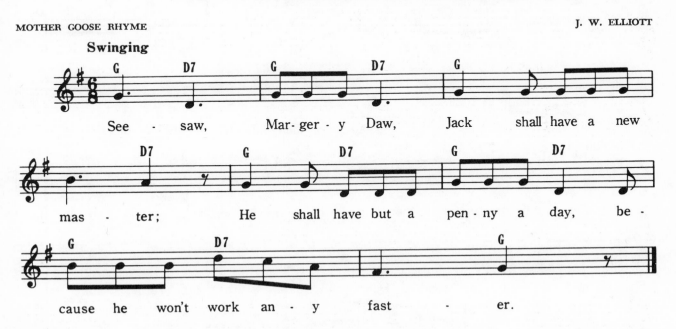

old Ken-tuck-y home, For the old Ken-tuck-y home, far a - way.

2. They hunt no more for the possum and the coon,
   On the meadow, the hill and the shore;
   They sing no more by the glimmer of the moon,
   On the bench by the old cabin door;
   The day goes by like a shadow o'er the heart,
   With sorrow where all was delight,
   The time has come when all people have to part,
   Then my old Kentucky home, good night.

America took this song to its heart in 1853. It is one of the few written by Stephen Foster which was inspired by the state it honors. Foster actually was visiting in Kentucky when he wrote it. The state regarded him as an honored son by adoption because of the beautiful song which brought Kentucky to national attention by virtue of its overwhelming popularity. Some authorities believe Foster's words were influenced by a poem he had read. Whatever its source of inspiration, many people consider *My Old Kentucky Home* a song of the first rank.

See-Saw, Margery Daw

MOTHER GOOSE RHYME   J. W. ELLIOTT

Swinging

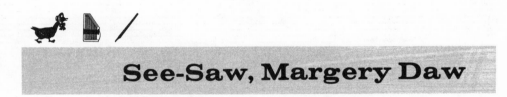

See - saw, Mar-ger - y Daw, Jack shall have a new

mas - ter; He shall have but a pen-ny a day, be -

cause he won't work an - y fast - er.

This Mother Goose play song may be dramatized by extended arms to form a see-saw. Its rhythm is also suitable for skipping.

Keep in the Middle of the Road

Fervently

SPIRITUAL

1. I hear those an - gels a - call - ing me,

Keep in the mid-dle of the road; They are wait - ing there in a

great big crowd, Keep in the mid - dle of the road; I

see them stand 'round a big white gate, We must

trav - el a - long 'fore we get too late. It is no use for to

sit down and wait. Keep in the mid - dle of the road.

Chorus

Then, chil - dren keep in the mid - dle of the road, Then, chil - dren keep in the

mid - dle of the road. Don't you look to the right, don't you

look to the left, But keep in the mid - dle of the road.

Keep in the Middle of the Road

2. I have no time for to stop and talk,
   Keep in the middle of the road,
   'Cause the road is rough and it's hard to walk,
   Keep in the middle of the road;
   I'll fix my eye on the golden stair,
   And I'll keep on going until I get there,
   'Cause my head is set for a crown to wear, so
   Keep in the middle of the road.

3. The world is filled with sinful things,
   Keep in the middle of the road,
   When the feet are sore put on the wings,
   Keep in the middle of the road;
   When you lie down on the road to die
   And you see those angels in the sky,
   You can put on wings and get up and fly, so
   Keep in the middle of the road.

4. I've come to join with the faithful band,
   Keep in the middle of the road,
   And we'll find our home in that happy land,
   Keep in the middle of the road;
   So turn your face from the world of sin
   And then just knock on the door
   And they will welcome you right in,
   Oh, you never will get this same chance again, so
   Keep in the middle of the road.

This conversation spiritual of faith and optimism was a great favorite on southern plantations. Traditionally, it is sung at a lively tempo, and the mood is happy. It employs the call-answer technique found in African tribal songs. The soloist (leader) or a small group of voices sings a phrase or statement, and the entire group responds, "Keep in the middle of the road."

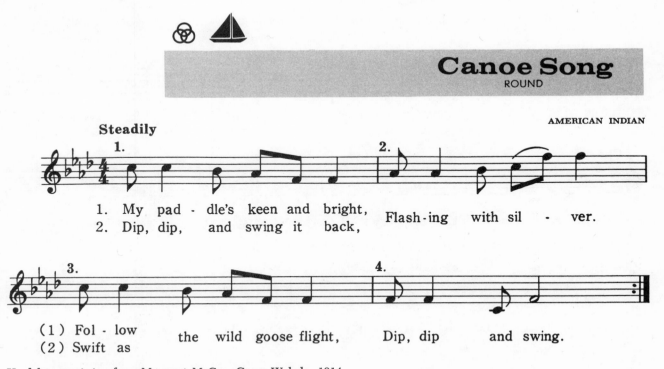

Canoe Song
ROUND

AMERICAN INDIAN

Steadily

1. My pad - dle's keen and bright,
2. Dip, dip, and swing it back,

Flash-ing with sil - ver.

(1) Fol - low the wild goose flight,
(2) Swift as

Dip, dip and swing.

Used by permission from Margaret McGee, Camp Wohelo, 1914.

The canoe is the traditional means of transportation by water for the Indian. This song often is acted out, as it is sung, to accentuate the rhythm. Originally animal skins or birch bark was stretched over the canoe framework to make the boat. Today canvas, laminated wood, and aluminum are commonly used. The basic design of the canoe is that of the Chippewa Indians.

Santa Lucia

TEODORO COTTRAU
TR. THOMAS OLIPHANT

TEODORO COTTRAU

Romantically

1. Now 'neath the sil - ver moon, o - cean is glow - ing,

O'er the calm bil - low, soft winds are blow - ing;

Here balm - y breez - es blow, pure joys in - vite us,

And as we gent - ly row, all things de - light us.

Chorus

Hark, how the sail - or's cry joy - ous - ly ech - oes nigh;

San - ta Lu - ci - a, San - ta Lu - ci - a,

Home of fair po - e - sy, realm of pure har - mon - y,

Santa Lucia

San - ta___ Lu - ci - a, San - ta Lu - ci - a!

2. When o'er thy waters soft winds are playing,
   Thy spell can soothe us, all cares allaying,
   To thee, sweet Napoli, what charms are given,
   Where smiles creation, toil blest by heaven.

1. Sul mare luccica l'astro d'argento,
   Placida è l'onda, prospero è il vento,
   Sul mare luccica l'astro d'argento,
   Placida è l'onda, prospero è il vento,
   Venite all'agile barchetta mia
   Santa Lucia, Santa Lucia,
   Venite all'agile barchetta mia
   Santa Lucia, Santa Lucia.

This world-famous boating song originated in Naples, Italy. It is a favorite of both Neapolitan fishermen and Venetian gondoliers. Santa Lucia is the guardian saint of the Neapolitans and this barcarole is sung in her honor. The words and music for *Santa Lucia* were written by Teodoro Cottrau (1827-1879). It was published in Naples in 1849. An early American edition with an English translation by Thomas Oliphant was published in Baltimore, but the date of this publication is unknown.

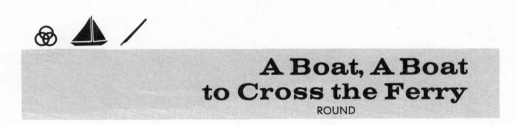

A Boat, A Boat to Cross the Ferry
ROUND

JOHN JENKINS

Buoyantly

A boat, a boat to cross the fer - ry, And we'll go o - ver

and be mer - ry, And as we float, sing hey down der - ry.

John Jenkins was born in Maidstone, England, in 1592, and died in 1678. He was an active member of the music world throughout his life, and served as one of the royal musicians. He played several music instruments, and wrote many works for viols and for organ. He also wrote many light pieces which he called "Rants." Of his many compositions for various instruments and vocal works, *A Boat, A Boat To Cross The Ferry* is almost the only one generally known today.

Sourwood Mountain

Rhythmically

APPALACHIA

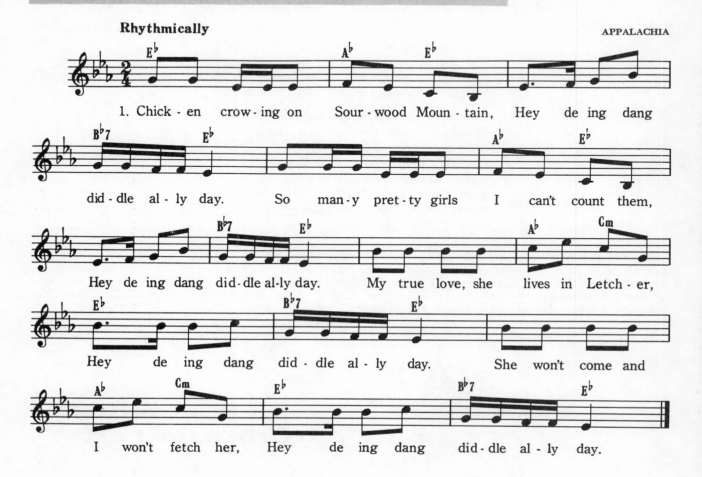

1. Chick-en crow-ing on Sour-wood Moun-tain, Hey de ing dang did-dle al-ly day. So man-y pret-ty girls I can't count them, Hey de ing dang did-dle al-ly day. My true love, she lives in Letch-er, Hey de ing dang did-dle al-ly day. She won't come and I won't fetch her, Hey de ing dang did-dle al-ly day.

2. My true love's a blue-eyed daisy, Hey, etc.
   If I don't get her I'll go crazy, Hey, etc.
   Big dogs bark and little ones bite you, Hey, etc.
   Big girls court and little ones slight you, Hey, etc.

3. My true love lives by the river, Hey, etc.
   A few more jumps and I'll be with her, Hey, etc.
   My true love lives up the hollow, Hey, etc.
   She won't come and I won't follow, Hey, etc.

This very old humor song was preserved in the isolation of the southern mountains. The words varied with the immediate area in which it was sung. It most often was sung in unison. It also was a rollicking fiddle tune for the rural dances. Appalachia was a world apart nestled in the southern mountains. During the seventeenth century many immigrants from the British Isles settled there. They kept to themselves partly from choice, partly because of the inaccessibility of the rugged terrain, and partly because transportation was primitive. Songs were handed down orally through the generations. Many which died out a century or more ago in the British Isles still are sung regularly in the mountain areas of the south. It has been said that nearly every folk song sung in the British Isles still can be found in these mountain regions. This may very well be true. Music there is a vital and living thing. Most homes have at least one musical instrument and everyone sings — from the youngest to the oldest inhabitant.

Red River Valley

COWBOY

Intensely

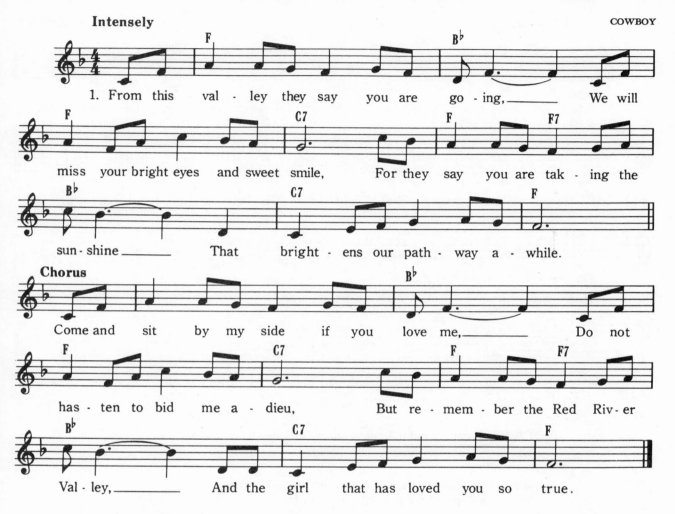

1. From this valley they say you are going,_____ We will miss your bright eyes and sweet smile, For they say you are taking the sunshine_____ That brightens our pathway awhile.

Chorus

Come and sit by my side if you love me,_____ Do not hasten to bid me adieu, But remember the Red River Valley,_____ And the girl that has loved you so true.

2. Won't you think of the valley you're leaving?
Oh, how lonely and sad it will be;
Oh, think of the fond heart you're breaking
And the grief you are causing to me.

3. I have promised you darling that never
Will a word from my lips cause you pain,
And my life, it shall be yours forever
If you only will be mine again.

4. As you go to your home by the ocean,
May you never forget those sweet hours
That we spent in the Red River Valley
And the love that was ours 'mid the flowers.

The cowboys of the Red River country took a song, *The Bright Sherman Valley*, which had been adapted from a New York State song, *In The Bright Mohawk Valley*, and modified it to their own locale as the *Red River Valley*. The course of the Red River is estimated at approximately 1,550 miles. It is the southernmost of the great tributaries of the Mississippi River. It courses through hundreds of miles of rich prairie land where great cattle domains were established. On the long drives to market points, cowboys sang endlessly to break the monotony and fatigue of the journey and to quiet the cattle. This cowboy love song with its myriad verses was a favorite on the trail.

Weevily Wheat

ENGLAND

Energetically

1. Your weevil-y wheat's not fit to eat, Nei-ther is your bar-ley; What I want is the best of rye To bake a cake for Char-ley.

Chorus

Rise you up in the morn-ing, All to-geth-er ear-ly; You need not be at all a-fraid, In-deed I love you dear-ly.

since it is E this is in E minor key

2. Charley's sweet and Charley's neat, Charley is a dandy;
   Charley is a nice young man, he feeds the girls on candy.

3. Charley is a brave young man, Charley is a soldier;
   Sword and pistol by his side, his musket on his shoulder.

4. Over the river to feed my sheep, over the river to Charley,
   Over the river to feed my sheep, and measure up my barley.

5. The higher up the cherry tree, the riper grows the cherry;
   The sooner boys and girls will court, the sooner they will marry.

Weevily Wheat originally was a jester's song which referred to Charles II of England, and was sung to an old English country dance tune. In the United States it became a play party game song and square dance tune. The weevils about which it tells are members of the beetle family with heads which end in projecting snouts. The grubs or larvae hatch from eggs, and are very destructive to many crops. They are difficult to control with sprays, and are controlled by burning infected plants, grain, and fruit, and by digging up the ground in which they spend the winter.

Over the River and Through the Wood

LYDIA MARIA CHILDS

U. S.

With animation

1. O - ver the riv - er and through the wood, To grand - fa - ther's house we go;_____ The horse knows the way to car - ry the sleigh, Through the white and drift - ed snow._____ O - ver the riv - er and through the wood, Oh, how the wind does blow!_____ It stings the toes and bites the nose, As o - ver the ground we go.

2. Over the river and through the wood and straight to the barnyard gate,
   We seem to go so very slow, and it's so hard to wait,
   Over the river and through the wood, now grandmother's cap I spy.
   Hurrah for the fun, the pudding's done, hurrah for the pumpkin pie.

3. Over the river and through the wood, now soon we'll be on our way,
   There's feasting and fun for every one, for this is Thanksgiving day,
   Over the river and through the wood, get on, my dapple grey,
   The woods will ring with songs we sing, for this is Thanksgiving day.

Gratitude for a bountiful harvest inspired the Pilgrims to observe the first Thanksgiving day in 1621, and the continued annual observation of this celebration is a significant part of the American heritage. *Over the River And Through The Wood* is a traditional Thanksgiving song.

Reuben and Rachel

U. S.

In jest

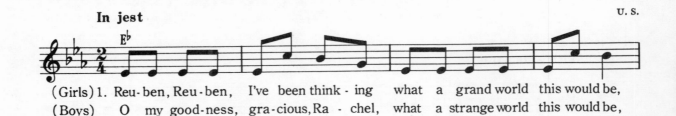

(Girls) 1. Reu-ben, Reu-ben, I've been think-ing what a grand world this would be,
(Boys) O my good-ness, gra-cious, Ra - chel, what a strange world this would be,

If the men were all trans-port-ed far be-yond the North-ern Sea.
If the men were all trans-port-ed far be-yond the North-ern Sea.

2. (*girls*) Reuben, Reuben, I've been thinking
What a fine life girls would lead
If they had no men about them,
None to tease them, none to heed.

   (*boys*) Rachel, Rachel, I've been thinking
Men would have a merry time
If at once they were transported
Far beyond the salty brine.

3. (*girls*) Reuben, Reuben, I've been thinking
If we went beyond the seas,
All the men would follow after
Like a swarm of bumble-bees.

   (*boys*) Rachel, Rachel, I've been thinking
If we went beyond the seas,
All the girls would follow after
Like a swarm of honey-bees.

4. (*girls*) Reuben, Reuben, I've been thinking
Life would be so easy then,
What a lovely world this would be
If there were no tiresome men.

   (*boys*) Rachel, Rachel, I've been thinking
Life would be so easy then,
What a happy world this would be
If you'd leave it to the men.

Reuben and Rachel

5. (*girls*) Reuben, Reuben, stop your teasing,
If you've any love for me,
I was only just a-fooling,
As, of course, I thought you'd see.

(*boys*) Rachel, if you'll not transport us
I will take you for my wife,
And I'll split with you my money
Every payday of my life.

All America was singing or whistling this conversation folk song in 1870. It may be sung as a duet, or with the girls singing the part of Rachel and the boys singing Reuben's lines. It also may be sung as a round using only the first verse, with the second part entering after the first part has sung one measure. Each group should sing its own words two times.

The Riddle Song

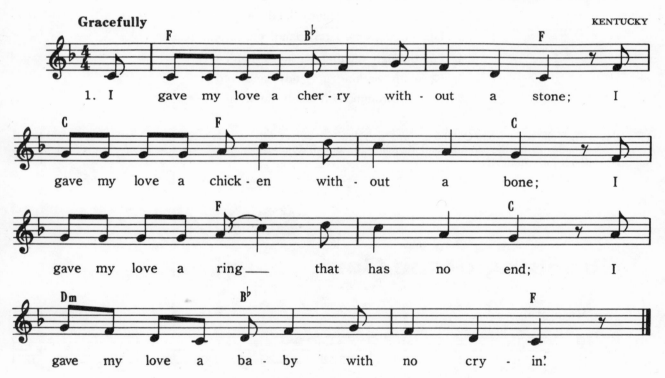

2. How can there be a cherry without a stone?
How can there be a chicken without a bone?
How can there be a ring that has no end?
How can there be a baby with no cryin'?

3. A cherry, when it's blooming, it has no stone;
A chicken, when it's peeping, it has no bone;
A ring, when its a-rolling, it has no end;
A baby, when it's sleeping, there's no cryin'.

This folk riddle song comes to us from the Kentucky mountains. An early version of this song was found in an English manuscript dating from the fifteenth century.

Sandy Land

OKLAHOMA

Briskly

1. Make my liv-ing in sand-y land, Make my liv-ing in sand-y land,

Make my liv-ing in sand-y land, La-dies, fare you well.

2. Raise potatoes in sandy land, etc.
3. Dig potatoes in sandy land, etc.
4. I'm through digging in sandy land, etc.
5. Gave up working in sandy land, etc.
6. I'm all through with sandy land, etc.

This play-party folk song from Oklahoma was popular for community singing at social gatherings. Additional verses were made up as the singing and dancing continued. It also is used as a circle game dramatized by the dancers as the words indicate.

Shucking of the Corn

TENNESSEE

Resolutely

1. I have a ship on the o-cean,_____ All

lined with sil-ver and gold,_____ Be-

Shucking of the Corn

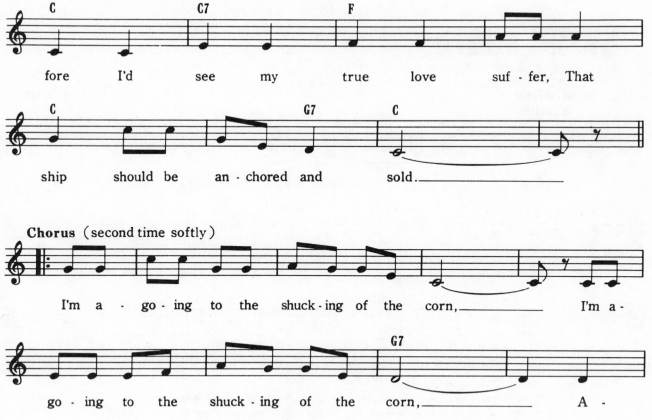

fore   I'd   see   my   true   love   suf - fer,   That

ship   should   be   an - chored   and   sold.

Chorus (second time softly)

I'm a - go - ing   to the   shuck - ing of   the   corn,_____   I'm a -

go - ing   to the   shuck - ing   of the   corn,_____   A -

shuck - ing   of   the   corn   and   a -   blow - ing   of   the

horn,   I'm a - go - ing to the   shuck - ing of   the   corn._____

2. The wind blows cold in Cairo,
   The sun refuses to shine,
   Before I'd see my true love suffer,
   I'd work all the summer time.

From *Joyful Singing*, Cooperative Recreation Service, Delaware, Ohio. Used by permission.

This southern folk song was particularly popular at social gatherings and cornhuskings. Neighborhood husking bees were festive occasions which brought friends together to work and play. The husking was followed by refreshments and dancing.

Jack and Jill

MOTHER GOOSE RHYME

J. W. ELLIOTT

Hastily

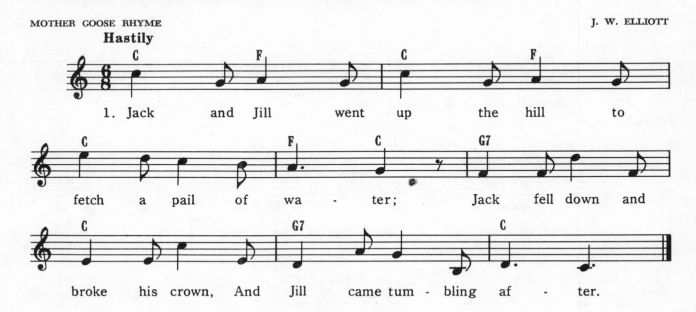

1. Jack and Jill went up the hill to fetch a pail of wa - ter; Jack fell down and broke his crown, And Jill came tum - bling af - ter.

2. Up Jack got, and home he ran as fast as he could caper,
   There his mother bound his head with vinegar and brown paper.

This song first appeared in print in a late eighteenth century English publication, *Mother Goose's Melody*. The exact publication date is in doubt. Some set it about 1765, but no copies remain to substantiate this date. Recent scholars believe publication occurred at the time of entry in *Stationer's Register* December 28, 1780, when T. Carnan applied for printer's rights. Copies of the second London edition in 1791 have been preserved. This marks the beginning of the association of "Mother Goose" with traditional nursery rhymes.

Blow Ye Winds

CHANTEY

Vigorously

'Tis ad - ver - tised in Bos - ton, New York, and Buf - fa - lo, Five hun - dred brave A - mer - i - cans, A - whal - ing for to go___, sing - ing

Blow Ye Winds

Blow, ye winds, in the morn-ing, Blow, ye winds, heigh-ho,

Haul a-way your run-ning gear, And blow, ye winds, heigh-ho.

Whaling was a major industry in early America. Whale oil was in demand and brought high prices. Sailors signed on whaling vessels for a share of the profit. The venture was dangerous, and some whaling voyages lasted for several years. To amuse themselves on these long trips, sailors made up songs about their activities and adventures. *Blow Ye Winds* is one of the stories American sailors told in song. The melody is an old English ballad which originally may have been a dancing song.

Jacob's Ladder

With faith

SPIRITUAL

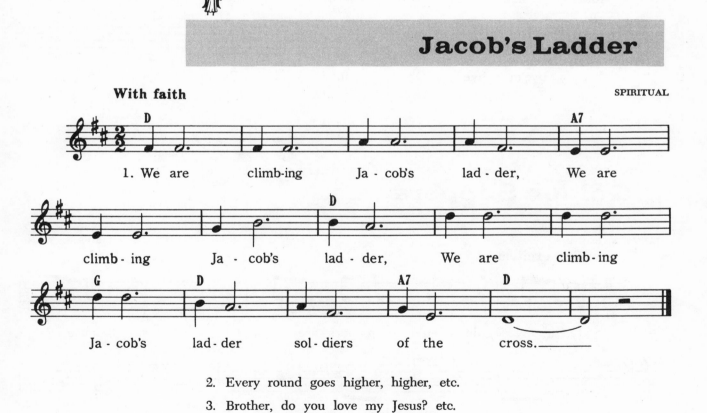

1. We are climb-ing Ja-cob's lad-der, We are

climb-ing Ja-cob's lad-der, We are climb-ing

Ja-cob's lad-der sol-diers of the cross.

2. Every round goes higher, higher, etc.

3. Brother, do you love my Jesus? etc.

4. If you love Him, you must serve Him, etc.

5. We are climbing higher, higher, etc.

This spiritual was born of religious expressions of Negroes in the south, and has been sung by people the country over who have been charmed by its direct simplicity.

Bye'm Bye

Playfully

TEXAS

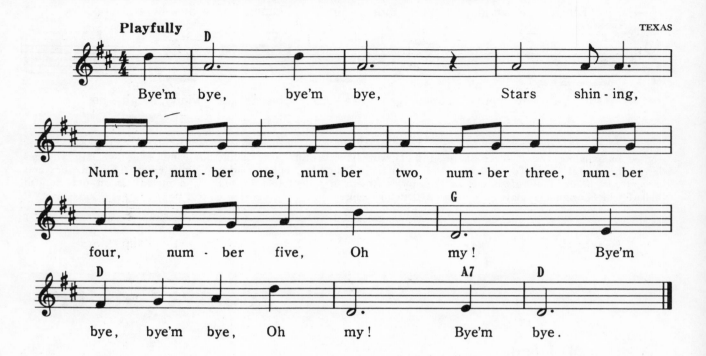

Bye'm bye, bye'm bye, Stars shin-ing,

Num-ber, num-ber one, num-ber two, num-ber three, num-ber

four, num-ber five, Oh my! Bye'm

bye, bye'm bye, Oh my! Bye'm bye.

Golden Slippers

JAMES A. BLAND

JAMES A. BLAND

With excitement

1. Oh, my gold-en slip-pers are ___ laid a-way, 'Cause I

don't 'spect to wear 'em till my wed-ding day, And my

long tailed coat that I loved so well, I will

120

Golden Slippers

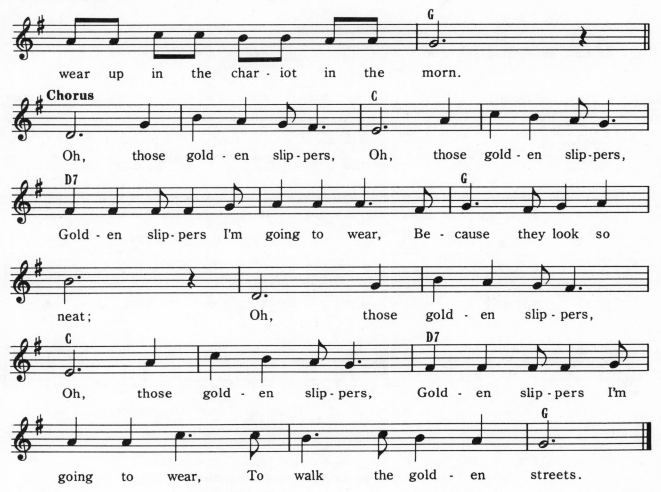

wear up in the char - iot in the morn.

Chorus

Oh, those gold - en slip - pers, Oh, those gold - en slip - pers,

Gold - en slip - pers I'm going to wear, Be - cause they look so

neat; Oh, those gold - en slip - pers,

Oh, those gold - en slip - pers, Gold - en slip - pers I'm

going to wear, To walk the gold - en streets.

2. There's the long white robe that I bought last June,
That I must go and change because it fits too soon,
And the old grey horse that I always drive,
I will hitch up to the chariot in the morn.

3. And my banjo still is hanging on the wall,
For it hasn't had a tune-up since away last fall,
But the folks all say we'll have a fine old time,
When we ride up in the chariot in the morn.

4. So it's goodbye, children, I will have to go
Where the rain can't fall and the wind won't blow,
And your ulster coats you never there will need
When we ride up in the chariot in the morn.

5. Now, your golden slippers must be shiny clean,
And your gloves the very whitest that were ever seen,
And be sure you're ready when it's time to go,
When we ride up in the chariot in the morn.

James A. Bland (1854-1911) was a well-known song writer who specialized in minstrel tunes. He was born in Flushing, New York. His father was one of the first Negroes in America to receive a college education, and one of the first Negroes to serve as an examiner in the United States Patent Office. James Bland was a page in the House of Representatives, and was educated at Howard University in law. He sang with the minstrels for several years, and during that time wrote *Carry Me Back to Old Virginny* (1878). *In The Evening By The Moonlight, Golden Slippers* (1879), and *Hand Me Down My Walking Cane* (1880). He called himself "the best Ethiopian song writer in the world." He went to Europe in 1882 where he was popular and prosperous, and a great favorite of English royalty. He returned to the United States in 1901 to find himself a forgotten man. He died in 1911, completely impoverished. In 1940, Virginia designated *Carry Me Back To Old Virginny* the official song of the state.

Rock of Ages

M. JASTROW G. GOTTLIEB

SYNAGOGAL MELODY

Earnestly

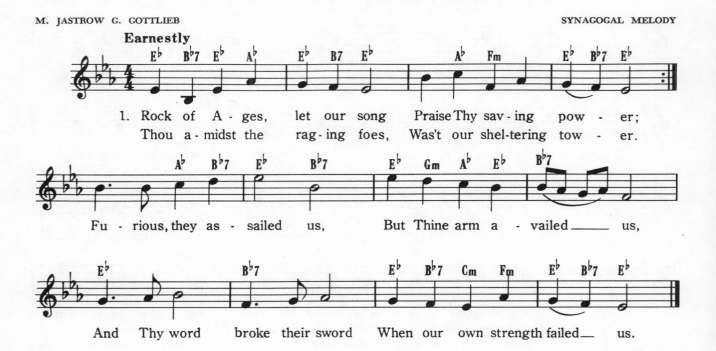

1. Rock of A - ges, let our song Praise Thy sav - ing pow - er;
Thou a - midst the rag - ing foes, Was't our shel-tering tow - er.

Fu - rious, they as - sailed us, But Thine arm a - vailed___ us,

And Thy word broke their sword When our own strength failed___ us.

2. Kindling new the holy lamps, Priests approved in suffering,
Purified the nation's shrine, brought to God their offering.
And his courts surrounding hear, in joy abounding,
Happy throngs singing songs with a mighty sounding.

3. Children of the martyr race, whether free or fettered,
Wake the echoes of the songs where ye may be scattered.
Yours the message cheering that the time is nearing
Which will see all men free, tyrants disappearing.

1. Mooz tzur y'shuosi l'ho noe l'shabeyah,
Tikon bes t'filosi v'shom toda n'zabeyah.
L'es tohin matbeyah mitzor ham'nabeah,
Oz egmor b'shir mizmor, hanukas hamizbeyah.

From the *Union Hymnal*. Used by permission of the Central Conference of American Rabbis.

Hanukkah ("dedication") is an eight-day Jewish celebration commemorating the rededication of the Temple at Jerusalem in 165 B.C. after the Maccabees had defeated the Syrian Greek armies in a religious war of libera-tion. Hanukkah is therefore known as the Feast of Dedication. It also is known as the Feast of Lights. A single candle is lit the first night before the *Menorah* (a special candelabra), and prayers are offered. Each night one additional candle is lit until on the last night eight candles are burning. Each night of the eight-day festi-val *Rock of Ages*, the traditional hymn, is sung in homes and synagogues. During Hanukkah, gifts are exchanged and games are played.

On Top of Old Smoky

U. S.

Mournfully

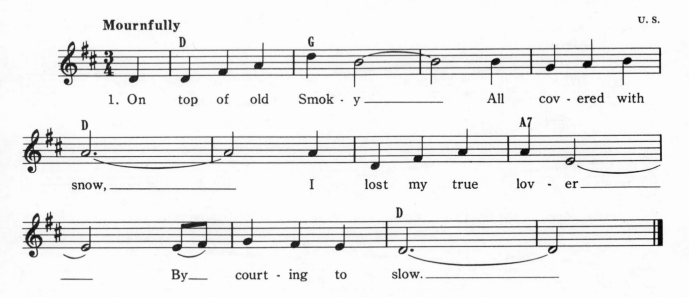

1. On top of old Smok - y ___ All cov - ered with snow, ___ I lost my true lov - er ___ By ___ court - ing to slow. ___

2. Oh, courting is pleasure and parting is grief,
   But a false hearted lover is worse than a thief.

3. A thief will just rob you of all that you save,
   But a false-hearted lover will lead to the grave.

4. The grave will decay you and turn you to dust,
   Not one in a million a poor girl (boy) can trust.

5. They'll kiss you and squeeze you and tell you more lies
   Than the rain drops from heaven, or stars from the skies.

6. They'll swear that they love you your heart for to please,
   But as soon as your back's turned, they'll love who they please.

7. It's raining and hailing this cold, stormy night,
   Your horses can't travel for the moon gives no light.

8. So put up your horses, and give them some hay,
   And come sit beside me as long as you stay.

9. My horses aren't hungry, they don't want your hay,
   I'm anxious to leave so I'll be on my way.

10. (repeat the first verse).

This well-known courting song developed in the mountain areas of southern and eastern United States. The verses sung to it are endless, and singers composed them as they sang the song.

Pussy Cat

MOTHER GOOSE RHYME

J. W. ELLIOTT

Lightly

Pus - sy cat, pus - sy cat where have you been?

I've been to Lon - don to vis - it the queen.

Pus - sy cat, pus - sy cat, what did you there? I

fright - ened a lit - tle mouse un - der her chair.

Birthday of a King

W. H. NEIDLINGER

Nobly

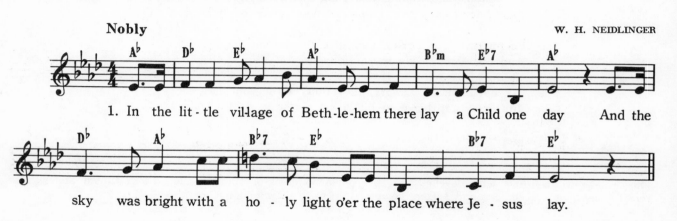

1. In the lit - tle vil - lage of Beth - le - hem there lay a Child one day And the

sky was bright with a ho - ly light o'er the place where Je - sus lay.

Birthday of a King

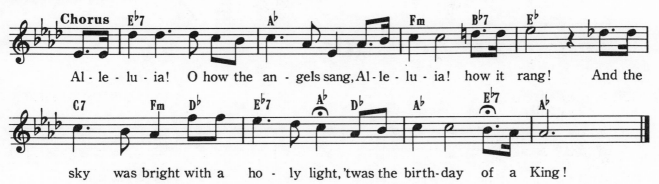

Chorus

Al - le - lu - ia! O how the an - gels sang, Al - le - lu - ia! how it rang! And the

sky was bright with a ho - ly light, 'twas the birth-day of a King!

2. 'Twas a humble birthplace, but oh, how much God gave to us that day!
    From a manger bed what a path hath led; what a perfect holy way!

Born in Brooklyn, New York, in 1863, Neidlinger was an organist, choral conductor, and voice teacher in the United States and Europe. He wrote some 200 sacred and secular songs, but he is best known for his books of children's songs. The great success of his *Small Songs for Small Singers* (1896), which became a standard work for kindergarten, turned his attention to the study of child psychology. He abandoned music in favor of this absorbing interest, and established a school in New Jersey for retarded children.

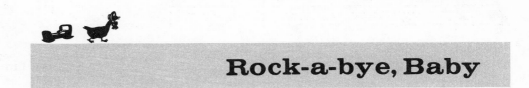

Rock-a-bye, Baby

MOTHER GOOSE RHYME   LULLABY

With lazy motion

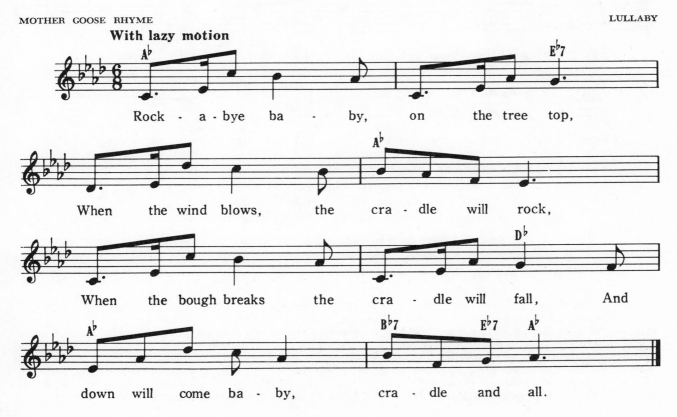

Rock - a - bye ba - by, on the tree top,

When the wind blows, the cra - dle will rock,

When the bough breaks the cra - dle will fall, And

down will come ba - by, cra - dle and all.

Ring, Ring the Banjo

STEPHEN C. FOSTER

STEPHEN C. FOSTER

Zestfully

C

1. The time is nev-er drear-y if a fel-low nev-er
come a-gain Su-san-na, by the gas-light of the

G7   C   F

groans; The la-dies nev-er wea-ry with the
moon, We'll strum the old pi-an-o when the

C   G7   1. C   2. C

rat-tle of the bones. Then
ban-jo's out of tune.

Chorus   G7

Ring, ring the ban-jo! I like that good old song;

C   F   C   G7   C

Come a-gain my true love, O where've you been so long?

2. Oh, never count the bubbles when there's water in the spring,
There's no one who has trouble when he has this song to sing,
The beauties of creation will never lose their charm
While I roam the old plantation with my true love on my arm.

3. My love, I'll have to leave you while the river's running high,
But I will not deceive you, so don't you wipe your eye,
I'm going to make some money, but I'll come another day,
I'll come again, my honey, if I have to work my way.

Stephen Foster (1826-1864) was born in Lawrenceville, Pennsylvania, on the Fourth of July, the same day that John Adams and Thomas Jefferson died. When he was six, his mother wrote that he had a drum and that he "marches around with a feather in his hat and a girdle round his waist, whistling *Auld Lang Syne.*" Years later, his brother Morrison wrote, "Melodies appeared to dance through his head continually. . ." and observed that often young Stephen would get out of bed at night, light a candle, and write down notes of a melody, and then go back to bed and to sleep. However, his family was unsympathetic with his musical aspirations. His father worked himself into a partnership with a mercantile firm, became a wealthy man, and turned his wealth over

Ring, Ring the Banjo

to the United States when the treasury was depleted during the War of 1812. His mother, Eliza Tomlinson, was the daughter of an aristocratic Wilmington family. They wanted better things for Stephen Foster than the uncertain future of a musician. However, his talent and determination were too great to be swayed, and Stephen Foster wrote music the whole country loved and has never ceased to sing. Memorials to him have been established in Bardstown, Kentucky; Greenfield Village, Michigan; and in Pittsburgh, Pennsylvania. The latter memorial is on the campus of the University of Pittsburgh, and houses the priceless collection of Fosteriana owned by Josiah Kirby Lilly. *Ring, Ring The Banjo* is lighthearted in character and marked with a syncopated rhythm.

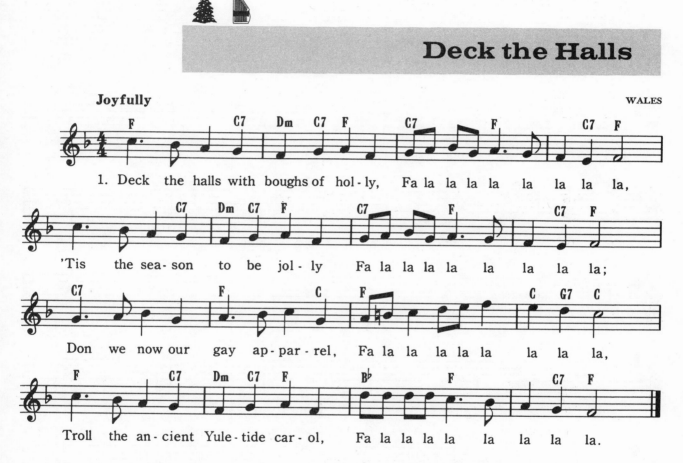

Deck the Halls

Joyfully

WALES

1. Deck the halls with boughs of hol-ly, Fa la la la la la la la la,
'Tis the sea-son to be jol-ly Fa la la la la la la la la;
Don we now our gay ap-par-rel, Fa la la la la la la la la,
Troll the an-cient Yule-tide car-ol, Fa la la la la la la la.

2. See the blazing Yule before us,
Fa la la la la la la la la,
Strike the harp and join the chorus,
Fa la la la la la la la la;
Follow me in merry measure,
Fa la la la la la la la la,
While I tell of Yuletide treasure,
Fa la la la la la la la la.

3. Fast away the old year passes,
Fa la la la la la la la la,
Hail the new, ye lads and lasses,
Fa la la la la la la la la;
Sing we joyous all together,
Fa la la la la la la la la,
Heedless of the wind and weather,
Fa la la la la la la la la.

All the gaiety of the Christmas season is suggested in this secular carol, a great favorite in all English speaking lands. Both the words and music are old and traditional. No reference is made to the birth of the Christ Child, but many seasonal customs associated with the event are described. In many countries greens have been used for centuries as decorations. Holly was considered sacred, and mistletoe was believed to have come from heaven since it had no roots in the ground. Laurel represented good luck, and the Yule log and its burning came from a Norse custom honoring Thor. Old ring dances often were done during the singing of this carol.

The Sidewalks of New York

CHARLES B. LAWLOR
JAMES W. BLAKE

CHARLES B. LAWLOR
JAMES W. BLAKE

Waltz tempo

1. Down in front of Ca - sey's

Old brown wood - en stoop,

On a sum - mer's eve - ning, We

formed a mer - ry group;

Boys and girls to - geth - er,

We would sing and waltz, While

To - ny played the or - gan on the

side - walks of New York.

128

The Sidewalks of New York

2. Things have changed since those times, some are up in "G,"
   Others, they are wanderers, but they all feel just like me,
   They'd part with all they've got, could they once more walk
   With their best girl and have a twirl on the sidewalks of New York.

This popular American song in waltz time is equally suitable for dancing and dramatization. It was written by Charles B. Lawlor, a vaudeville figure, in collaboration with James W. Blake, a hat salesman. It was published in 1894, and was first sung by Lottie Gilson in the Bowery at the London Theatre.

The Quaker's Wife

MAY SARSON

SCOTLAND

1. The Quak-er's wife sat down to bake with all_ her bairns a-bout her. She made_ them all a sug-ar cake, and the mil-ler wants his mout-er. Sug-ar and spice and all things nice, and all things ver-y good in it; The Quak-er, he_ sat down to play a tune_ up-on the spin-et.

Chorus

Mer-ri-ly danced the Quak-er's wife, and mer-ri-ly danced the Quak-er;

Mer-ri-ly danced the Quak-er's wife, and mer-ri-ly danced the Quak-er.

2. The Quaker's wife sat down to spin and merrily turned the wheel, O,
And then the Quaker he looked in to say he'd like a meal, O;
Now, if you feed your good man well he'll love you all your life, O,
And then to all the world he'll say "there never was such a wife, O."

In this old Scottish dance song, the *bairns* are children and the *mouter* is the fee charged by the miller for grinding the grain.

130

Rig-a-jig-jig

U. S.

Animated

1. As I was walk - ing down the street, Heigh -
o, heigh-o, heigh - o, heigh-o! A pret - ty girl I
chanced to meet, Heigh - o, heigh- o, heigh - o!

Chorus

Rig - a - jig - jig and a - way we go, a - way we go, a -
way we go, Rig - a - jig - jig and a - way we go, Heigh-
o, heigh-o, heigh - o! Heigh - o, heigh- o, heigh-
o, heigh- o, heigh - o, heigh-o, heigh - o, heigh-o!

Rig - a - jig - jig and a - way we go, Heigh- o, heigh-o, heigh-o!

2. I said to her, "What is your trade?"
Heigh-o, heigh-o, heigh-o, heigh-o!
Said she, "I am a weaver's maid,"
Heigh-o, heigh-o, heigh-o!

This American game song has an excellent rhythm for skipping or walking, and often is used for rhythmic dramatization.

131

Frog Went A - Courting

With humor

1. A frog went a-court-ing and he did ride, uh, huh!
A frog went a-court-ing and he did ride, uh, huh!
A frog went a-court-ing and he did ride, a
sword and pis-tol by his side, uh, huh!

2. He rode right to Miss Mousie's door, uh, huh!
   He rode right to Miss Mousie's door, uh, huh!
   He rode right to Miss Mousie's door
   Where he had often gone before, uh, huh!

3. He took Miss Mousie on his knee,
   Said, "Miss Mousie, will you marry me?" uh, huh! etc.

4. "Without my Uncle Rat's consent
   I couldn't marry the president!" uh, huh! etc.

5. Uncle Rat gave his consent,
   So they got married and off they went, uh, huh! etc.

6. Now, where will the wedding supper be?
   Away down yonder by the hollow tree, uh, huh! etc.

7. Who's going to make the wedding gown?
   Old Miss Toad from the lily pond, uh, huh! etc.

8. Now, what will the wedding supper be,
   Two big green peas and a blackeyed pea, uh, huh! etc.

9. Now, the first to come was a big white moth,
   She spread down a white table cloth, uh, huh! etc.

10. If you want this song again to ring,
    Make it up yourself and start to sing, uh, huh! etc.

Frog Went A-Courting

This story song from England was popular in colonial times, and flowered in Appalachia. Children often panto-mime the words as they sing the song or dance to its rhythm. In the English version, the frog is said to refer to the Duke of Anjou who was courting Queen Elizabeth. There is another version of the same song which is quite different in character. Another song, *Frog He Would A-Wooing Go*, bears marked similarity to *Frog Went A-Courting*.

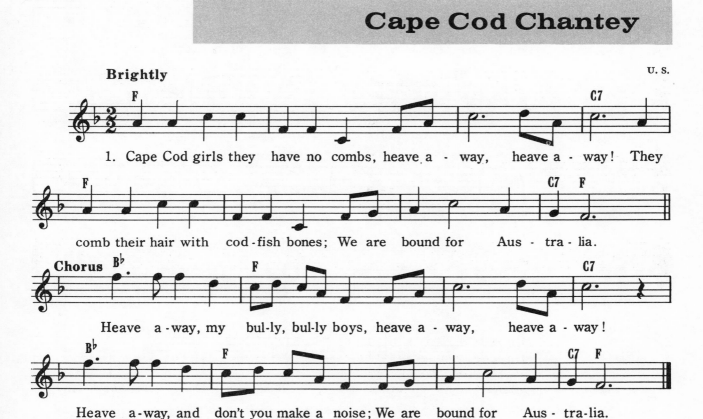

Cape Cod Chantey

U. S.

Brightly

1. Cape Cod girls they have no combs, heave a - way, heave a - way! They comb their hair with cod - fish bones; We are bound for Aus - tra - lia.

Chorus

Heave a - way, my bul - ly, bul - ly boys, heave a - way, heave a - way!

Heave a - way, and don't you make a noise; We are bound for Aus - tra - lia.

2. Cape Cod boys they have no sleds, heave away, heave away!
   They slide down hill on codfish heads;
   We are bound for Australia.

3. Cape Cod cats they have no tails, heave away, heave away!
   They blew away in heavy gales;
   We are bound for Australia.

The words which are different in each verse may be sung by a solo voice; the chorus and the words which are the same in all verses by the entire group.

On early American sailing ships a large spool-shaped cylinder which turned on an inner shaft was used to wind anchor cables on. This was called a *capstan*. The chanteyman would sing a verse of a chantey to set the work pace. The sailors, posted around the capstan, would sing the refrain in rhythm with their motions. The chantey-man was a most important member of the crew. He was hired for his powerful voice and ability to make up endless verses to any song to keep the sailors working together until the job was completed. This is a typical capstan chantey.

My Bonnie

H. J. FULLER

H. J. FULLER

With yearning

1. My Bon - nie lies o - ver the o - cean, _____ My

Bon - nie lies o - ver the sea, _____ My

Bon - nie lies o - ver the o - cean _____ O

bring back my Bon - nie to me. _____

Chorus

Bring back bring back, O bring back my

Bon - nie to me, to me; Bring back,

bring back, O bring back my Bon - nie to me. _____

2. O blow, ye winds, over the ocean,
   And blow, ye winds, over the sea,
   O blow, ye winds, over the ocean,
   And bring back my Bonnie to me.

3. Last night as I lay on my pillow,
   Last night as I lay on my bed,
   Last night as I lay on my pillow,
   I dreamed that my Bonnie was dead.

134

There Are Many Flags

MARY H. HOWLISTON

U. S.

With fervor

There are man-y flags in man-y lands, There are

flags of eve-ry hue; But there

is no flag how ev-er grand, Like our

own Red, White__ and__ Blue. Then hur -

rah for the flag, our coun-try's flag, Its

stripes and white stars too, For there

is no flag in an-y land Like our

own Red, White__ and__ Blue.

Dixie

DANIEL D. EMMETT

DANIEL D. EMMETT

1. I__ wish I was__ in the land of cot - ton,
In__ Dix - ie Land__ where__ I was born in,

Old times there are not for - got - ten, Look a -
Ear - ly on one frost - y morn - ing, Look a -

way! Look a - way! Look a - way! Dix - ie Land.
way! Look a - way! Look a - way! Dix - ie Land.

Chorus

Then I wish I was in Dix - ie, Hoo - ray! Hoo - ray! In

Dix - ie Land I'll take my stand To live and die in Dix - ie; A -

way, a - way, a - way down south in Dix - ie, A -

way a - way a - way down south in Dix - ie.

2. There's buckwheat cakes and Indian batter,
   Makes you fat or a little fatter,
   Look away! Look away! Look away! Dixie Land;
   Then hoe it down and scratch your gravel,
   To Dixie Land I'm bound to travel,
   Look away! Look away! Look away! Dixie Land.

136

Dixie

This rollicking song was written for Bryant's Minstrels by Daniel D.Emmett who sang it in New York in 1859. It was an immediate hit. Emmett, a former circus man, was a northerner with northern sympathies, but southerners loved him for his songs of the South. Originally entitled *I Wish I Was In Dixie Land*, the song was introduced in New Orleans in 1860 when it was sung in a burlesque of Pocahontas. Southerners immediately took it to their hearts. *Dixie* was sung at the inauguration of Jefferson Davis as the Confederate President at Montgomery, Alabama, February 18, 1861. It became the marching song of the Confederate armies. In 1865 the song was covered with fresh glory when President Abraham Lincoln requested its performance during a serenade shortly before his assassination.

Rise Up, Shepherd, and Follow

CHRISTMAS SPIRITUAL

2. If you take close heed of the angel's words,
    Rise up, shepherd, and follow,

You'll forget your flocks, and forget your herds,
Rise up, shepherd, and follow.

This is the story of the nativity as the Negro people sang it. It is one of the few spirituals based on the Christmas story. Traditionally, the leader or solo voice sings the story, the group responds with the refrain. This call and answer technique is found in African tribal songs, and may be where the custom originated.

Joshua Fought the Battle of Jericho

With determination

SPIRITUAL

Josh - ua fought the bat - tle of___ Jer - i - cho,___

Jer - i - cho,___ Jer - i - cho;___ Josh - ua fought the bat - tle of___

Jer - i - cho,___ and the walls came tum - bling down.

Verse

1. You may talk a - bout your kings of Gid - e - on, You may

talk a - bout your men___ of___ Saul, But there's none like good old

Josh - ua at the bat - tle of Jer - i - cho.

Key - D minor

2. Now the Lord commanded Joshua:
   "I command you, and obey you must;
   You just march straight to those city walls
   And the walls will turn to dust."

3. Straight up to the walls of Jericho
   He marched with spear in hand,
   "Go blow that ram's horn," Joshua cried,
   "For the battle is in my hand."

4. Then the lamb ram sheep horns began to blow,
   And the trumpets began to sound,
   And Joshua commanded, "Now children, shout!"
   And the walls came tumbling down.

Joshua succeeded Moses and led the Israelites into the Promised Land. The story of the siege of Jericho is recorded in the Bible, Book of Joshua, Chapter 6. The story is retold in poetic form and with a degree of poetic license in this spiritual.

Old Dog Tray

STEPHEN C. FOSTER

STEPHEN C. FOSTER

Sentimentally

1. The morn of life is past, And eve-ning comes at last; It brings me a dream of a once hap-py day, Of mer-ry forms I've seen Up-on the vil-lage green, A sport-ing with my old dog Tray.

Chorus
Old dog Tray's ev-er faith-ful, Grief can-not drive him a-way; He's gen-tle, he is kind; I'll nev-er, nev-er find A bet-ter friend than old dog Tray.

2. The forms I called my own have vanished one by one,
The loved ones, the dear ones have all passed away;
The happy smiles have flown, the gentle voices gone,
I've nothing left but old dog Tray.

3. When thoughts recall the past, his eyes on me are cast;
I know that he feels what my breaking heart would say,
Although he cannot speak, I'll vainly, vainly seek
A better friend than old dog Tray.

Stephen Foster was a sentimental man, and often a melancholy man. Both sentiment and sadness are evident in *Old Dog Tray.* Tray is said to have been a puppy of Foster when he was a boy, and his constant companion. The man continued to love the dog, and years later wrote the song in his memory. It was published in 1853, just 11 years before Foster died.

139

Susie, Little Susie

ADELHEID WETTE
TR. CONSTANCE BACHE

E. HUMPERDINCK

Brightly

1. Su - sie, lit - tle Su - sie, pray what is the news?

The geese are run-ning bare - foot be - cause they've no shoes!

The cob - bler has leath - er and plen - ty to spare,

Why___ can't he make the poor goose a new pair?___

2. Eia popeia, pray what's to be done?
   Who'll give me milk and sugar, for bread I have none?
   I'll go back to bed and I'll lie there all day,
   Where there's nought to eat then there's nothing to pay!

This folk-like melody is from the first scene of the fairy opera *Hansel And Gretel*. Hansel and his sister Gretel live in a small house in the forest. As the scene opens, Hansel is sitting by the door making brooms, and Gretel is by the fireplace knitting a stocking. In the opera, Gretel sings the first verse and Hansel the second. Engelbert Humperdinck (1854-1921) was born in Germany near Bonn. He received world recognition as a composer with the production of *Hansel And Gretel* in Weimar in 1893. The text was written by Humperdinck's sister, Adelheid Wette. The delightful fairy opera has been described as a "fine work in the operatic repertoire to which one can take a child with the definite certainty of gratitude." Although Humperdinck composed other works and other operas, his fame rests almost entirely upon *Hansel And Gretel*.

Loch Lomond

With feeling

SCOTLAND

1. By— yon bon-nie banks and by yon bon-nie braes, Where the
sun shines bright on Loch Lo - mond, Where me and my true love were
ev-er wont to gae, On the bon-nie, bon-nie banks of Loch Lo - mond.

Chorus

Oh! ye'll take the high road, and I'll take the low road, And
I'll be in Scot-land a-fore ye, But me and my true love we'll
nev-er meet a-gain On the bon-nie, bon-nie banks of Loch Lo - mond.

2. 'Twas there that we parted in yon shady glen
On the steep, steep side of Ben Lomond,
Where in purple hue the highland hills we view,
And the moon coming out in the gloaming.

3. The wee birdies sing, and the wild flowers spring,
And in sunshine the waters are sleeping,
But the broken hearts kens nae second spring again,
Though the waeful may cease frae their greeting.

The words of this song often are attributed to Lady John Scott. The melody to which they are sung is an old Jacobite air. Loch (lake) Lomond is a beautiful lake of Scotland which is renowned for its breath-taking scenery. Located in the southern highlands, it is almost entirely surrounded with hills. One of these is Ben Lomond, a peak 3,192 feet high. The lake reaches a depth of 600 feet and abounds with such fish as salmon, trout, and pike. Its surface is studded with many small islands.

Sweet and Low

ALFRED TENNYSON

JOSEPH BARNBY

Serenely

1. Sweet and low, sweet and low, Wind of the west-ern sea;

Low, low, breathe and blow, Wind of the west-ern sea;

O-ver the roll-ing wa-ters go, Come from the dy-ing

moon and blow, Blow him a-gain to me,

While my lit-tle one, while my pret-ty one sleeps.

2. Sleep and rest, sleep and rest,
Father will come to thee soon,
Rest, rest on mother's breast,
Father will come to thee soon,
Father will come to his babe in the nest,
Silver sails all out of the west,
Under the silver moon,
Sleep, my little one, sleep, my pretty one, sleep.

The brilliant English composer, Sir Joseph Barnby (1838-1896), composed this song. He adapted it to the words of a poem, *Princess*, by Alfred, Lord Tennyson (1809-1892), poet laureate of England. Barnby also was an outstanding conductor and organist, and he held important musical posts in England which included: conductor of the London Music Society, Principal of the Guildhall School of Music, Director of Music at Eaton College, Conductor of Albert Hall Choral Society, and conductor of many music festivals. He organized many choral groups and concert series, and served as organist at the finest churches in England. He was knighted in 1892.

Going to Boston

U. S.

Blithely

1. Good-by girls, we're going to Bos-ton Good-by girls, we're going to Bos-ton
   (Boys)

Good-by girls, we're going to Bos-ton, Ear-ly in the morn - ing.

Sad-dle up girls, and let's go with them, Sad-dle up girls, and let's go with them,
(Girls)

Sad-dle up girls, and let's go with them, Ear-ly in the morn - ing.

Chorus

Won't we look pret-ty in the ball - room, Won't we look pret-ty in the ball-room,
(Both)

Won't we look pret-ty in the ball - room, Ear-ly in the morn - ing?

2. Out of the way, you'll get run over, etc.

3. Swing your partner, on to Boston, etc.

4. Aren't we lovely when we're dancing? etc.

5. Now we skip around the circle, etc.

6. This is how we go to Boston, etc.

This American play party game is popular with groups of all ages. Youngsters sing, dance, skip, and run to its rhythm, and youngsters of all ages find it an excellent square dance tune.

Every Time I Feel the Spirit

SPIRITUAL

With conviction

Eve - ry time I ___ feel the spir - it ___ mov - ing
in my heart ___ I will pray. Eve - ry time I ___ feel the
spir - it ___ mov - ing in my heart ___ I will pray.

Verse

1. Up - on the moun - tain ___ when my Lord spoke, Out of His
mouth came ___ fire and smoke. Up - on the moun - tain ___ when my Lord
spoke, Out of His mouth came ___ fire and smoke.

2. Looked all around me, it sure looked fine;
   I asked my Lord if it were mine.
   Looked all around me, it sure looked fine;
   I asked my Lord if it were mine.

A general realization of the musical powers of the Negroes, and of their vast fund of moving and appealing music, came when the Jubilee Singers of Fisk University made their first concert tour to raise funds for their school. They met with tremendous success in America, and crossed to Europe where they were equally well received. Their success seemed complete when they were invited to appear before Queen Victoria. *Every Time I Feel The Spirit* is one of the livelier and more highly syncopated Negro gospel songs.

Faith of Our Fathers

FREDERICK W. FABER

HENRY F. HEMY

Earnestly

1. Faith of our fa - thers, liv - ing still
In spite of dun - geon, fire ___ and sword;
Oh, how our hearts ___ beat high ___ with joy,
When - e'er we hear that glo - ri - ous word!

Chorus
Faith of our fa - thers, ho - ly faith,
We will be true to thee till death.

2. Faith of our fathers, we shall strive to win all people unto thee,
And through the ways of righteousness mankind will surely then be free.

3. Faith of our fathers, we shall love both friend and foe what e'er our strife,
And preach Thy ways as best we know by kindly words and upright life.

This hymn was conceived as a pledge of faithfulness by its composer. Frederick William Faber, who was born in England in 1814. He wrote 150 hymns during the last 18 years of his life. *Faith Of Our Fathers* (1849) has been used widely in all communions, and is sung frequently by men in the armed forces.

Home, Sweet Home

JOHN H. PAYNE

HENRY R. BISHOP

2. I gaze on the moon as I tread the drear wild,
   And feel that my mother now thinks of her child;
   As she looks on that moon from our own cottage door,
   Through the woodbine whose fragrance shall cheer me no more.

3. An exile from home splendor dazzles in vain,
   Oh, give me my lowly thatched cottage again;
   The birds singing gaily, that came at my call,
   Give me them, and that peace of mind dearer than all.

John Howard Payne (1791-1852), who wrote *Home, Sweet Home* which probably is the most renowned tribute to home, said, "The world has literally sung my song until every heart is familiar with the melody, yet I have

146

Home, Sweet Home

been a wanderer from my boyhood." He roamed through Europe as composer, actor, and play translator. He wrote the libretto for the opera *Clari, Or The Maid of Milan* in 1823. The opera faded into obscurity, but one aria gained world fame — *Home, Sweet Home*. It became so significant a song that its centenary birthday was observed in the United States and in England.

Cradle Song

CLAUDIUS
TR. THEODORE BAKER

FRANZ SCHUBERT

Calmly

1. Sweet - ly slum - ber 'neath the or - chard shad - ows,

Near thee murm - 'ring soft, the brook - let flows;

Winds of spring - time gen - tly lull thee,

Moth - er's dar - ling moth - er's op' - ning rose.

2. Sweetly slumber, o'er thine eyelids tender
   Orchard blossoms waft their fragrant snows;
   May they wake not, may they bring thee
   Angel visions, dewy deep repose!

3. Sweetly slumber, while I bear thee homeward;
   Heaven grows darker, cold an east wind blows;
   In these arms sleep softly, darling,
   Mother's love no change, no coldness knows.

1. Schlafe, schlafe holder süsser Knabe,
   Leise wiegt dich deiner Mutter Hand;
   Sanfte Ruhe, milde Labe
   Bringt dir schwebend dieses Wiegenband.

Franz Schubert was born near Vienna in 1797. He was one of fourteen children, and his father was a schoolmaster. Young Franz was greatly talented in music, and became a member of the Vienna Court Choir when he was eleven years old. He never married and had no children of his own, but he loved young people and wrote many beautiful songs for them.

Oh Dear, What Can the Matter Be

Rather quickly

ENGLAND

Oh   dear !   What   can   the   mat - ter   be?

Oh   dear !   What   can   the   mat - ter   be ?   Oh   dear !

What   can   the   mat - ter - be ?   John - ny's   so   long   at   the   fair. _____

Verse

1. He   prom - ised   to   buy   me   a   trin - ket   to   please   me,   And

then   for   a   kiss,   O   he   vowed   he   would   tease   me,   He

prom - ised   to   bring   me   a   bunch   of   blue   rib - bons   To

tie   up   my   bon - nie   brown   hair. _____   So   it's

2. He promised to bring me a basket of posies,
   An arm full of lilies, a bunch of red roses,
   A pretty straw hat to set off the blue ribbons
   That tie up my bonnie brown hair; so it's, etc.

Jingle Bells

JAMES PIERPONT

JAMES PIERPONT

Gaily

G

1. Dash-ing through the snow, in a one-horse o-pen sleigh,

Am   D   D7   G

O'er the fields we go, Laugh-ing all the way;— Bells on bob-tail ring,

C   Am   D   D7   G

Mak-ing spir-its bright, Oh, what fun it is to sing a sleigh-ing song to night.

Chorus   C   G

Jin-gle bells, Jin-gle bells, Jin-gle all the way, Oh, what fun it is to ride in a

A7   D7   G

one-horse o-pen sleigh!____ Jin-gle bells, Jin-gle bells,

C   G   D7   G

Jin-gle all the way, Oh, what fun it is to ride in a one-horse o-pen sleigh!

2. A day or two ago, I thought I'd take a ride,
And soon Miss Fannie Bright was seated by my side;
The horse was lean and lank, misfortune seemed his lot,
He got into a drifted bank, and we, we got upsot.

3. Now the ground is white, go it while you're young,
Take the girls tonight, and sing this sleighing song;
Just get a bobtailed nag, two-forty for his speed,
Then hitch him to an open sleigh, and crack! you'll take the lead.

This sleighing song written in 1857 is a favorite of the Christmas season even though it contains no reference to the traditional symbols of Christmas.

Soldier, Soldier

ENGLAND

This song was very popular and widely sung after the demobilization of soldiers following the Civil War.

The Cuckoo

AUSTRIA

Smoothly

1. Oh, I went to the flow-ing spring, Where the wa-ter's so blue; And I heard there the cuck-oo bird, As she sang clear and true.

Chorus

Ho lay ah, Ho lay ah ree lee ah, Ho lay ah cuck-oo Ho lay ah ree lee ah, Ho lay ah cuck-oo. Ho lay ah ree lee ah, Ho lay ah cuck-oo, Ho lay ah ree lee ah hoo.

2. When I've married my lady fair what can I then desire?
   Oh, a home she'll be caring for, and some wood for the fire.

The cuckoo bird has a long, slender body which is a dull grayish-brown on top and white below. The European species builds no nest of its own. It lays eggs in the nests of other birds, leaving the eggs to be incubated by the foster bird. The American variety hatches and rears its own young. The call of the cuckoo sounds somewhat like its name.

151

Dame Get Up

Lilting

ENGLAND

1. Dame, get up— and bake your pies, bake your pies, bake your pies,

Dame, get up— and bake your pies on Christ-mas day in the morn - ing.

Key - G minor
(B♭ major key signature)
Harmonic alternation

2. Dame, why do your maidens cry? etc.
3. Dame, what causes your ducks to die? etc.
4. Dame, why is it your ducks can't fly? etc.

This old Mother Goose game song is written in minor mode. Verses often are made up by the singers as the song progresses.

Sweet Betsy from Pike

Crisply

WESTERN U. S.

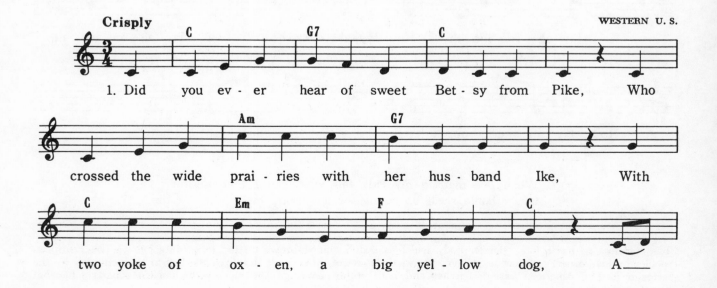

1. Did you ev - er hear of sweet Bet - sy from Pike, Who

crossed the wide prai - ries with her hus - band Ike, With

two yoke of ox - en, a big yel - low dog, A—

Sweet Betsy from Pike

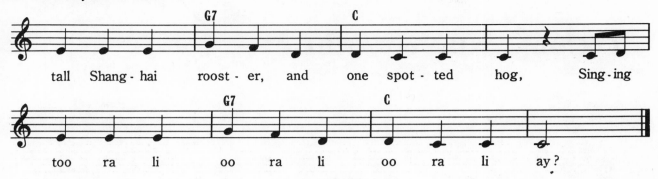

tall Shang - hai roost - er, and one spot - ted hog, Sing - ing
too ra li oo ra li oo ra li ay?

2. One evening quite early they camped on the Platte,
   Up close to the road on a green grassy flat,
   Poor Betsy, sore footed, lay down for repose,
   And Ike sat and gazed at his Pike County rose,
   Singing too ra li oo ra li oo ra li ay.

3. The alkali desert was burning and bare,
   And Ike cried in fear, "We are lost, I declare!
   My dear old Pike County, I'll come back to you!"
   Vowed Betsy, "You'll go by yourself if you do."
   Singing too ra li oo ra li oo ra li ay.

4. Their wagon broke down with a terrible smash,
   And over the prairie rolled all kinds of trash,
   Poor Ike got discouraged, and Betsy got mad,
   The dog drooped his tail and looked terribly sad.
   Singing too ra li oo ra li oo ra li ay.

5. 'Twas out on the desert that Betsy gave out,
   And down in the sand she lay rolling about,
   Poor Ike, half distracted, looked down in surprise,
   Saying "Betsy, get up, you'll get sand in your eyes!"
   Singing too ra li oo ra li oo ra li ay.

6. Then Betsy got up and gazed out on the plain,
   And said she'd go back to Pike County again,
   But Ike heaved a sigh, and they fondly embraced,
   And they headed on west with his arm 'round her waist.
   Singing too ra li oo ra li oo ra li ay.

7. They swam the wide rivers and crossed the high peaks,
   They camped on the prairie for weeks upon weeks,
   They fought with the Indians with musket and ball,
   And they reached California in spite of it all.
   Singing too ra li oo ra li oo ra li ay.

This song crossed the country with prospectors heading for western gold, and "Sweet Betsy" came to represent every girl who might have made the perilous trip. This song is typical of the exaggerated humor and satire sometimes found in songs of the frontier. Carl Sandburg wrote of *Sweet Betsy From Pike*, "It has the stuff of a realistic novel. It is droll and don't-care, bleary and leering, as slippery and lackadaisical as some of the comic characters of Shakespeare." The melody was brought to this country under the name of *Villikins And His Dinah*, a copy of which is in the British Museum in the form of a very old manuscript.

O Come, All Ye Faithful
(ADESTE FIDELES)

TR. F. OAKLEY

JOHN FRANCIS WADE

Triumphantly

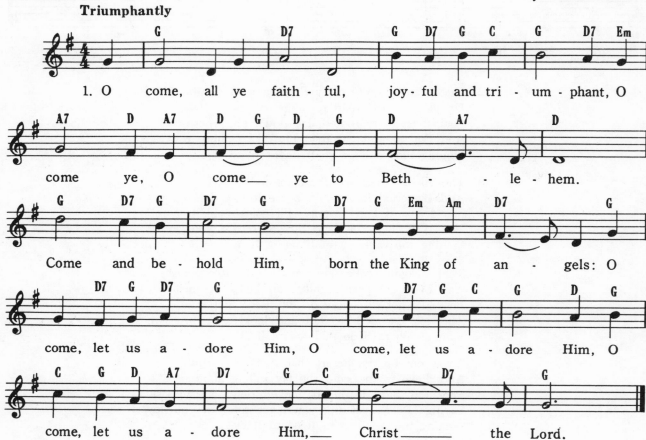

1. O come, all ye faith-ful, joy-ful and tri-um-phant, O
come ye, O come__ ye to Beth - - le-hem.
Come and be-hold Him, born the King of an - gels: O
come, let us a - dore Him, O come, let us a - dore Him, O
come, let us a - dore Him,__ Christ__ the Lord.

2. Sing, choirs of Angels, sing in exaltation,
   Sing, all ye citizens of heaven above;
   Glory to God, In the highest glory,
   Oh, come, let us adore Him, O come, let us adore Him,
   Oh, come, let us adore Him, Christ, the Lord.

3. Yea, Lord, we greet Thee, born this happy morning,
   Jesus, to Thee be all glory given;
   Word of the Father now in flesh appearing,
   Oh, come, let us adore Him, O come, let us adore Him,
   Oh, come, let us adore Him, Christ, the Lord.

1. Adeste, fideles, laeti triumphantes, Venite, venite in Bethlehem.
   Natum videte, Regem angelorum, Venite, adoremus,
   Venite, adoremus, Venite, adoremus Dominum.

For many years people were in doubt as to the origin of this wonderful old Christmas carol, but recently its beginnings have come to light and seem quite conclusive. John Francis Wade was an Englishman who lived at Douai, France. He copied music for a livelihood and composed hymns as a hobby. He took the words for

O Come, All Ye Faithful

this Christmas hymn from an old Latin chant sung by certain religious orders during processionals, and the melody appears in an edition of Wade's manuscripts, *Cantus Diversi*. It enjoyed great popularity at the Portuguese Embassy Chapel in London, and still is listed in some hymnals as the *Portuguese Hymn*. It was first sung in Latin, and for this reason sometimes is listed in hymnals as *Adeste Fideles,* the first two words of the Latin text.

Frog Went Courting

Jestfully

KENTUCKY

1. Frog went court-ing, he did ride, Rink-tum bod-dy mitch-a-cam-bo.

Sword and buck-ler by his side, Rink-tum bod-dy mitch-a-cam-bo.

Chorus

Kim - an - i - ro, down to Cai - ro, Kim - an - i - ro,

Cai - ro; Strad - a - lad - da - lad - a - bod - dy,

Lad - da - bod - dy - link - tum, Rink - tum bod - dy mitch - a - cam - bo.

2. To the lady mouse said he, "Will you kindly marry me?" etc.

3. Who can make the wedding gown? Old Miss Rat from London town, etc.

4. Then there came a big Tom Cat, So long frog and mouse and rat! etc.

In the English version of this southern mountain nonsense song, the frog is said to refer to the Duke of Anjou who was courting Queen Elizabeth. Anjou (An' joo) was an old province of western France surrounding the city of Angers. Its name has been used by several royal houses, notably by the Plantagenets. Another version of *Frog Went Courting* was popular in the same southern mountain area, but bears little resemblance to this version.

Early to Bed

Swinging

ROUND

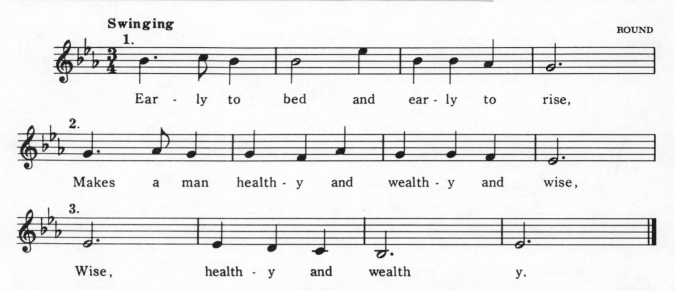

Ear - ly to bed and ear - ly to rise,

Makes a man health - y and wealth - y and wise,

Wise, health - y and wealth y.

This early American round echoes the advice given by Benjamin Franklin in his *Poor Richard's Almanac* and probably was inspired by the old proverb stated in the song. Franklin (1706-1790), in addition to being a world famous scientist, was widely acclaimed as a philosopher. He was founder of the American Philosophical Society, and established the first circulating library in America in 1731. His writings rank high in American literature for their shrewd, lucid comments on a wide variety of subjects.

The Star-Spangled Banner

FRANCIS SCOTT KEY

JOHN STAFFORD SMITH

Proudly

1. Oh,____ say can you see, by the dawn's ear - ly

light, What so proud - ly we hailed at the twi - light's last

gleam - ing, Whose broad stripes and bright stars, through the

The Star-Spangled Banner

2. On the shore dimly seen through the mists of the deep,
   Where the foe's haughty host in dread silence reposes,
   What is that which the breeze, o'er the towering steep,
   As it fitfully blows, half conceals, half discloses?
   Now it catches the gleam of the morning's first beam,
   In full glory reflected now shines in the stream,
   'Tis the Star-Spangled Banner, O long may it wave
   O'er the land of the free and the home of the brave.

3. O thus be it ever when free men shall stand
   Between their loved homes and the war's desolation!
   Blest with vict'ry and peace may the heaven-rescued land
   Praise the power that hath made and preserved us a nation!
   Then conquer we must, when our cause it is just,
   And this be our motto, "In God is our trust,"
   And the Star-Spangled Banner in triumph shall wave
   O'er the land of the free and the home of the brave.

The young district attorney for Washington, D. C., Francis Scott Key, was detained in the harbor by the British during the bombardment of Fort McHenry in 1814. Fearful that the fort would fall during the attack which continued through the night, Key expressed his relief and pride in a poem written on the spot to be sung to the tune *Anacreon in Heaven*. Actor Ferdinand Durang sang the song for the first time in a Baltimore tavern. It found instant favor with all who heard it, but it was not officially designated as the national anthem until 1931.

The Derby Ram

ENGLAND

Boastfully

1. As I went down to Der - by, All on a sum - mer's day, 'Twas there I saw the big - gest ram 'twas ev - er fed on hay.

Chorus

And sing tith - er - y - i - re - our - y - ann, Sing tith - er - y - i - o - day.

2. The wool on that ram's back, sir, it reached unto the sky,
   And eagles built their nests there, I heard their young ones cry.

3. The wool on that ram's belly, it dragged down to the ground,
   They sold it there in Derby for forty thousand pounds.

4. The horns on that ram's head, sir, they reached up to the moon,
   A man went up in March but didn't get back down till June.

5. He had four feet to walk, sir, he had four feet to stand,
   And every foot he had, sir, took at least an acre of land.

6. The wool on that ram's tail, sir, I've heard the weaver say,
   It spun full forty yards, sir, and some was thrown away.

This English song with its folk humor of high exaggeration was a favorite of George Washington, it is said. Derby (pronounced and sometimes spelled darby) is the county seat of Derbyshire, England. It is pleasantly situated in a wide and fertile valley open to the south. Oats and turnips are important crops, and the area is famous for the sheep raised there. Country fairs are held, and competition for prizes is keen among animal raisers. This may have been one raiser's opinion of his prize ram — or the story may have grown with the telling as settlers brought it to America where it enjoyed equal popularity with the favor it enjoyed in England.

Did You Ever See a Lassie
(ACH DU LIEBER AUGUSTIN)

GERMANY

Quickly

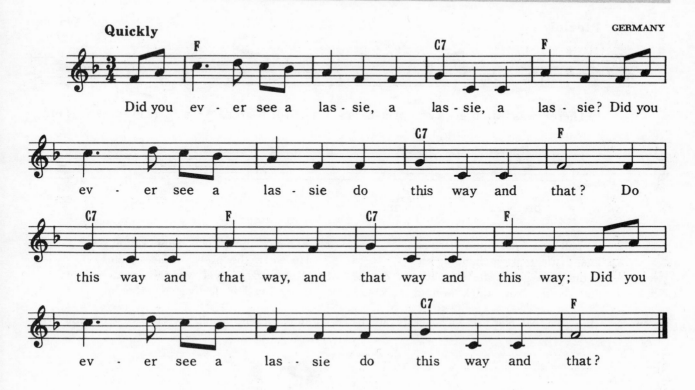

Did you ev - er see a las - sie, a las - sie, a las - sie? Did you

ev - er see a las - sie do this way and that? Do

this way and that way, and that way and this way; Did you

ev - er see a las - sie do this way and that?

1. Ach, du lieber Augustin, Augustin, Augustin,
   Ach, du lieber Augustin, Alles ist hin.
   Geld ist hin, Mad'l ist hin, All's ist hin, Augustin;
   Ach, du lieber Augustin, Alles ist hin.

2. Ach, du lieber Augustin, Augustin, Augustin,
   Ach, du lieber Augustin, Alles ist hin.
   Boch ist weg, Stock ist weg, Auch ich bin in dem Dreck;
   Ach, du lieber Augustin, Alles ist hin.

(Translation)

1. O, my dear old Augustin, Augustin, Augustin,
   O, my dear old Augustin, robbed I have been.
   Money's gone, girl is gone, everything else is gone;
   O, my dear old Augustin, robbed I have been.

2. Goat is gone, staff is gone, and I am in a fix;

This English country dance song, based on a German folk song, was brought to this country by early settlers and flourished in New England. The music moves in waltz time — three beats or pulses to a measure — and the rhythm is not as vigorous or demanding as many country dance tunes.

The Sleeping Princess

SWEDEN

Placidly

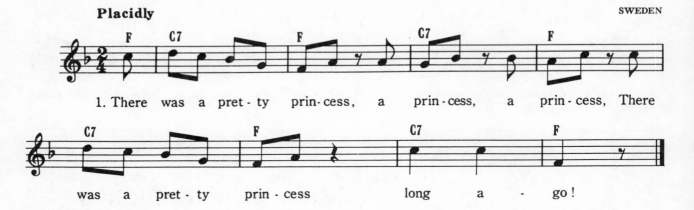

1. There was a pret-ty prin-cess, a prin-cess, a prin-cess, There

was a pret-ty prin-cess long a - go!

2. A spell was cast upon her, etc.
3. The castle was enchanted, etc.
4. A hundred years she slept there, etc.
5. The thorns grew thick around it, etc.

6. A handsome prince came riding, etc.
7. He woke the pretty princess, etc.
8. They had a royal wedding, etc.
9. They lived their lives together, etc.

The words set to this old Swedish folk melody are based on an old legend familiar to children the world over.

Ten Little Indians

U. S.

Quickly

1. One lit - tle, two lit - tle, three lit - tle In - dians

Four lit - tle, five lit - tle, six lit - tle In - dians,

Seven lit - tle, eight lit - tle nine lit - tle In - dians,

160

Ten Little Indians

Ten lit - tle In - dian boys.

2. Ten little, nine little, eight little Indians,
Seven little, six little, five little Indians,
Four little, three little, two little Indians,
One little Indian boy.

This familiar counting song not only adds and takes away numbers, but is suitable for games, dances and pantomime.

Cotton Needs Picking

VIRGINIA

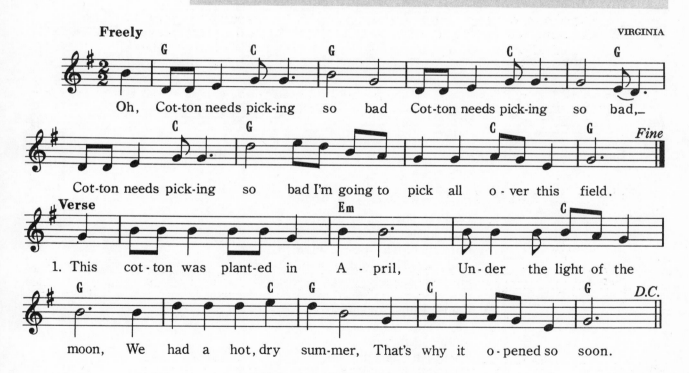

Freely

Oh, Cot-ton needs pick-ing so bad Cot-ton needs pick-ing so bad,—

Cot-ton needs pick-ing so bad I'm going to pick all o - ver this field.

Verse

1. This cot - ton was plant-ed in A - pril, Un - der the light of the

moon, We had a hot, dry sum-mer, That's why it o - pened so soon.

2. Oh, hurry up, hurry up, children,
Pick that cotton today;
The sky it looks so cloudy,
A storm is coming this way.

This was a popular work song in the cotton fields. Such songs served to lighten spirits as well as to pace the work. Cotton is the basis for the cloth most widely used throughout the world. A four or five foot shrub, the cotton plant bears blossoms which produce a boll of about two-thirds seed and one-third fiber. The plant needs rich soil, moderate irrigation, and much sun. Eli Whitney's cotton gin invented in 1793 removed the seeds from the fiber and gave the cotton industry great impetus. Until recently all cotton was picked by hand. In 1927 the Rust brothers invented a machine to do the picking. The United States ranks among the chief cotton-producing countries.

Come Thou Almighty King

Regally

FELICE GIARDINI

1. Come Thou al - might - y King, Help us Thy praise_____ to sing. Help us to praise, Fa - ther all glo - ri - ous, O'er all vic - to - ri - ous, Come and reign o - ver us, An - cient of days.

2. Come, Thou incarnate Word,
   Gird on Thy mighty sword,
   Our prayer attend!
   Come, and Thy people bless,
   And give Thy word success;
   Spirit of holiness, on us descend!

3. Come, Holy Comforter,
   Thy sacred witness bear,
   In this glad hour!
   Thou, who almighty art,
   Now rule in every heart,
   And ne'er from us depart, Spirit of power!

Giardini (1716-1796) was a distinguished Italian dramatic composer and violinist. He concertized with great success, and settled in Paris where he became a favorite of the court and aristocracy. In 1750 he became leader of the Italian Opera, and in 1756 became its manager. He died in Russia during a tour with his opera troup. *Come Thou Almighty King* is a hymn of the Holy Trinity and is sung to music known as the *Italian Hymn* written ·by Giardini. The words, written in 1756, were widely attributed to the famous hymnist, Charles Wesley. Evidence failed to support this assignment, and the hymn does not appear in any of Wesley's publications. The hymn, once sung to the tune of the British national anthem, *God Save Our Gracious King,* has been translated into many languages and is sung in many nations.

Carrousel

SWEDEN

Cheerfully

1. How we love to ride the car - rou - sel,

'Round and 'round ad - vanc - ing, on our po - nies pranc - ing. Cam - els, ze - bras,

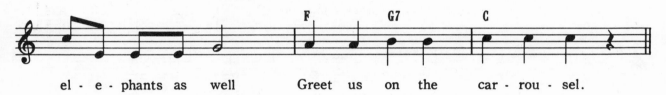

el - e - phants as well Greet us on the car - rou - sel.

Chorus

Ha, ha, ha, Hap - py are we.

An - der - son and Hen - der - son and Lund - strom and me.

2. While we're riding on the carrousel,
   Up and down we're bouncing, in the saddle jouncing,
   Any time you hear the starting bell
   Join us on the carrousel.

From *This Is Music* — Book III by William R. Sur, William R. Fisher, Mary R. Tolbert, and Adeline McCall. Copyright © 1961 by Allyn and Bacon, Inc. Used by permission.

For the first seven measure of the song the girls circle left two steps to a measure — boys with hands on girls' shoulders. On the eighth measure the dancers stamp in place. At the chorus, dancers slide left four times each measure. On the repeat, they slide right. On the final measure, partners change places, then repeat the dance.

Diddle, Diddle Dumpling

MOTHER GOOSE RHYME

Saucily

Did - dle, did - dle dump - ling, my son John
Went to bed with his stock - ings on; One shoe off and
one shoe on, Did - dle, did - dle dump - ling, my son John.

This nursery rhyme was first sung in American music halls by Arthur Lloyd, who claimed its authorship on the published copy.

Santy Maloney

ENGLAND

Lively

1. Can you dance, San - ty Ma - lon - ey? Can you dance, San - ty Ma - lon - ey?
Can you dance, San - ty Ma - lon - ey, As we go round a - bout?

Santy Maloney

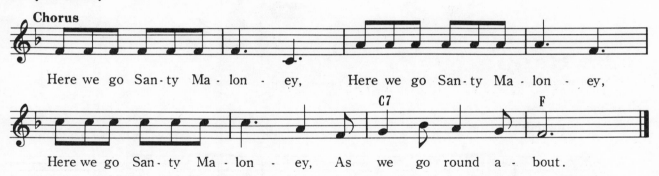

Here we go San-ty Ma-lon-ey, Here we go San-ty Ma-lon-ey,

Here we go San-ty Ma-lon-ey, As we go round a-bout.

2. Put your two hands on your shoulders, (3 times)
   As we go round about.

3. Put your two hands out before you, (3 times)
   As we go round about.

4. Put your two hands in your pockets (3 times)
   As we go round about.

5. Put your two hands back behind you, (3 times)
   As we go round about.

The group forms a circle and skips while singing verse 1 and the first chorus. The group stops and performs the actions described while singing the other verses, and then resumes skipping each time the chorus is sung. Create additional verses and sing them with appropriate actions.

The Farmer in the Dell

ENGLAND

1. The far-mer in the dell,___ The far-mer in the dell,

Hi! ho! the der-ry oh, The far-mer in the dell.___

2. The farmer takes a wife	6. The dog takes the cat
3. The wife takes the child	7. The cat takes the rat
4. The child takes the nurse	8. The rat takes the cheese
5. The nurse takes the dog	9. The cheese stands alone

This ring choosing game originally was an English country dance. It starts with "the farmer" in the center of the ring. The "taken" player drops out of the ring and joins the farmer in the center. After all the choosing is completed, the "cheese," who stands alone, becomes the farmer, and the game begins again.

La Raspe

TR. MAURICE TALBOT

MEXICO

Spanish rhythm

With click-ing of cas-ta-nets and jin-gle of tam-bou-rine, All work of the day for-got, and danc-ing to-night is queen. We're danc-ing a dance from old Mex-i-co, La la la la la la; Our steps light and gay, and our hearts a-glow, La la la la la la.

La Raspe is a traditional Mexican song-dance. The rhythm and words establish the style of the dance. The tune is lively and gay; the dance steps are light and springy.

The Keeper

Moving along

ENGLAND

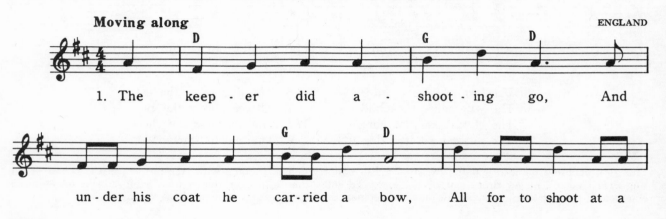

1. The keep-er did a-shoot-ing go, And un-der his coat he car-ried a bow, All for to shoot at a

166

The Keeper

mer-ry lit-tle doe A - mong the leaves so— green, O.

Chorus Jack-ie boy! Sing ye well! Hey down,
Mas - ter! Ver-y well! Ho down,

der - ry, der-ry down, A - mong the leaves so— green, O. To my
hey, down, down, Hey down,

To my ho, down, down, Ho down
der - ry, der - ry down A - mong the leaves so— green, O.

2. The first doe he shot at he missed,
   The second doe he trimmed he kissed,
   The third doe went where nobody wist,
   Among the leaves so green, O.

3. The fourth doe she did cross the plain;
   The keeper fetched her back again;
   Where she is now she may remain,
   Among the leaves so green, O.

4. The fifth doe she did cross the brook,
   The keeper fetched her back with his crook;
   Where she is now you must go and look
   Among the leaves so green, O.

5. The sixth doe she ran over the plain,
   But he with his hounds did turn her again,
   And it's there he did hunt in a merry, merry vein
   Among the leaves so green, O.

This familiar old English folk song is often used as a tone matching song. Part of the group sings the first part of the song in unison. The others "echo" the tones in the last section of the song.

Kookaburra
ROUND

M. SINCLAIR

AUSTRALIA

KEY–D

Fast

1. SOL SOL SOL SOL LA LA LA SOL MI SOL MI

0 5 5 5 5 6 6 5 3 5 3

Kook - a - bur - ra sits on an old gum tree.____

2. MI MI MI MI FA FA FA MI DO MI DO

3 3 3 3 4 4 4 3 1 3 1

Mer - ry, mer - ry king of the bush is he.____

3. DO LA TI DO LA SOL SOL LA SOL FA 4. MI DO DO DO DO

8 6 7 8 6 5 5 6 5 4 3 1 1 1 1

Laugh, kook-a - bur - ra, laugh, kook-a - bur - ra, Gay your life must be.

Words and music from *The Ditty Bag*, copyright, 1946, by Janet E. Tobitt. Used by permission.

The kookaburra is a large kingfisher of Australia and New Guinea. It sometimes is called a laughing jackass because of the weird, raucous laugh-like sound it makes.

Sing a Song of Sixpence

MOTHER GOOSE RHYME

J. W. ELLIOTT

Lively

1. Sing a song of six - pence, a pock - et full of rye;

Four and twen - ty black - birds baked in a pie;

When the pie was o - pened, the birds be - gan to sing;

Sing a Song of Sixpence

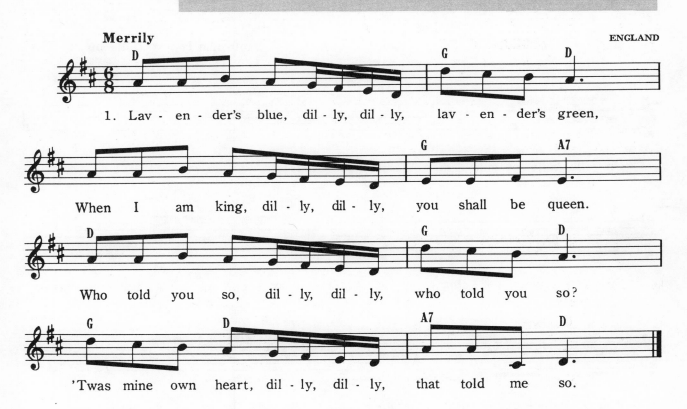

Was-n't that a dain-ty dish to set be-fore a king?

2. The king was in the counting house counting out his money;
The queen was in the parlor eating bread and honey;
The maid was in the garden hanging out the clothes;
Along came a blackbird and nipped off her nose.

Lavender's Blue

Merrily

ENGLAND

1. Lav - en - der's blue, dil - ly, dil - ly, lav - en - der's green,

When I am king, dil - ly, dil - ly, you shall be queen.

Who told you so, dil - ly, dil - ly, who told you so?

'Twas mine own heart, dil - ly, dil - ly, that told me so.

2. Call up your men, dilly, dilly, set them to work,
Some with a hoe, dilly, dilly, some with a fork;
Some to pitch hay, dilly dilly, some to hoe corn,
While you and I, dilly dilly, keep ourselves warm.

This English folk song once was a choosing game song. It refers to the choosing of the king and the queen during Twelfth-night, the evening which preceded Twelfth-day, when games and feasting marked the celebration. Twelfth-day, the twelfth day after Christmas, formerly was observed as the official end of the Christmas season.

Kentucky Babe

RICHARD BUCK

ADAM GEIBEL

Quietly

1. Skeet - ers are a - hum - ming on the hon - ey - suck - le vine,

Sleep, Ken - tuck - y Babe! Sand - man is a - com - ing to this

lit - tle babe of mine, Sleep, Ken - tuck - y Babe!

Sil - v'ry moon is shin - ing in the heav - ens up a - bove,

Bob - o - link is pin - ing for his lit - tle la - dy love.

You are might - y luck - y, Babe of old Ken - tuck - y,

Kentucky Babe

Close your eyes in sleep._____

Chorus

Fly a - way, Fly a - way Ken-tuck - y Babe,

fly a - way to rest, Fly a - way,

Lay your lit - tle sleep - y head on your mam - my's breast.

Um_____ Um_____

Close your eyes in sleep._____

2. Daddy's in the cane-break with his little dog and gun,
Sleep, Kentucky Babe,
Possum for your breakfast when your sleeping time is done,
Sleep, Kentucky Babe,
Bogie man will catch you sure unless you close your eyes,
Waiting just outside the door to take you by surprise,
Best be keeping shady, drowsy little lady,
Close your eyes in sleep.

This song was published in 1896. The melody was written by Adam Geibel, a German organist, and the words composed by Richard Buck. It attained immediate popularity and received wide performance by glee clubs across the country. It soon became a standard with barbershop quartets and remained a permanent part of their repertoire.

O Hanukkah

With feeling

JEWISH FOLK SONG

O Ha-nuk-kah, O Ha-nuk-kah, come light the me-no-rah,

Let's have a par-ty, we'll all dance the ho-rah, Gath-er round the ta-ble, we'll

give you a treat, S'vi-vo-nim to play with, le-vi-vot to eat, And

while we are play-ing, The can-dles are burn-ing low.

One for each night, they shed a sweet light, To re-

1. mind us of days long a-go,

2. mind us of days long a-go.

Reprinted from *Gateway to Jewish Song* by Judith K. Eisenstein, published by Behrman House, Inc., 1261 Broadway, New York 1, N.Y.

Hanukkah is the Hebrew word meaning "dedication." The Hebrew Hanukkah, or Feast of Lights, is an eight-day celebration commemorating the rededication of the Temple at Jerusalem (165 B.C.) after the Maccabees had defeated the Syrian Greek armies in a religious war of liberation. During the festival, a candle is lit for each day. A special candle, called the *shamos*, is used to light the others. Hanukkah falls at approximately the same time as Christmas, and is celebrated with parties, entertainments, and the exchange of gifts. The *menorah*, a candelabra which holds the eight candles, is not only in synagogues but in homes as well. The *horah* mentioned in *O Hanukkah* is a Jewish ring dance, *s'vivonim* is the spinning top children play with, and *levivot* is a special pastry eaten at Hanukkah.

Children's Prayer

ADELHEID WETTE
TR. CONSTANCE BACHE

E. HUMPERDINCK

Prayerfully

When at night I go to sleep, Four - teen an - gels

watch do— keep,— Two my head are guard - ing,

Two my feet are guid - ing, Two are on my right hand,

Two are on my left hand, Two who warm - ly cov - er,

Two who o'er me hov - er, Two to whom tis

giv - en to guide my steps to hea - - ven.

This familiar evening paper is from Engelbert Humperdinck's fairy tale opera, *Hansel And Gretel*. It was written in 1893, and was an immediate success. This was due both to the excellence of the opera and the native folk music which inspired it. Within a year it was in the repertoire of every opera house in Germany and was enjoying great success in other countries. In the opera, this prayer is sung as a duet by Hansel and Gretel in the dusky woods just before they fall asleep. The angels about which they sing come and keep watch over them.

The Donkey

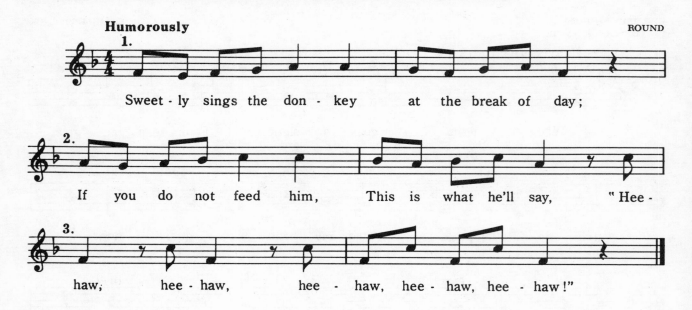

Humorously   ROUND

1. Sweet - ly sings the don - key   at the break of day;

2. If you do not feed him,   This is what he'll say,   " Hee -

3. haw;   hee - haw,   hee - haw, hee - haw, hee - haw!"

The donkey, usually gray in color, was tamed before the horse in the deserts of Egypt and Western Asia. They still run wild in the Nubian deserts and in the interior of Asia and are agile and courageous. They are smaller than the horse, with long hair only at the end of the tail. The donkey is highly prized as a domestic animal, especially in Syria and Egypt, where it yields milk and leather.

God Rest You Merry, Gentlemen

Brightly   ENGLAND

| Em | B7 | Em | Am | Em | C |

1. God rest you mer - ry,   gen - tle - men, let   noth - ing you dis -

| B7 | Em | B7 | Em | Am | Em | C |

may,   Re - mem-ber Christ our   Sav - iour was   born on Christ - mas

God Rest You Merry, Gentlemen

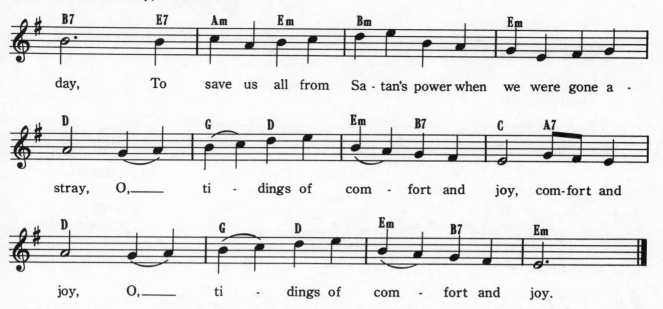

day,   To   save us all from   Sa - tan's power when we were gone a -

stray,   O,____   ti - dings of   com - fort and   joy,   com-fort and

joy,   O,____   ti - dings of   com - fort and   joy.

2. From God our heavenly Father
A blessed angel came,
And unto certain shepherds
Brought tidings of the same,
How that in Bethlehem was born
The son of God by name,
O, tidings of comfort and joy,
Comfort and joy,
O, tidings of comfort and joy.

3. "Fear not, then," said the angel,
"Let nothing you affright,
This day is born a Saviour
Of a pure Virgin bright,
To free all those who trust in Him
From Satan's power and might,"
O, tidings of comfort and joy,
Comfort and joy,
O, tidings of comfort and joy.

4. But when to Bethlehem they came
Whereat this Infant lay,
They found Him in a manger
Where oxen feed on hay,
His mother, Mary, kneeling,
Unto the Lord did pray,
O, tidings of comfort and joy,
Comfort and joy,
O, tidings of comfort and joy.

5. Now to the Lord sing praises,
All you within this place,
And with true love and brotherhood
Each other now embrace,
This holy tide of Christmas
All others doth deface,
O, tidings of comfort and joy,
Comfort and joy,
O, tidings of comfort and joy.

This joyful carol is rated the most popular Christmas carol in the land of its origin, England, and it has become a favorite in all English-speaking countries. Charles Dickens refers to it in his famous story, *A Christmas Carol.* The miser, Scrooge, was counting his money when a poor lad paused to cheer the man and sang out "God Rest You Merry, Gentleman, Let nothing you dismay!" Scrooge chased him away, but later came under the spell of the season and echoed a hearty "amen" to Tiny Tim's Christmas prayer, "God Bless Us Everyone." The melody is an old, traditional one originally harmonized by the noted composer and organist, Sir John Stainer. For centuries carolers have gone from door to door singing this lovely old Yule message of faith and good will.

Clementine

U. S.

Whimsically

G

1. In a cav - ern, in a can - yon, Ex - ca - vat - ing for a

D7   **G**   **D7**   **G**

mine, Dwelt a min - er, for - ty - nin - er, And his daugh - ter Clem - en - tine.

Chorus

Oh, my dar - ling, Oh, my dar - ling, Oh, my dar - ling Clem - en -

D7   **G**   **D7**   **G**

tine! You are lost and gone for - ev - er, Dread-ful sor - ry, Clem-en-tine!

2. Light she was, and like a fairy,
   And her shoes were number nine,
   Herring boxes without topses,
   Sandals were for Clementine.

3. Drove she ducklings to the water
   Every morning just at nine,
   Hit her foot against a splinter,
   Fell into the foaming brine.

4. Ruby lips above the water
   Blowing bubbles soft and fine;
   As for me, I was no swimmer
   And I lost my Clementine.

5. How I missed her, how I missed her,
   How I missed my Clementine,
   Then I kissed her little sister,
   And forgot dear Clementine.

The origin of this song is unknown. It was not written by Stephen Foster, as was believed at one time. Some authorities attribute the words and music to Percy Montrose, but without conclusive evidence. *Clementine* probably was written about 1883. It soon became a favorite on college campuses, and its popularity spread throughout the country.

176

Prayer of Thanksgiving

TR. THEODORE BAKER

NETHERLANDS

With gladness

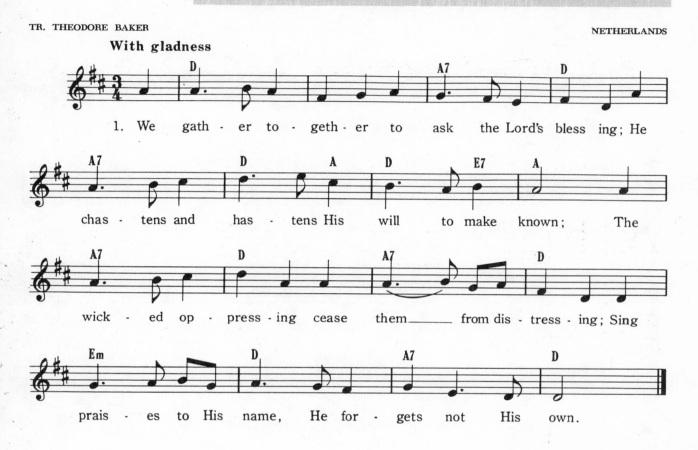

1. We gath-er to-geth-er to ask the Lord's bless-ing; He chas-tens and has-tens His will to make known; The wick-ed op-press-ing cease them from dis-tress-ing; Sing prais-es to His name, He for-gets not His own.

2. Beside us to guide us, our God with us joining,
   Ordaining, maintaining His kingdom divine;
   So from the beginning the fight we were winning,
   Thou, Lord, was at our side, let the glory be Thine.

3. We all do extol Thee, Thou leader in battle,
   And pray that Thou still our Defender will be.
   Let Thy congregation escape tribulation,
   Thy name be ever praised, and Thy people be free.

This song came to America with Dutch settlers and became a favorite among the colonists. Dutch merchants had planted a trading post in North America as early as 1612. A Dutch colony was established in 1613. Known as New Netherland, it included the territory which under subsequent British colonization was New York, New Jersey, and Delaware. Most of the wealth of New Netherland came from the fur trade. New Amsterdam was the name given to the Dutch Colonial town on Manhattan Island which later became New York City. When England took possession, the name was changed in honor of the Duke of York who was given a grant of the territory.

Little David, Play on Your Harp

SPIRITUAL

Spiritedly

Lit-tle Da - vid, play on your harp, Hal - le - lu! Hal - le -

lu! Lit - tle Da - vid play on your harp, Hal - le -

lu! Lit-tle Da - vid play on your harp, Hal - le - lu! Hal - le -

lu! Lit-tle Da - vid play on your harp, Hal - le - lu!

Verse

1. Lit - tle Da - vid was a shep-herd boy, He

killed Go - li - ath and shout-ed for joy.

2. Oh, Joshua was the son of Nun, he never would quit till his work was done.

This is the musical version of David and Goliath as the Negroes sang it. The moving and simple spiritual is based on the Biblical record of the young shepherd boy, David, who agreed to fight the Philistine giant, Goliath armed with only a sling shot (I Samuel 17:4,49). In this spiritual, as in many others, the solo voice or leader starts each line of the verse, and the entire group joins in the refrain. *Little David, Play On Your Harp* is one of the more highly syncopated spirituals and is lively in character.

When Johnny Comes Marching Home

LOUIS LAMBERT

March tempo

1. When John-ny comes march-ing home a-gain, hur-rah,_____ hur-rah!_____ We'll give him a heart-y wel-come then, hur-rah,_____ hur-rah!_____ The_ men will cheer,_ the boys will shout, the la-dies they_ will all turn out, And we'll all feel gay when John-ny comes march-ing home._____

2. The old church bell will peal with joy, hurrah, hurrah!
   To welcome home our darling boy, hurrah, hurrah!
   The village lads and lassies say,
   With roses they will strew the way,
   And we'll all feel gay when Johnny comes marching home.

Patrick Gilmore, an Irishman in the Union Army band, wrote the words of this marching song early in the Civil War period under the pen name "Louis Lambert." The melody was from an Irish, antiwar folk song although Gilmore claimed he adapted it from a "well-known Negro air."

Little Jack Horner

MOTHER GOOSE RHYME

J. W. ELLIOTT

Moderately

Lit - tle Jack Hor - ner sat in a cor - ner

eat - ing a Christ - mas pie,_____ He put in his thumb and

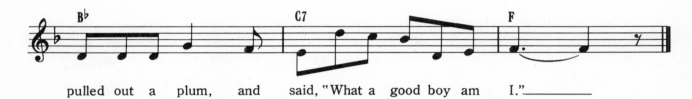

pulled out a plum, and said, "What a good boy am I."_____

Good King Wenceslas

JOHN M. NEALE

ENGLAND

With dignity

1. Good King Wen - ces - las looked out, On the Feast of Ste - phen,

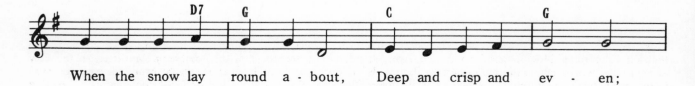

When the snow lay round a - bout, Deep and crisp and ev - en;

180

Good King Wenceslas

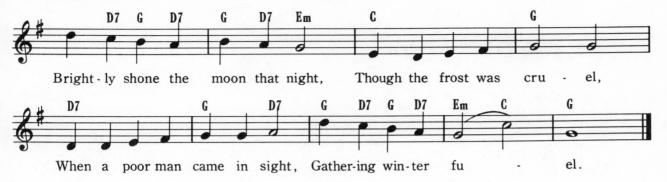

Bright - ly shone the moon that night, Though the frost was cru - el,

When a poor man came in sight, Gather-ing win-ter fu - el.

2. "Hither, page, and stand by me,
   If thou knowest it, telling,
   Yonder peasant, who is he,
   Where and what his dwelling?"
   "Sire, he lives a good league hence
   Underneath the mountain,
   Right against the forest fence
   By Saint Agnes' fountain."

3. "Bring me flesh, and bring me wine,
   Bring me pine logs hither,
   Thou and I will see him dine
   When we bear them thither."
   Page and monarch forth they went,
   Forth they went together,
   Through the rude wind's wild lament
   And the bitter weather.

4. "Sire, the night is darker now,
   And the wind blows stronger;
   Fails my heart, I know not how,
   I can go no longer."
   "Mark my footsteps, my good page,
   Tread thou in them boldly,
   Thou shalt find the winter's rage
   Freeze thy blood less coldly."

5. In his master's steps he trod,
   Where the snow lay dinted,
   Heat was in the very sod
   Which the saint had printed.
   Therefore, Christian men, be sure,
   Wealth or rank possessing,
   Ye who now will bless the poor
   Shall yourselves find blessing.

This popular carol is not about the wondrous birth of the Christ Child but about the love and kindness He brought to the world. It is based on the life of Wenceslas the Holy, who ruled Bohemia in the tenth century and was renowned for his great kindness to the needy. Reputed to have been particularly generous with his subjects at Christmas and on St. Stephen's Day, December 26, Wenceslas is honored in Bohemia as protecting saint and national benefactor.

Las Mañanitas

As a serenade

MEXICO

As of old, we bring a song, a greet - ing gay at ear - ly dawn; Wak - en, friend, and join our sing - ing, O hear the mu - sic we bring.

I'll step out of doors at dawn - ing, I'll climb up a mag - ic stair, And bring down the stars of morn - ing to make a crown for your hair.

Estas son las mañanitas que cantaba el Rey David,
Pero no eran tanbonitas como las cantan aquí.
Despierta, mi bién, despierta, mira que ya amaneció;
Ya los pajarillos cantan, la luna ya se metió.
Despierta, mi bién, despierta, mira que ya amaneció;
Ya los pajarillos cantan, la luma ya se metió.
Estas son las mañanitas que cantaba el Rey David,
Pero no eran tanbonitas como las cantan aquí.

This birthday serenade usually is sung early in the day as a beginning to the birthday celebration. The melody is a Mexican folk tune.

Little Boy Blue

MOTHER GOOSE RHYME

Gently

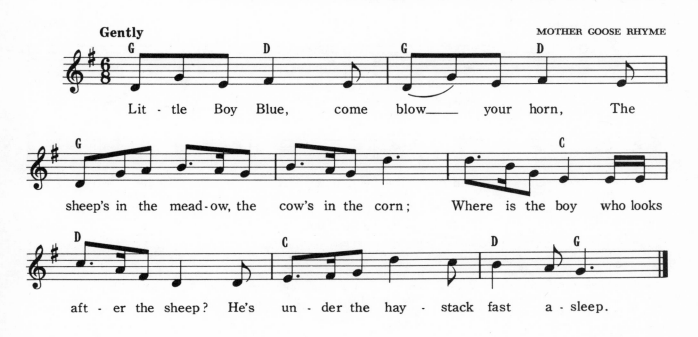

Lit - tle Boy Blue, come blow___ your horn, The sheep's in the mead-ow, the cow's in the corn; Where is the boy who looks aft - er the sheep? He's un - der the hay - stack fast a - sleep.

Taps

U. S. ARMY BUGLE CALL

Restfully

Day is done, gone the sun, From the lake, from the hill, from the sky. All is well, safe - ly rest, God is nigh.

Taps are sounded in the armed forces as a signal for everyone to put lights out and retire for the night. Taps also are sounded at funerals of military personnel. Various sets of words have been sung to this famous bugle call.

Go In and Out the Window

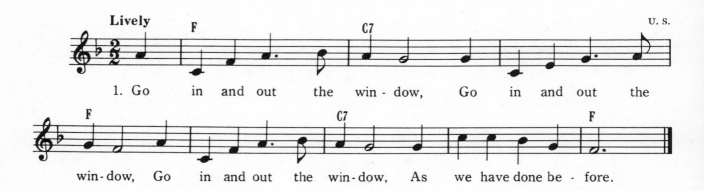

Lively   F   C7   U. S.

1. Go in and out the win - dow, Go in and out the

F   C7   F

win - dow, Go in and out the win - dow, As we have done be - fore.

2. Go forth and choose your partner, etc.
3. Go underneath the arches, etc.

This is an old circle singing game. Most frequently, the players form a circle and join hands. Arms are raised, and the player designated "it" weaves in and out as the song progresses. During the second verse, he chooses a partner. The couple then weaves in and out, and the second player becomes "it." Verses may be added to the song to indicate additional activities.

When the Train Comes Along

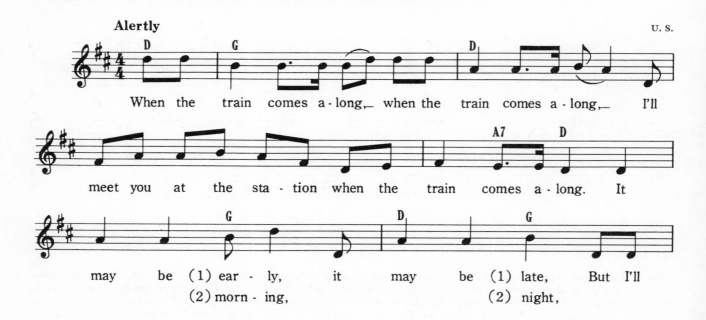

Alertly   D   G   D   U. S.

When the train comes a - long,— when the train comes a - long,— I'll

                        A7   D

meet you at the sta - tion when the train comes a - long. It

            G   D   G

may be (1) ear - ly, it may be (1) late, But I'll
      (2) morn - ing,   (2) night,

When The Train Comes Along

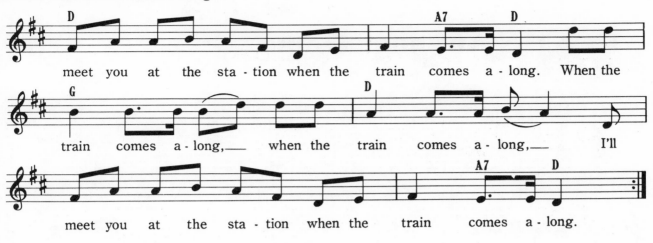

meet you at the sta-tion when the train comes a-long. When the

train comes a-long,— when the train comes a-long,— I'll

meet you at the sta-tion when the train comes a-long.

3. Raining, wet.
4. Snowing, cold.

This American folk song lends itself to dramatization, or it may be used as a statement-answer song.

Goodby, Old Paint

COWBOY

Regretfully

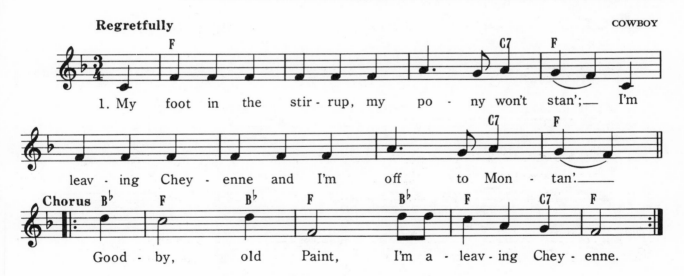

1. My foot in the stir-rup, my po-ny won't stan';— I'm

leav-ing Chey-enne and I'm off to Mon-tan'.—

Chorus Good-by, old Paint, I'm a-leav-ing Chey-enne.

2. I'm riding old Paint and I'm leading old Fan;
Goodby little Annie, I'm off for Montan'.

3. Oh, keep yourself by me as long as you can;
Goodby little Annie, I'm off for Montan'.

This cowboy song was used as the closing number at pioneer dances. Verses were made up by the dancers and sung to postpone the evening's ending as long as possible. This is another of the favorite cowboy songs selected by the distinguished American composer, Aaron Copland, for inclusion in his ballet suite, *Billy The Kid* (1938). By virtue of such compositions by Copland, Roy Harris, and George Antheil, many of the early American ballads and cowboy songs have reached concert halls throughout the country.

Hey, Ho, Anybody Home
ROUND

ENGLAND

Stoically

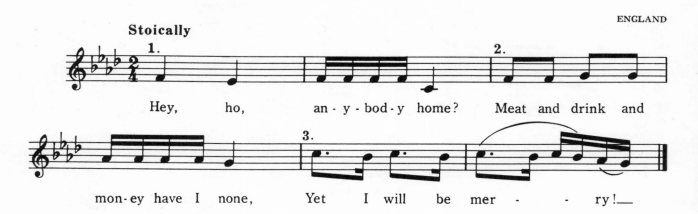

Hey, ho, an-y-bod-y home? Meat and drink and

mon-ey have I none, Yet I will be mer - - ry!—

This old English round is written in the minor mode. The words of the first phrase also are sung and published as "Heigh, ho, nobody home."

Dona Nobis Pacem

ROUND

Peacefully

Do - na no - bis pa - cem pa - cem,

do - na — no - bis pa - - cem.

Do - na no - bis pa - cem,

do - na no - bis pa - - cem.

186

Dona Nobis Pacem

Do - na   no - bis___ pa - cem,

do - na   no - bis   pa - - cem.

The words to this Latin canon mean "give to us peace." It dates from the sixteenth century, but the composer is unknown.

My Hat
(MEIN HUT)

GERMANY

Moderate waltz time

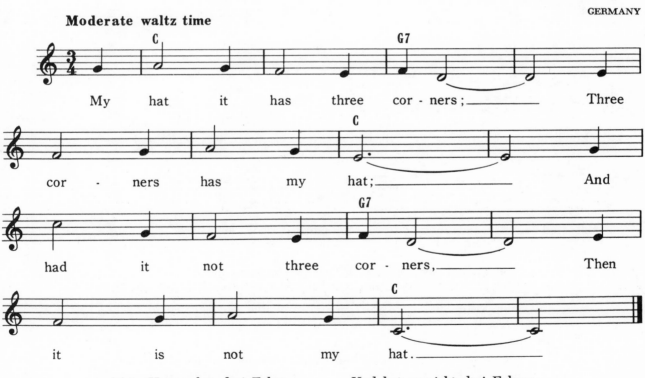

My hat it has three cor - ners;___ Three

cor - ners has my hat;___ And

had it not three cor - ners,___ Then

it is not my hat.___

Mein Hut er hat drei Ecken;   Und hat er nicht drei Ecken;
Drei Ecken hat mein Hut;   Denn das ist nicht mein Hut.

Strolling musicians frequent the streets of European cities where they are most popular. People stop to listen to the music, dance to it when they are so inclined, and sing along with the musicians. This nonsense song was a favorite of street bands because it attracted an audience. It often is sung with gestures — the singer points to himself on the word "my," his head on "hat," holds up three fingers on "three," makes a corner with his two index fingers on "corners" — etc. Another variation is to omit words systematically and in perfect rhythm, beginning with every other word, and dropping words until only one or two words remain to be sung. The gestures may be substituted for the omitted words.

Skye Boat Song

HAROLD BOULTON

SCOTCH HIGHLANDS

Boldly

Speed, bon-nie boat, like a bird on the wing,

"On-ward," the sail-ors cry; Car-ry the lad that's

born to be king o - ver the sea to Skye.

Verse

1. Loud the winds howl, loud the waves roar, thun-der clouds rend the air;

Baf-fled our foes stand by the shore, fol-low they will not dare.

2. Though the waves leap, soft shall ye sleep, ocean's a royal bed.
   Rocked in the deep, Flora will keep watch by your weary head.

3. Many's the lad fought on that day, well the claymore could wield,
   When the night came, silently lay, dead on Culloden's Field.

4. Burned are our homes, exile and death scatter the loyal men;
   Yet ere the sword cool in the sheath, Charlie will come again.

This is an old Highland rowing song. Skye is one of the Hebrides Islands west of Scotland. The group has an area of approximately 2,900 square miles. Charles Edward Stewart (1720-1788) is Bonnie Prince Charlie, the lad "born to be king." After his defeat in the Battle of Culloden Moor April 16, 1746, he escaped to Skye and safety. He was called "The Young Pretender" to distinguish him from his father, James Francis Edward Stuart, "The Old Pretender." The melody of *Skye Boat Song* is pentatonic, that is, based on a five-tone scale with pitches which correspond with the pattern produced by the black keys of the piano. Pentatonic scales are very ancient, dating back to 2000 B.C. in China. They occur in nearly all early musical cultures including, in addition to that of the Scotch, those of the Celts, Africans, American Indians, and the Polynesians. Pentatonic scales preceded the modern scales, like major and minor, in the evolution of music.

Nobody Knows the Trouble I've Seen

SPIRITUAL

With deep feeling

No - bod - y knows the trou - ble I've seen,

No - bod - y knows but Je - sus. No - bod - y knows the

trou - ble I've seen, glo - ry hal - le - lu - jah! *Fine*

Verse

1. Some - times I'm up, some - times I'm down, oh yes, Lord. Some -

times I'm al - most to the ground, oh yes, Lord.

2. Although you see me going along slow, Oh, yes, Lord,
   I have great trials here below, Oh, yes, Lord.

3. One day when I was walking along, Oh, yes, Lord,
   Heaven opened wide, and love came down, Oh, yes, Lord.

4. Why does old Satan hate me so? Oh, yes, Lord,
   He had me once, then let me go, Oh, yes, Lord.

5. I never will forget the day, Oh, yes, Lord,
   When Jesus washed my sins away, Oh, yes, Lord.

This song was performed by the Fisk University Jubilee Singers on a concert fund-raising tour in 1871. The group programmed the southern Negro songs and spirituals which had been part of their heritage since their childhood. The lovely songs and the fervor with which they were sung charmed audiences, and soon the songs were being sung everywhere.

189

The Little Mohee

U. S.

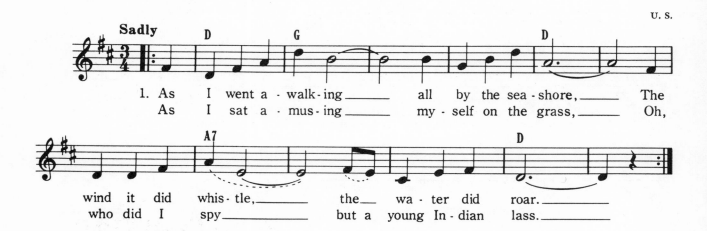

Sadly

1. As I went a-walk-ing_____ all by the sea-shore,_____ The
   As I sat a-mus-ing_____ my-self on the grass,_____ Oh,

wind it did whis-tle,_____ the__ wa-ter did roar._____
who did I spy_____ but a young In-dian lass._____

2. She came and sat by me, took hold of my hand
   And said, "You're a stranger and in a strange land.
   But if you will follow you're welcome to come
   And dwell in the cottage where I call it my home."

3. The sun was fast sinking far over the sea,
   As I wandered along with my little Mohee.
   Together we wandered, together we roam,
   'Til I came to the little cottage where she called it her home.

4. She asked me to marry and offered her hand
   Saying, "My father's the chieftain all over this land.
   My father's a chieftain and ruler can be,
   I'm his only daughter, my name is Mohee."

5. "Oh no, my dear maiden, that never can be,
   I have a dear sweetheart in my own countree.
   I will not forsake her, I know she loves me,
   Her heart is as true as any Mohee."

6. It was early one morning, Monday morning in May,
   I broke her poor heart by the words I did say,
   "I'm going to leave you, so fare you well, my dear,
   My ship's sails are now spreading, over home I must steer."

7. The last time I saw her she knelt on the strand,
   Just as my boat passed her she waved me her hand,
   Saying, "When you get over with the girl that you love,
   Oh remember the Mohee, in the cocoanut grove."

8. And when I had landed with the girl that I love,
   Both friends and relations gathered 'round me once more,
   I gazed all about me, not one did I see
   That really did compare with the little Mohee.

The Little Mohee

> 9. And the girl I had trusted had proved untrue to me,
> So I says, "I'll turn my courses back over the sea,
> I'll turn my courses and backward I'll flee,
> I'll go and spend my days with the little Mohee."

Words and melody from Loraine Wyman's *Lonesome Tunes*, copyrighted 1916; by special permission of the publisher, H. W. Gray Company, New York.

"Lonesome Songs" were called so because they were sung as unaccompanied solos. They were marked by fluctuating rhythm and free intonation, and by virtue of these had a special and quaint charm. In the southern mountains of the United States, everyone sang. Few homes were without instruments of some sort. Most often they were banjos, fiddles, or guitars. These people seemed particularly gifted in making ballads, and a rich storehouse of these were either preserved or created in this region. *The Little Mohee* has marked similarity to another southern mountain lonesome ballad and courting song, *On Top Of Old Smoky*.

Zum Gali Gali

ISRAEL

2. Avodah le 'man hechalutz;
   Hechalutz le 'man avodah.

3. Hechalutz le 'man hab'tulah;
   Hab'tulah le 'man hechalutz.

4. Hashalom le 'man ha'amim;
   Ha'amim le 'man hashalom.

Sing the chant twice as an introduction and repeat it continuously as a background for the verses. The chant may be sung by itself as an interlude between verses and as a closing strain, repeated several times, gradually fading out. The words concern the labor of pioneers. Phonetic pronunciation produces a reasonably authentic sound.

Hickory Dickory Dock

MOTHER GOOSE RHYME

J. W. ELLIOTT

Animated

Hick - o - ry dick - o - ry dock, The

mouse ran up the clock; The clock struck one, the

mouse ran down, Hick - o - ry dick - o - ry dock.

This song appeared in *Tommy Thumb's Pretty Song Book*, the earliest recorded collection of English nursery rhymes as such, published about 1744.

Come, Ye Thankful People, Come

HENRY ALFORD

GEORGE J. ELVEY

Purposefully

1. Come, ye thank-ful peo-ple, come, Raise the song of Har-vest-home;

All is safe-ly gath-ered in, Ere the win-ter storms be-gin;

Come, Ye Thankful People, Come

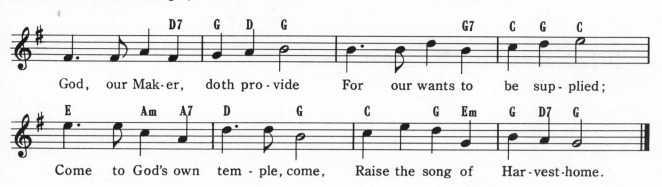

God, our Mak-er, doth pro-vide For our wants to be sup-plied;

Come to God's own tem-ple, come, Raise the song of Har-vest-home.

2. All the world is God's own field,
Fruit unto His praise to yield;
Wheat and tares together sown,
Unto joy or sorrow grown;

First the blade and then the ear,
Then the full corn will appear;
Lord of harvest, grant that we
Wholesome grain and pure may be.

This harvest hymn is sung widely during the Thanksgiving season by religious and secular groups. The music was written by the noted English composer, Sir George J. Elvey, who served as organist at St. George's Chapel, Windsor Castle, for nearly half a century. His first service there was to William IV, and then to Queen Victoria, who knighted him. Words to the hymn were written by Henry Alford, and it was first published in 1844.

Hey Diddle Diddle

MOTHER GOOSE RHYME

J. W. ELLIOTT

Lively

Hey did-dle did-dle, the cat and the fid-dle, The

cow jumped o-ver the moon,___ The lit-tle dog laughed_ to

see such sport, And the dish ran a-way with the spoon.___

This song appeared in print for the first time in a late eighteenth century English publication, *Mother Goose's Melody*. The original date of publication is in doubt; the time of entry in *Stationer's Register* was December 28, 1780, when T. Carnan applied for printer's rights. The second edition (1791) has been preserved.

The Friendly Beasts

Reverently

ENGLAND

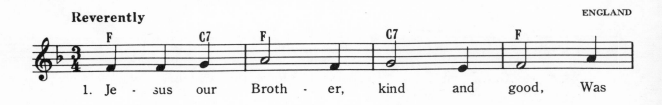

1. Je - sus our Broth - er, kind and good, Was

hum - bly born in a sta - ble rude, And the

friend - ly beasts a - round Him stood,

Je - sus our Broth - er, kind and good.

2. "I," said the donkey, shaggy and brown,
   "I carried His Mother uphill and down;
   I carried His Mother to Bethlehem town,
   I," said the donkey, shaggy and brown.

3. "I," said the cow, all white and red,
   "I gave Him my manger for His bed,
   I gave Him my hay to pillow His head,
   I," said the cow, all white and red.

4. "I," said the sheep with curly horn,
   "I gave him my wool for a blanket warm,
   He wore my coat on Christmas morn,
   I," said the sheep with curly horn.

5. "I," said the dove from rafters high,
   "Cooed him to sleep so he would not cry,
   We cooed him to sleep, my mate and I,
   I," said the dove from rafters high.

6. Thus, every beast who loved Him well
   In the stable rude was glad to tell
   Of the gift he gave Emmanuel,
   Of the gift he gave Emmanuel.

This English story of the Nativity is unusual in that it is told from the point of view of animals and their contribution to the Baby. The tune is a medieval French melody.

194

Vive L'amour

With animation

U. S.

1. Let eve·ry good fel·low now join in a song,
Vi·ve la com·pa·gnie! Suc·cess to each oth·er and
pass it a·long, Vi·ve la com·pa·gnie!

Chorus

Vi·ve la, vi·ve la, vi·ve l'a·mour,
Vi·ve la vi·ve la vi·ve l'a·mour Vi·ve l'a·mour,
Vi·ve l'a·mour, Vi·ve la com·pa·gnie!

2. A friend on the left and a friend on the right, Vive la compagnie!
In willing endeavor our hands we unite, Vive la compagnie!

3. Should time or occasion compel us to part, Vive la compagnie!
These days shall forever enliven the heart, Vive la compagnie!

The composer of this famous song of good fellowship is unknown. It was published in Baltimore in 1844, and a copy of it exists in the Grosvenor Library in Buffalo. Familiar and easy to sing, *Vive L'Amour* is a favorite of glee clubs, barbershop quartets, and at parties. The Rutgers University Band plays it every time the football team makes a touchdown. So popular has it become on college campuses across the country that it often is designated a "college song."

The Sheepshearing

ENGLAND

Sturdily

1. How de - light - ful to see in these eve - nings in spring, the__ sheep go - ing home to the fold.____ The__ mas - ter doth sing as he views eve - ry thing, and his dog goes be - fore him where told,____ and his dog goes be - fore him where told.____

2. Now as for those sheep, they're delightful to see,
   They're a blessing to man on his farm.
   For their meat it is good, it's the best of all food,
   And the wool it will clothe us up warm,
   And the wool it will clothe us up warm.

From *100 English Folk Songs* by Cecil Sharp, copyrighted by Oliver Ditson Company 1916, used by permission.

The sheep is one of the most useful animals to man. Its wool provides clothing, its skin is made into leather, its flesh is an excellent food, and its milk, thicker than the milk of cows, is used in some countries to make butter and cheese. Sheep ordinarily live from twelve to fifteen years. If they are being raised for fleece, they are shorn each year in the spring. One breed to be found in England, the Leicester, has fleece which weighs from seven to eight pounds. England is among the leading sheep-raising countries. There, sheep dogs, small collies, tend the sheep. Feasts often are held at the time the sheep are sheared. This English folk song honoring the custom is sung at the celebrations.

She'll Be Coming 'Round the Mountain

U. S.

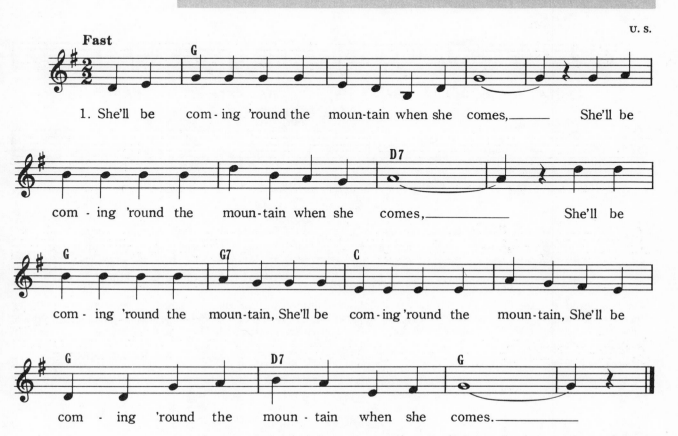

1. She'll be com-ing 'round the moun-tain when she comes,_____ She'll be com-ing 'round the moun-tain when she comes,_____ She'll be com-ing 'round the moun-tain, She'll be com-ing 'round the moun-tain, She'll be com-ing 'round the moun-tain when she comes._____

2. She'll be driving six white horses when she comes, etc.

3. Oh, we'll all go out to meet her when she comes, etc.

4. Oh, we'll kill the old red rooster when she comes, etc.

5. And we'll all have chicken dumplings when she comes, etc.

Appropriate sounds and actions can be performed during the long notes in the melody, for example:

Coming 'round the mountain — whoo-hoo.
Driving six white horses — giddy-up.
All go out to meet her — hi, y'all.
Kill the old red rooster — oh, boy.
All have chicken dumplings — yum, yum.

At the end of each verse the sounds and actions of the previous verses can be repeated in reverse order: *yum, yum, oh, boy, hi, y'all, giddy-up, whoo-hoo* for the last verse.

As railroads expanded across the country they inspired an abundance of music. *She'll Be Coming 'Round The Mountain* is one of the best known songs of the period. Mountaineers adapted their words to the melody of an old Negro spiritual, *When The Chariot Comes*. Western railroad gangs sang it in the 1890's, and it became a game and action song which often is pantomimed.

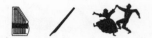

Hey, Betty Martin

Briskly

U. S.

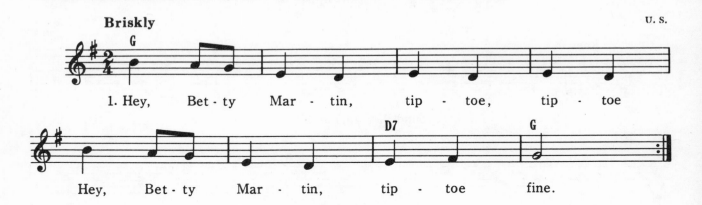

1. Hey, Bet - ty Mar - tin, tip - toe, tip - toe

Hey, Bet - ty Mar - tin, tip - toe fine.

2. Can't find a boy, a boy to please her,
Can't find a boy to please her mind;
She hopes to find a boy to please her,
She hopes to find a certain kind.

3. I found a boy, boy to please me,
I found a boy to please my mind;
I found a boy, a boy to please me,
I found a boy, a certain kind.

This song from the stages of London was a well-known fiddle tune for country dances in New England. Steps danced to it by adroit dancers were similar to steps of the Highland Fling. The song was popular with soldiers of the War of 1812, and often was played by the fife and drum corps. Both "hey" and "high" are used in the title and in the song today.

Up on the Housetop

BENJAMIN R. HANBY   BENJAMIN R. HANBY

Gaily

1. Up   on the house - top the rein - deer pause,

Out jumps good old San - ta Claus; Down through the chim - ney with

Up on the Housetop

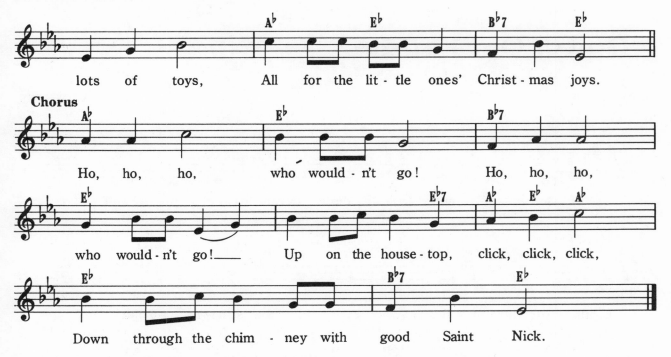

lots of toys, All for the lit-tle ones' Christ-mas joys.

Chorus

Ho, ho, ho, who would-n't go! Ho, ho, ho,

who would-n't go!___ Up on the house-top, click, click, click,

Down through the chim-ney with good Saint Nick.

2. First comes the stocking of little Nell, oh, dear Santa, fill it well,
   Give her a dolly that laughs and cries, one that can open and close its eyes.

3. Here is the stocking of little Will, look at what a glorious fill,
   Here is a hammer and lots of tacks, bat and a ball and a whip that cracks.

This song dates from the mid-nineteenth century. It was written by Benjamin Russel Hanby, who also wrote *Darling Nelly Gray.*

Mother's Knives and Forks

NURSERY RHYME

JANET GAYNOR

Moderately

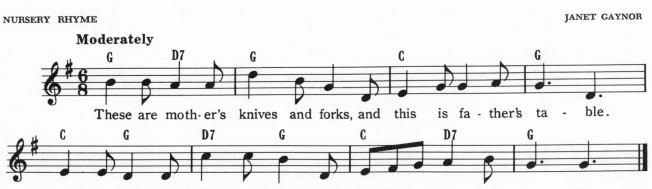

These are moth-er's knives and forks, and this is fa-ther's ta-ble.

This is sis-ter's look-ing glass, and this is the ba-by's cra-dle.

This old nursery rhyme is also a finger play song. To make the knives and forks, fold hands with fingers inter-laced and pointing upwards; flatten fingers against the hands to make the table; turn hands, still folded, with thumbs straight up to form the looking glass; lower thumbs and cup folded hands to form the cradle.

God of Our Fathers

DANIEL C. ROBERTS

G. W. WARREN

With power

1. God of our fa-thers Whose al-might-y hand,

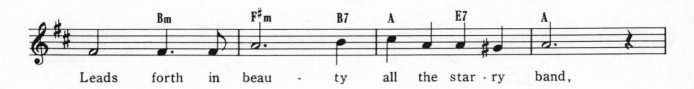

Leads forth in beau-ty all the star-ry band,

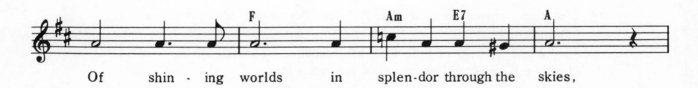

Of shin-ing worlds in splen-dor through the skies,

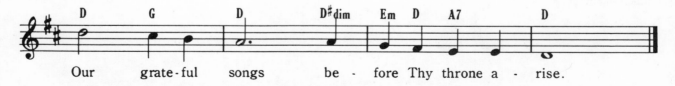

Our grate-ful songs be-fore Thy throne a-rise.

2. Thy love divine hath led us in the past,
   In this free land by Thee our lot is cast;
   Be thou our Ruler, Guardian, Guide and Stay,
   Thy word our law, Thy paths our chosen way.

3. From war's alarms, from deadly pestilence,
   Be Thy strong arm our ever sure defense;
   Thy true religion in our hearts increase,
   Thy bounteous goodness nourish us in peace.

4. Refresh Thy people on their toilsome way,
   Lead us from night to never ending day;
   Fill all our lives with love and grace divine,
   And glory, laud, and praise be ever Thine.

The year 1876 was the hundredth anniversary of the Declaration of Independence, and the entire country cele-brated the event. Philadelphia, where the original document was signed, sponsored a Centennial Exposition. In the small village of Brandon, Vermont, the Rev. Daniel Crane Roberts (1841-1907), a veteran of the Union Army in the Civil War, wrote a poem in honor of the occasion. The words were sung to the tune of *The Russian Hymn*. It first was published in a hymnal in 1894. George W. Warren, a New York City organist, wrote the music to which *God Of Our Fathers* is sung today, and it is found in most hymnals published in the United States.

Three Blue Pigeons

Happily

U. S.

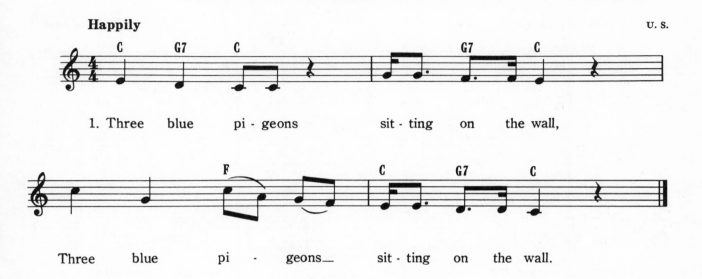

1. Three blue pi - geons sit - ting on the wall,

Three blue pi - geons— sit - ting on the wall.

    Spoken: One flew away.
           O-o-oh!

2. Two blue pigeons sitting on the wall, two blue pigeons sitting on the wall.
    Another flew way.
    O-o-o-oh!

3. One blue pigeon sitting on the wall, one blue pigeon sitting on the wall.
    And the third flew away!
    O-o-o-o-oh!

4. No blue pigeons sitting on the wall, no blue pigeons sitting on the wall.
    One flew back.
    Whee-ee-ee!

5. One blue pigeon sitting on the wall, one blue pigeon sitting on the wall.
    Another flew back.
    Whee-ee-ee-ee!

6. Two blue pigeons sitting on the wall, two blue pigeons sitting on the wall.
    And the third flew back!
    Whee-ee-ee-ee-ee!

7. Three blue pigeons sitting on the wall, three blue pigeons sitting on the wall.

This old American folk counting song offers an excellent opportunity for group response. The spoken words may be said either by one person or the entire group. The "O-o-o-oh" may be done with exaggerated emotion by the entire group or designated individuals.

Home

Sentimentally

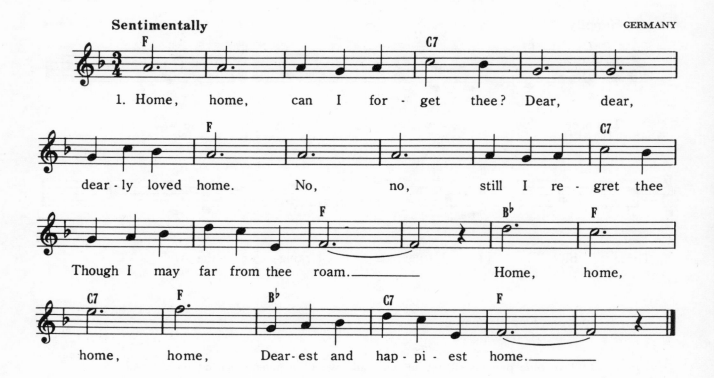

1. Home, home, can I for-get thee? Dear, dear, dear-ly loved home. No, no, still I re-gret thee Though I may far from thee roam._____ Home, home, home, home, Dear-est and hap-pi-est home._____

2. Home, home, why did I leave thee?
Dear, dear friends, do not mourn.
Home, home, once more receive me,
Quickly to thee I'll return.
Home, home, home, home,
Dearest and happiest home.

1. Du, du, liegst mir im Herzen,
Du, du, liegst mir im Sinn;
Du, du, machst mir viel Schmerzen,
Weisst nicht wie gut ich dir bin.
Ja, ja, ja, ja,
Weisst nicht wie gut ich dir bin.

2. So, so, wie ich dich liebe,
So, so, liebe auch mich,
Die, die, zärtlichsten Triebe
Fühl' ich allein nur für dich.
Ja, ja, ja, ja,
Fühl' ich allein nur für dich.

This song about home is sung to an old German folk tune.

Night Herding Song

COWBOY

As a lullaby

1. O, slow up, do-gies, quit rov-ing a-round, You have wan-dered and tram-pled all o-ver the ground; O, graze a-long do-gies, and feed kind-a slow, And don't for-ev-er be on the go. O, move slow, do-gies, move slow,_____ Hi-o, hi-o,____ hi-o._____

2. Lay down, little dogies, and when you are down
You can stretch yourselves out, for there's plenty of ground,
Stay still, little dogies, for I'm awfully tired,
If you run off I will sure get fired.
O down, down, dogies, lay down,
Hi-o, hi-o, hi-o.

3. Now I've circle herded and night herded too,
And to keep you together's not easy to do,
So snore, little dogies, I'll welcome the sound,
And you'll be bunched when the daylight comes.
O, bunch up, dogies, bunch up,
Hi-o, hi-o, hi-o.

This is a lullaby for cattle. A "dogie" is a stray yearling steer or a motherless calf. These young orphans became restless, particularly at night, and often caused the herd to stampede in the darkness. Singing quieted and soothed them, and helped keep the cowboys awake during night watches. Harry Stephens, bronco buster and cowboy poet, claimed in a letter to a friend that he wrote this song while night herding in Yellowstone Park.

Long, Long Ago

THOMAS H. BAYLY

THOMAS H. BAYLY

Smoothly

1. Tell me the tales that to me were so dear, Long, long a-go,

long, long a-go; Sing me the songs I de-light-ed to hear,

Long, long a-go, long a-go. Now you are come all my

grief is re-moved, Let me for-get that so long you have roved,

Let me be-lieve that you love as you loved, Long, long a-go, long a-go.

2. Do you remember the place where we met
Long, long ago, long, long ago?
Ah, yes you told me you'd never forget,
Long, long ago, long ago.
Then, to all others, my smile you preferred,
Love, as you spoke, gave a charm with each word,
My heart remembers the praises I heard
Long, long ago, long ago.

3. You gave your promise to come back some day,
Long, long ago, long ago;
Through the long waiting, my heart seemed to say,
Long, long ago, long ago.
Now you have come, all my grief is removed,
Let me forget that so long you have roved,
Let me remember the way that you loved,
Long, long ago, long ago.

This ballad of love and loneliness was the song hit of the year in 1843.

204

One More River
(NOAH'S ARK)

With enthusiasm

SPIRITUAL

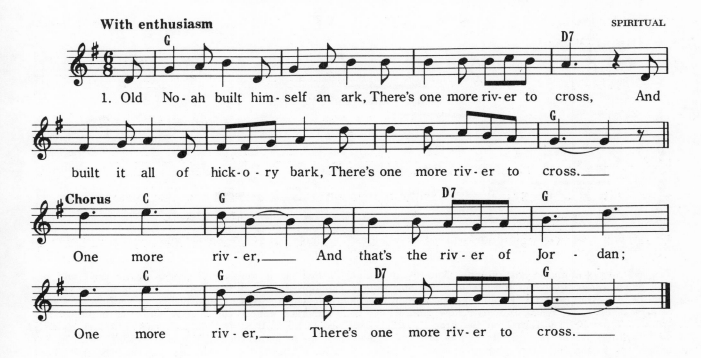

1. Old No-ah built him-self an ark, There's one more riv-er to cross, And built it all of hick-o-ry bark, There's one more riv-er to cross.

Chorus

One more riv-er,____ And that's the riv-er of Jor-dan; One more riv-er,____ There's one more riv-er to cross.____

2. The animals came two by two, there's one more river to cross,
   The elephant and kangaroo, there's one more river to cross.

3. The animals came three by three, there's one more river to cross,
   The baboon and the chimpanzee, there's one more river to cross.

4. The animals came four by four, there's one more river to cross,
   Old Noah got mad and hollered for more, there's one more river to cross.

5. The animals came five by five, there's one more river to cross,
   The bees came swarming from the hive, there's one more river to cross.

6. The animals came six by six, there's one more river to cross,
   The lion laughed at the monkey's tricks, there's one more river to cross.

7. When Noah found he had no sail, there's one more river to cross,
   He just ran up his old coat tail, there's one more river to cross.

8. Before the voyage did begin, there's one more river to cross.
   Old Noah pulled the gangplank in, there's one more river to cross.

9. They never knew where they were at, there's one more river to cross,
   'Til the old ark bumped on Ararat, there's one more river to cross.

This Negro spiritual is typical in its reference to the River Jordan which must be crossed before "the promised land" can be reached, but it is one of the few which tells the story in a lighter vein. Its origin is unknown.

Whippoorwill
ROUND

Evenly

U. S.

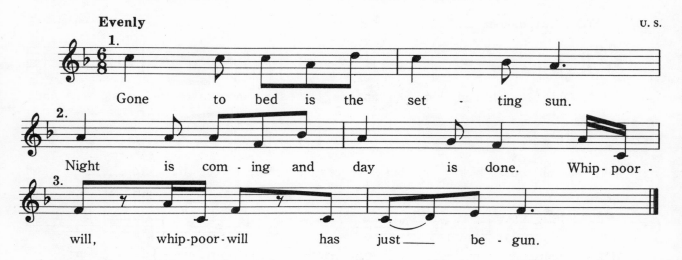

1.
Gone   to   bed   is   the   set - ting   sun.

2.
Night   is   com - ing   and   day   is   done.   Whip - poor -

3.
will,   whip - poor - will   has   just ____ be - gun.

The whippoorwill makes its presence known by calling its own name loudly and repeatedly, at dusk and before dawn, often preceding it by a low clucking sound. The noisy caller is somewhat a hermit in other ways. Few people ever see it for its plumage has a mottled coloration which serves as an excellent camouflage — a mixture of black, gray, beige, brown, yellow, and white, which merges almost completely with the natural background. It perches lengthwise on the branch, which conceals it still further. It builds no nest, but lays its eggs on indentures in the ground. Its haunts are low valleys and brooks and meadows where it captures with its big mouth the moths and other nocturnal insects which are its food. During the day it sleeps in thickets. It is about ten inches in length.

Lovely Evening

Calmly

ROUND

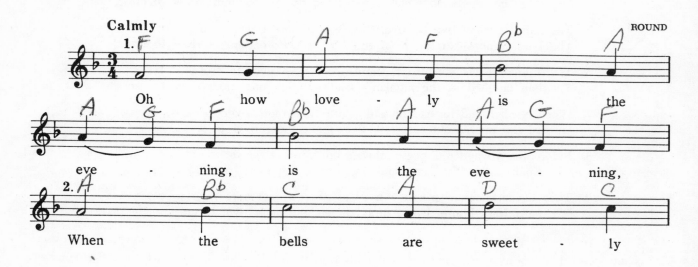

1. F   G   A   F   B♭   A

Oh   how   love - ly   is   the

A   G   F   B♭   A   A   G   F

eve - ning,   is   the   eve - ning,

2. A   B♭   C   A   D   C

When   the   bells   are   sweet - ly

Lovely Evening

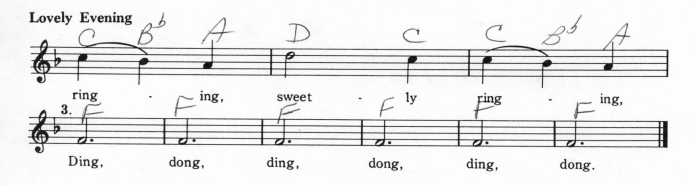

ring - ing,   sweet - ly   ring - ing,

Ding,   dong,   ding,   dong,   ding,   dong.

London Bridge

ENGLAND

Skipping rhythm

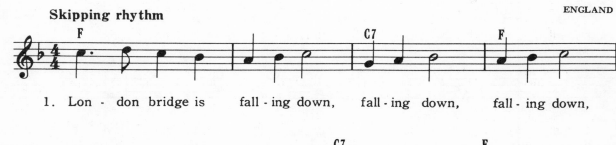

1. Lon - don bridge is fall - ing down, fall - ing down, fall - ing down,

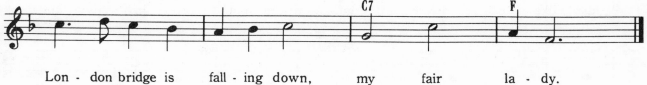

Lon - don bridge is fall - ing down, my fair la - dy.

2. Build it up with iron bars
3. Iron bars will rust and break
4. Build it up with sticks and stones
5. Sticks and stones will tumble down
6. Here's a prisoner I have found
7. Off to prison he (she) must go
8. Have the jailer lock him (her) up

This singing game can be used to choose up sides. The captains of the two teams join hands to form an arch. As the song is sung, the other players walk single file in a circle passing under the arch. On the final word of each verse the captains drop their arms and capture a player. The captured players alternately form lines behind their respective captains. The verses are repeated until all of the players have been selected.

London is the capital of the United Kingdom, and one of the largest cities in the world. It stands on both sides of the Thames River which is both tidal and navigable, and which narrows to 325 yards at the site of London Bridge. One of many fine bridges which now span the Thames, London Bridge first was built by the Romans. It was hauled down by Vikings in the eleventh century, but rebuilt. It was the only bridge across the river until 1750. The present bridge was built in 1831 of Aberdeen granite. The precise limit of the tides is marked by London Bridge, and when the tide ebbs from the bridge, the foreshores of this old city are worth searching for diverse relics which remain from nearly 2,000 years of continuous inhabitation.

The Humming Bird

EDWIN STAR BELKNAP   TIROL, AUSTRIA

Delicately

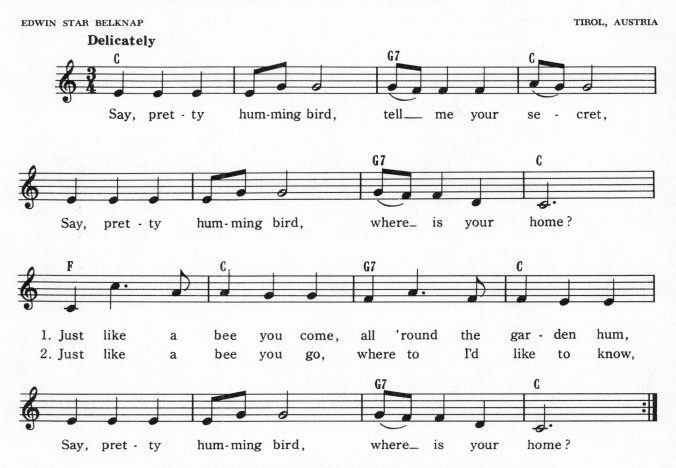

Say, pret-ty hum-ming bird, tell__ me your se - cret,

Say, pret-ty hum-ming bird, where__ is your home?

1. Just like a bee you come, all 'round the gar-den hum,
2. Just like a bee you go, where to I'd like to know,

Say, pret-ty hum-ming bird, where__ is your home?

From *The American Singer*, Book 5, copyright 1946, 1955, and 1960 by American Book Company. Used by permission.

Humming birds are among the bird world's best flyers. Only a blur can be seen and a humming be heard when they move their wings, hence their name. Their family consists of nearly 700 species which range in size from the giant hummer of the Andes Mountains (8 1/2 inches) to the fairy hummingbird of Cuba (2 1/4 inches), the world's smallest bird. Some 19 species and subspecies, which range in length from three to five inches, occur in the United States and Canada. The only note of the hummingbird is a single chirp, not louder than that of a cricket. The Ruby-Throated Hummingbird is found throughout the United States in the summer months. It is from three to four inches long, and the smaller males glisten with their green emerald and changeable amethyst coloring. They weigh only about as much as a penny, and a half-dollar would cover their nest. Nests are made of plant down, lichen, spider web, and saliva threads. Once or twice a year two tiny white eggs about one-half inch long are laid in the nest saddled on a tree branch between three and fifty feet high. The tiny bird has re-markable flying capacities, and can hover like a helicopter above a blossom to drink its nectar. It never lights to take food, but feeds while on the wing, using its long beak and long, forked tongue. It can fly backwards or forwards with equal ease, or swing back and forth in the air as if suspended on a string.

Vesper Hymn

THOMAS MOORE

RUSSIA

Fervently

1. Hark! the ves - per hymn is steal-ing, o'er the wa-ters soft and clear;

Near - er yet and near - er peal - ing, soft it breaks up - on the ear.

Ju - bi - la - te! Ju - bi - la - te! Ju - bi - la - te! A - men.

Far - ther now and far - ther steal-ing, soft it fades up - on the ear.

2. Now like moonlight waves retreating, to the shore it dies along;
Now like angry surges meeting, breaks the mingled tide of song.
Jubilate! Jubilate! Jubilate! Amen;
Jubilate! Jubilate! Jubilate! Amen.
Hark! Again like waves retreating, to the shore it dies along.

3. Once again sweet voices ringing, louder still the music swells;
While on summer breezes winging, comes the chime of vesper bells.
Jubilate! Jubilate! Jubilate! Amen;
Jubilate! Jubilate! Jubilate! Amen.
On the summer breezes winging, fades the chime of vesper bells.

Thomas Moore (1779-1852), Irish poet and balladeer, was born in Dublin. He went to England as a young man and became a literary and social success. His fame spread through a group of poems he wrote and set to Irish folk melodies. So great was his reputation as a poet that he was favorably compared with Scott and Byron. One poem, for which he was paid a very high price, was *Lalla Rookh*. It was translated into almost all European languages. *The Vesper Hymn* was written in 1818 and adapted to an old tune, *Russian Air*. Moore also wrote *The Last Rose of Summer, The Harp That Once Through Tara's Halls,* and *Believe Me, If All Those Endearing Young Charms*.

Happy Birthday

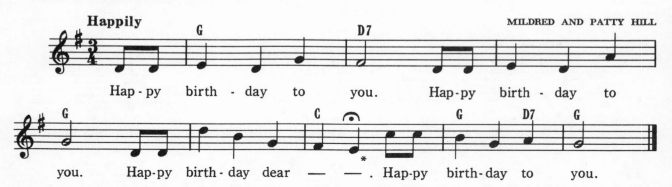

Happily

G   D7

MILDRED AND PATTY HILL

Hap-py birth-day to you. Hap-py birth-day to

G   C   G   D7   G

you. Hap-py birth-day dear — —. Hap-py birth-day to you.

*Sing the name of the person whose birthday is being celebrated.

Mildred and Patty Hill wrote a song, *Good Morning To You*, which was sung by all America. When the words of *Happy Birthday To You* were adapted to the original tune, it became the standard birthday greeting of the entire country.

Going to the Fair
(ACH JA)

Rapidly

F   C7

GERMANY

1. When my fa-ther and my moth-er are a-go-ing to the fair, Ach

F   F

ja! Ach ja! If they have-n't an-y mon-ey they're as

C7   F

rich as an-y there, Ach ja! Ach ja!

210

Going to the Fair

Chorus

Tra la la, tra la la, tra la la la la la la, Tra la

la, tra la ta, tra la la la la la la, Ach ja! Ach ja!

2. It is fun to join the people who are hurrying to the fair,
Ach ja! Ach ja!
And to know that friends and neighbors will be waiting for you there,
Ach ja! Ach ja!

"Ach ja!" means "oh, yes" in Germany where this dancing game song originated. The dance is performed with partners forming a double ring, girls on the inside. Bows are made to partners on the words "ach ja!" and each boys moves to the next girl, who becomes his partner.

He's Got the Whole World in His Hands

With conviction

SPIRITUAL

1. He's got the whole world— in His hands,— He's got the

whole world— in His hands,— He's got the whole world—

in His hands,— He's got the whole world in His hands.

2. He's got the wind and rain in His hands.
3. He's got that little baby in His hands.
4. He's got you and me in His hands.
5. He's got everybody in His hands.
6. He's got the whole world in His hands.

211

Eency, Weency Spider

ACTION SONG

Playfully

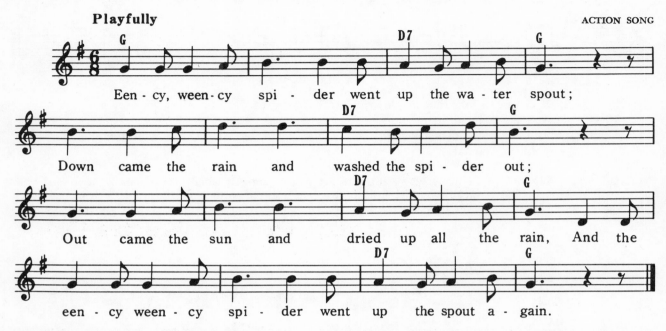

Een-cy, ween-cy spi-der went up the wa-ter spout;

Down came the rain and washed the spi-der out;

Out came the sun and dried up all the rain, And the

een-cy ween-cy spi-der went up the spout a-gain.

The words of this song suggest actions. The motion of the spider can be represented by touching the tip of the index finger on one hand to the tip of the thumb on the other and alternating them as the hands move up and down.

We're All Together Again

ENGLAND

With joy

We're all to-geth-er a-gain, we're here, we're

here! We're all to-geth-er a-gain, we're

here, we're here! Who knows

We're All Together Again

when we'll be all to-geth-er a-gain, sing-ing,

"All to-geth-er a-gain, we're here, we're here!"_____

Every four years an International Jamboree is attended by Boy Scouts from all over the world. This song from Great Britain is the theme song of these conclaves.

Polly, Put the Kettle On

MOTHER GOOSE RHYME   BRITISH ISLES

Simply

Pol-ly, put the ket-tle on, Pol-ly, put the ket-tle on,

Pol-ly, put the ket-tle on, We'll all have tea.

Su-key, take it off a-gain, Su-key, take it off a-gain,

Su-key take it off a-gain, They've all gone a-way.

This old nursery song has been assigned to several countries. Some believe the words are English and the tune Scottish. Others assign it to Germany, perhaps because the tune is very much like the *Hansel and Gretel Dance* in the opera of the same name by the German composer Humperdinck. In the eighteenth century it was a familiar nursery song and country dance known as *Jenny's Bawbee*. It made its appearance in the music halls about 1870. Children have made up countless verses to the song to represent their interests and activities. The rhythm is excellent for tapping, clapping, or dancing.

213

Now Is the Month of Maying

THOMAS MORLEY

1. Now is the month of May - ing, When mer - ry lads are play - ing, Fa la la la la la la la la, Fa la la la la la la.

Each with his bon - nie lass, A - danc - ing on the grass, Fa la la la la, fa la la la la la la la la la la la.

2. The spring, clad all in gladness, doth laugh at winter's sadness,
   Fa la la la la la la la la la, Fa la la la la la la la.
   And to the bagpipe's sound, the nymphs tread out their ground,
   Fa la la la la la, fa la la la la la la la la la la la la.

3. Fie, then, why sit we musing, youth's sweet delights refusing?
   Fa la la la la la la la la la, Fa la la la la la la la.
   Say, dainty nymphs, and speak, shall we play barley break?
   Fa la la la la, fa la la la la la la la la la la la la.

Thomas Morley (1557-1603), noted English composer, wrote this spring song. Morley wrote songs for Shakespeare's plays, including *It Was A Lover And His Lass* from *As You Like It*. In 1597 he wrote the first regular treatise on music published in England, *A Plaine And Easie Introduction To Practicall Musicke*, which was popular for 200 years and which remains one of the best general references on music of this period. The "fa la la's" are characteristic of the English madrigal style. Madrigals were written for unaccompanied voices. English madrigals were mines of pure poetry and some have been republished in modern times purely as poetry apart from the music. The first day of May, or May Day, is an eagerly awaited event after a long or difficult winter, as it signals spring. Traditionally, May Day celebrations include the erection of a Maypole decorated with flowers and foliage around which the celebrators dance. From among the dancers, a lady is chosen "Queen of the May" to reign over the celebration. May baskets filled with spring flowers also are a part of the festivities. In ancient Rome, it was considered unlucky to contract marriages during the month of May, a superstition which still prevails in some parts of Europe. In olden days, outdoor sports and activities were common on May Day, and in lesser degree remain so to the present time.

The Little Shoemaker

ALICE RILEY

JANET GAYNOR

Brightly

1. There's a lit-tle wee man in a lit-tle wee house Lives o-ver the way you see, And he sits at the win-dow and sews all day Mak-ing shoes for you and me.

Chorus

A - rap - a - tap - tap, a - rap - a - tap - tap, Hear the ham-mer's tit - tat - tee. A - rap - a - tap-tap, a - rap - a - tap-tap, Mak-ing shoes for you and me.

2. He puts his needle in and out, his thread flies to and fro,
   With his tiny awl he bores the holes; hear the hammer's busy blow.

This song is sung at a lively tempo, and with exaggerated pantomime as indicated by the words. It first was published in 1897 in *Songs Of The Child World*.

Music Alone Shall Live
ROUND

Moderately

GERMANY

All things shall per - ish un - der the sky;

Mu - sic a - lone shall live, Mu - sic a - lone shall live,

Mu - sic a - lone shall live, nev - er to die.

Himmel und Erde müssen vergehn;
Aber die Musica, aber die Musica,
Aber die Musica, bleiben bestehn.

Where Has My Little Dog Gone
(DER DEITCHER'S DOG)

SEPTIMUS WINNER

GERMANY

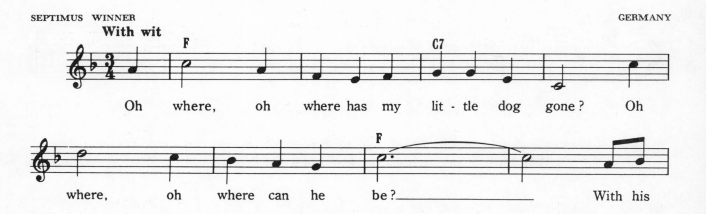

Oh where, oh where has my lit - tle dog gone? Oh

where, oh where can he be?_____ With his

Where has my Little Dog Gone

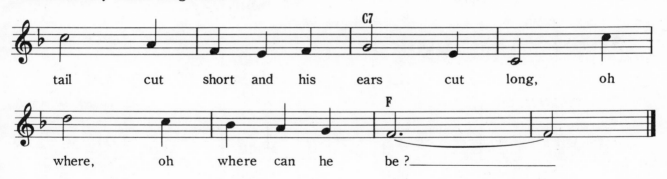

tail cut short and his ears cut long, oh
where, oh where can he be?

This was a music hall song written in 1864. It also was known as *Der Deitcher's Dog.* The words were written by Septimus Winner. The tune was from a German folk song, *Zu Lauterback hab' i mein Strumpf verlor'n.*

Donkey Riding

With gusto

CANADA

1. Were you ev-er in Que-bec, Stow-ing tim-ber on the deck?
Where there's a king with a gold-en crown, Rid-ing on a don-key.

Chorus
Hey, ho! A-way we go! Don-key rid-ing, don-key rid-ing.
Hey,— ho! A-way we go, Rid-ing on a don-key.

2. Were you ever off the Horn,
Where it's always fine and warm,
And seen the lion and the unicorn,
Riding on a donkey?

3. Were you ever in Cardiff Bay?
Where the folks all shout, "Hooray!
Here comes John with his three months' pay,
Riding on a donkey!"

Lumbering is an important industry in Canada. This work song was chanted in rhythm by stevedores as they loaded lumber on ships which sailed from Quebec to England. The "donkey" is a small engine which is used in loading lumber on the ships.

217

Johnny Schmoker

Moderately

PENNSYLVANIA DUTCH

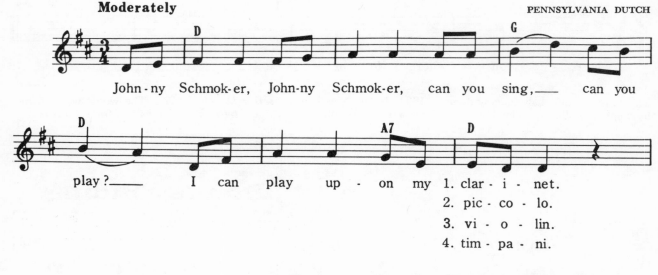

John - ny Schmok - er, John - ny Schmok - er, can you sing,— can you

play?— I can play up - on my 1. clar - i - net.
2. pic - co - lo.
3. vi - o - lin.
4. tim - pa - ni.

Doo - dle doo - dle - det, so sings my
Twee - dle twee - dle - o, so sings my
Fid - dle did - dle - din, so sings my
Boom - a boom - a - dee, so sings my

clar - i - net.
pic - co - lo.
vi - o - lin.
tim - pa - ni.

Johann Schmoker, Johann Schmoker,
Kannst du singen? Kannst du spielen?

1. Ich kann spielen auf meine Klarinette.
2. Ich kann spielen auf meine kleine Flöte.
3. Ich kann spielen auf meine Violine.
4. Ich kann spielen auf meine Pauken.

Doodle doodle-det, das ist meine Klarinette.
Tweedle tweedle-o, das ist meine kleine Flöte.
Fiddle diddle-din, das ist meine Violine.
Boom-a boom-a-dee, das ist meine Pauken.

On the first stanza go directly to the second ending. On the second and following stanzas sing the section between the repeat signs of all previous stanzas in reverse order before going to the second ending. Make up
sounds for additional instruments, and pretend to play the instruments as their sounds are imitated. This anony-
mous cumulative folk song was brought to this country by German immigrants. It was first published in 1863
under the title *Jemmy Boker*.

218

The Tailor and the Mouse

With spirit

ENGLAND

1. There was a tai-lor had a mouse, Hi did-dle um-kum fee - dle. They
lived to - geth - er in one house, Hi did-dle um - kum fee - dle.

Chorus
Hi did-dle um - kum ta - rum tan-tum, Through the town of Ram - say,
Hi did-dle um - kum, o - ver the lea, Hi did-dle um - kum fee - dle.

2. The tailor thought the mouse was ill,
   Hi diddle umkum feedle,
   Because he took an awful chill,
   Hi diddle umkum feedle.

3. The tailor thought his mouse would die,
   Hi diddle umkum feedle,
   And so he baked him in a pie,
   Hi diddle umkum feedle.

4. He cut the pie, the mouse ran out,
   Hi diddle umkum feedle,
   The mouse was in a terrible pout,
   Hi diddle umkum feedle.

5. The tailor gave him catnip tea,
   Hi diddle umkum feedle,
   Until a healthy mouse was he,
   Hi diddle umkum feedle.

This carefree English folk song is one of the few of such gaiety written in the minor mode. There are many variations in the words, which differ with locales. The song lends itself to dramatization.

Sing Together
ROUND

Hastily

ENGLAND

Sing, sing to - geth - er, mer - ri - ly, mer - ri - ly sing;

Sing, sing to - geth - er, mer - ri - ly mer - ri - ly sing;

Sing, sing, sing, sing.

This old English round is a popular ring dance tune.

Walking Song
(WEGGIS FAIR)

Walking rhythm

SWITZERLAND

1. From Lu - cerne to Weg - gis fair, Hol - di - ri - di - a, hol - di - ri - a,

Shoes and stock - ings we need not wear, Hol - di - ri - di - a, hol - di - a.

Chorus

Hol - di ri - di - a, hol - di - ri - di - a, hol - di - ri - a,

220

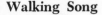

Walking Song

Hol - di - ri - di - a, hol - di - ri - di - a, hol - di - a.

2. When we row out across the bay, hol-di-ri-di-a, hol-di-ri-a,
   There we see lovely maidens gay, hol-di-ri-di-a, hol-di-a.

3. Weggis leads to a mountain high, hol-di-ri-di-a, hol-di-ri-a,
   Gaily singing as we go by, hol-di-ri-di-a, hol-di-a.

The melody of *Walking Song* is a Swiss folk melody. The song also is known as *Weggis Fair* and is published under this title.

When the Little Children Sleep

CARL REINECKE

Delicately

When the lit - tle chil - dren sleep, Lit - tle stars are wak - ing,

An - gels bright from heav - en come, And till morn is break - ing,

They will watch the live-long night, By their beds till morn-ing light, When the

lit - tle chil - dren sleep, When the lit - tle chil - dren sleep.

Carl Reinecke (1824-1910) was born in Altona, Germany, and was a pianist and writer. His first concert tour was to Denmark and Sweden in 1843. He then went to Leipzig where he was an associate of Mendelssohn and Schumann. From 1846 to 1848 he was court pianist to Christian VIII at Copenhagen. He entered the teaching field when he became a professor at the Cologne Conservatory. He was an eminent pianist and excelled as an interpreter of Mozart. He made concert tours almost yearly and was enthusiastically welcomed in England, Holland, Scandinavia, Switzerland, and throughout Germany. As a composer and teacher of composition, Reinecke was the leader in Leipzig for a quarter of a century.

Lullaby

Gently

JOHANNES BRAHMS

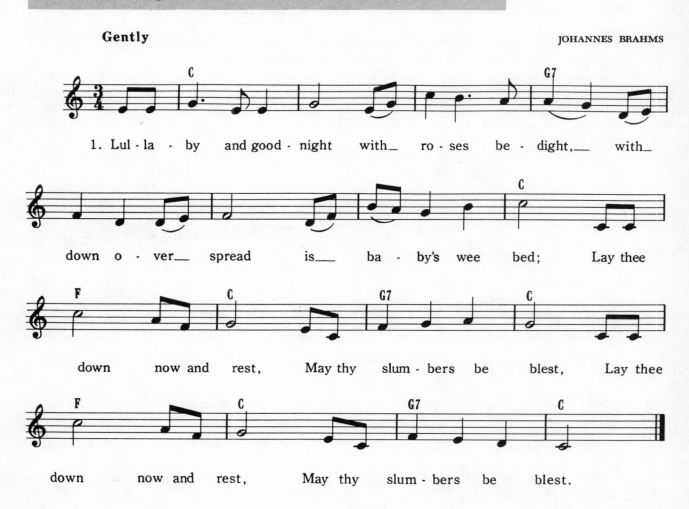

1. Lul - la - by and good - night with_ ro - ses be - dight,_ with_ down o - ver_ spread is_ ba - by's wee bed; Lay thee down now and rest, May thy slum - bers be blest, Lay thee down now and rest, May thy slum - bers be blest.

2. Lullaby and goodnight, thy mother's delight,
   Bright angels beside my darling abide.
   They will guard thee at rest, thou shalt wake on my breast,
   They will guard thee at rest, thou shalt wake on my breast.

1. Guten Abend, gut' Nacht, mit Rosen bedacht,
   Mit Näglein besteckt, schlupf unter die Deck.
   Morgen früh, wenn Gott will, wirst du weider geweckt;
   Morgen früh, wenn Got will, wirst du weider geweckt.

Johannes Brahms was born in Hamburg, Germany in 1833, and died in Vienna in 1897. He wrote many lovely children's songs. This one is reminiscent of an old Austrian folk tune. Musicians know Brahms for his monumental symphonies and concertos. Children remember him for his folk song settings and lullabies.

Silent Night

JOSEPH MOHR

FRANZ GRUBER

Peacefully

1. Si - lent night, ho - ly night! All is calm, all is bright.
Round yon vir - gin Moth-er and Child. Ho - ly In-fant so ten-der and mild,
Sleep in heav-en-ly peace,_____ Sleep_ in heav-en-ly peace.

2. Silent night, holy night!
   Shepherds quake at the sight.
   Glories stream from heaven afar,
   Heavenly hosts sing, "Alleluia!"
   Christ, the Saviour is born,
   Christ, the Saviour is born.

3. Silent night, holy night!
   Son of God, love's pure light!
   Radiant beams from Thy holy face
   With the dawn of redeeming grace,
   Jesus, Lord, at Thy birth,
   Jesus, Lord, at Thy birth.

1. Stille Nacht, Heilige Nacht! Alles schläft, einsam wacht
   Nur das traute, hochheilige Paar. Holder Knabe im lockigen Haar,
   Schlaf in himmlischer Ruh, Schlaf in himmlischer Ruh!

Joseph Mohr, the 26-year-old parish priest in the little Alpine village of Oberndorf in Austria, was deeply troubled Christmas Eve, 1818. The church organ was broken, and no one in the village could repair it. There would be no special music to mark the holy occasion, even though St. Nicholas Church always had special music on Christmas Eve. Franz Gruber, the schoolmaster who also served as church organist, had asked the priest for his help. Gruber suggested that Father Mohr write a poem which he, Gruber, could set to music. The priest agreed, and Gruber played the accompaniment to the "special music" on his guitar. When the organ repairman came to the village the following week, the performance of *Silent Night* was repeated for him. He was so impressed with the work he took it to some concert singers, the three Strasser sisters, who found it delightful and carried it throughout Europe on their concert tours. From there, it spread throughout the world.

Red Iron Ore

Swinging rhythm

GREAT LAKES CHANTEY

1. Come all you bold sail-ors that fol-low the lakes, On an i-ron ore ves-sel your liv-ing to make; I shipped in Chi-ca-go, bid a-dieu to the shore, Bound a-way to Es-ca-na-ba for red i-ron ore.

Chorus

Der-ry down, down, down, der-ry down.

2. In the month of September, the seventeenth day,
Oh, two and a quarter is all they would pay,
And on Monday morning the "Bridgeport" did take
The old ore ship, "C. E. Roberts," far out in the lake.

3. This packet she howled 'cross the mouth of Green Bay,
And before her cutwater she dashed the white spray,
We rounded the sand point, our anchor let go,
Then we furled in our canvas, and the watch went below.

4. Next morning we hove alongside the "Exile,"
And we soon were made fast to an iron ore pile,
They lowered their chutes and just like thunder did roar,
Then they spouted into us all that red iron ore.

5. Some sailors took shovels while others got spades,
And then some took wheelbarrows, each man to his trade,
Our clothes picked up red dust, and our fingers got sore,
We loathed Escanaba and that red iron ore.

Red Iron Ore

In 1844 mining engineer George Sturz found an important iron range, the Mesabi, on Lake Superior. Sailors on the Great Lakes logged their difficulties of hauling the red iron ore to eastern iron foundries in song. They adapted their tales to the melody of an old Irish sea chantey, *Derry Down Down Down, Derry Down*. The words record the actual names of ships and port cities.

Pop, Goes the Weasel

Cheerfully

ENGLAND

1. All around the cobbler's bench, Monkey chased the weasel, Monkey thought 'twas all___ in fun, Pop, goes the weasel. Penny for a spool___ of thread, Penny for a needle, That's the way the money goes, Pop, goes the weasel.

2. The painter needs a ladder and brush, the artist needs an easel,
The dancers need a fiddler's tune, pop, goes the weasel;
I've no time to wait or to sigh, or to tell the reason why,
Kiss me quick, I'm off, good-by, Pop goes the weasel.

Originally an old English singing game of unknown origin, this was a popular dance tune from the seventeenth century. It was introduced to New England as a contradance in which the partners form two facing lines and skip the dance figures. It became a favorite square dance tune, and many verses were improvised to fit dance figures. Legend has it that the song originally did not refer to the animals mentioned, but to a tool used by old London hatters and tailors called a "weasel," which they would pawn or "pop" when they were short of funds and needed money to tide them over until times were better for them.

Hansel and Gretel Dance

(PARTNER COME AND DANCE WITH ME)

ADELHEID WETTE
TR. CONSTANCE BACHE

E. HUMPERDINCK

Sprightly

Part - ner come and dance with me, Both my hands I of - fer thee

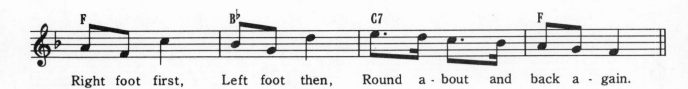

Right foot first, Left foot then, Round a - bout and back a - gain.

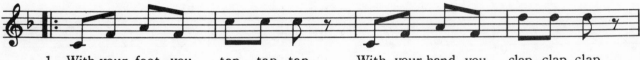

1. With your foot you tap, tap, tap, With your hand you clap, clap, clap,
2. With your head you nick, nick, nick, With your fin - gers click, click, click,

Right foot first, Left foot then, Round a - bout and back a - gain.

Copyright, 1895, by B. Schott's Söhne, Mayence.

This dance song is from the opera *Hansel And Gretel*. The actions of the dance are described in the words of the song. In the opening scene of the opera, first produced in Munich in 1893, the boy Hansel (mezzo-soprano) and his sister Gretel (soprano) are broom-making and knitting, respectively. They are very hungry as there is nothing in the house to eat. They tell each other about their sad plight, and Gretel quotes an old saying of her father:

(Gretel)   "When past bearing is our grief, God the Lord will send relief."
(Hansel)   "Yes, yes, that sounds very fine, but alas, off maxims we cannot dine!
             Oh, Gretel, it would be such a treat if we had something nice to eat."

Then Gretel tells him a secret — a kind neighbor has brought a jug of fresh milk for their supper. Hansel sticks his finger in the cream and samples it, dreaming of a rice blanc mange he hopes his mother will make for them. Gretel scolds him for not doing his work, but he tells her he would rather dance. Gretel is delighted at the thought and sings an old song their grandmother used to sing to them, and they begin the dance.

226

O Little Town of Bethlehem

PHILLIPS BROOKS

LEWIS H. REDNER

1. O lit-tle town of Beth-le-hem how still we_ see thee lie; A-bove thy deep and dream-less sleep the si-lent_ stars go by. Yet in thy dark streets shin-eth the ev-er-last-ing light; The hopes and fears of all the years are met in thee to-night.

2. For Christ is born of Mary and gathered all above
   While mortals sleep, the angels keep their watch of wondering love.
   O morning stars, together proclaim the holy birth,
   And praises sing to God the King and peace to men on earth.

3. How silently, how silently the wondrous gift is given;
   So God imparts to human hearts the blessings of his heaven.
   No ear may hear His coming, but in this world of sin
   Where meek souls will receive Him, still the dear Christ enters in.

4. O holy Child of Bethlehem descend to us, we pray,
   Cast out our sin and enter in, be born in us today.
   We hear the Christmas angels the great glad tidings tell,
   O come to us, abide with us our Lord Emmanuel!

Phillips Brooks (1835-1893), brilliant young minister of Episcopal Church of the Holy Trinity in Philadelphia, was graduated from Harvard when he was only 19 years old. He had planned to teach, but turned to the ministry because of his deep religious convictions. His greatest wish was to visit the Holy Land, and so Christmas Eve of 1865 found him in the Church of the Nativity in Jerusalem. When he returned to Philadelphia, he told the children of his parish about the experience, and wrote it in verse for them. The church organist, Lewis Redner (1831-1901), also was a composer. He agreed to write the music for the verse. One night the melody came to him. "It was like a gift from heaven," he said. Rev. Brooks eventually became Bishop of Massachusetts and one of the greatest preachers of his age.

Skip to My Lou

SOUTHERN U. S.

2. Lost my partner, what'll I do?

3. I'll get another one, prettier than you.

4. Can't get a red bird, a blue bird'll do.

There are innumerable verses for this southern mountain song. The four above are representative, and it is fun to invent new ones in a similar vein. *Skip To My Lou* was an extremely popular fiddling tune at parties. Participants added to the fun by making up words to suggest actions as they danced. Often they danced it as a circle game with partners. A single person in the center would "steal" a partner, the odd dancer would proceed to the center, and the dance would continue. Songs such as this were instituted by the more religious pioneers as a substitute for the more familiar forms of dancing.

Old Joe Clark

Quick dance rhythm

1. I used to live on the moun-tain top, Now I live in town,
I'm stay-ing at the big ho-tel, Court-ing Bet-sy Brown.

Chorus

Fare you well, old Joe Clark, Good-by Bet-sy Brown,

Fare you well, old Joe Clark, Fare-well to the town.

2. Old Joe Clark had a house twenty stories high,
   And every story in that house was filled with chicken pie.

3. Once I had a muley cow, muley, when she's born,
   Took a buzzard a million years to fly from horn to horn.

4. Joe Clark had a yellow cat, she'd neither sing nor pray,
   Stuck her head in the buttermilk jar and washed her sins away.

5. I went down to Joe Clark's house, he asked me in to stay,
   He slept on a feather bed, and I slept in the hay.

6. Wish I had a pretty little girl, I'd put her on a shelf,
   And every time she winked her eye I'd climb up there myself.

7. Joe Clark had a violin, he fiddled all the day,
   Let anybody start to dance and Joe would start to play.

This old Appalachian mountain fiddle tune was a popular play party and square dance song. Dancers stepped to the rhythm of the nonsense jingles they improvised, and scores of verses were made up as the dance progressed. *Old Joe Clark* often was played on the harmonica and guitar as well as the fiddle. Its date of origin is unknown.

Rio Grande

AMERICAN CHANTEY

Vigorously

1. O say, were you ev-er in Ri-o Grande? A-
(Chanteyman)   (Sailors)
way,_____ Ri-o,_____ It's there that the riv-er runs
down gold-en sand, And we're bound for the Ri-o Grande._____
(Chanteyman)
(Sailors)

Chorus
And a-way,_____ Ri-o,_____ A-
way,_____ Ri-o,_____ So fare___ you well, my
bon-nie young girl, And we're bound for the Ri-o Grande._____

2. Oh, New York City is no place for me, away, Rio,
   I'll pack my bags and then I'll go out to sea,
   We're bound for the Rio Grande.

3. The anchor's aweigh and the sails they are set,
   The girls we are leaving we'll never forget, etc.

4. So pack up your sea bag and get under way,
   Perhaps we'll return again another day, etc.

Rio Grande

5. A jolly good mate and a jolly good crew,
   A jolly good ship and a good skipper, too, etc.

6. Now you lovely ladies, we would let you know,
   That the time has come, and we're about to go, etc.

7. Sing goodby to Sally, and goodby to Sue,
   And to all you listening, it's goodby, too, etc.

This outward-bound capstan chantey dates from the time of the Mexican War (1846-1848). Mexico strongly protested the proposed annexation of Texas, and the situation was complicated by the extravagant boundaries the Texans claimed. As a part of Mexico, Texas' southwestern border was generally conceded to be the Nueces River, but on becoming independent the new state laid claim to a new border, the Rio Grande from its mouth to its source, then north to the forty-second parallel. President Polk, hoping for peace, sent a minister to Mexico, John Slidell of Louisiana, to purchase the territory. The Slidell mission failed, and war broke out. It was settled by the Treaty of Guadalupe Hidalgo. By its terms Mexico accepted the Rio Grande boundary, and ceded New Mexico and California and all the territory between them to the United States. During the war, many merchant ships hired out for the dangerous task of delivering contraband south of the Rio Grande. American sailors pronounced the Mexican name Rio Grande (large river) "rye-o-grand."

The More We Get Together

GERMANY

The more we get to-geth-er, to - geth - er, to - geth - er, The more we get to-geth-er, the hap-pier we'll be. For your friends are my friends and my friends are your friends. The more we get to-geth-er the hap-pier we'll be.

Frog He Would A - Wooing Go

Mirthfully

ENGLAND

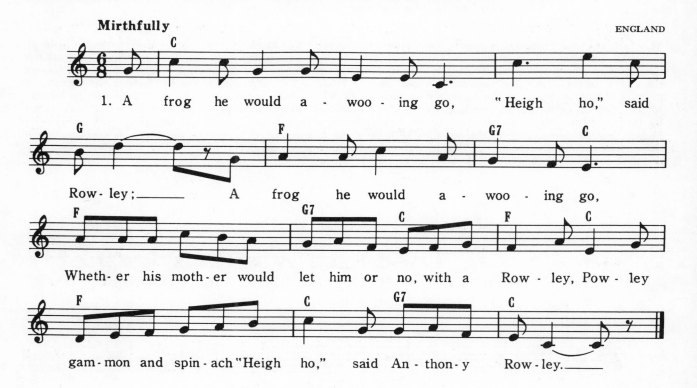

1. A frog he would a - woo - ing go, "Heigh ho," said Row - ley;____ A frog he would a - woo - ing go, Wheth - er his moth - er would let him or no, with a Row - ley, Pow - ley gam - mon and spin - ach "Heigh ho," said An - thon - y Row - ley.____

2. Then off he set in his top hat, "Heigh ho," said Rowley,
   Then off he set in his top hat, and on the road he met a rat,
   With a Rowley, Powley, gammon and spinach, "Heigh ho," said Anthony Rowley.

3. And soon they came to Mouses' Hall, "Heigh ho," said Rowley,
   And soon they came to Mouses' Hall, they gave a knock, they gave a call,
   With a Rowley, Powley, gammon and spinach, "Heigh ho," said Anthony Rowley.

4. "Pray, Mrs. Mouse, are you within? Heigh ho," said Rowley,
   "Pray, Mrs. Mouse, are you within?" "Yes, kind sir, I am just starting to spin,"
   With a Rowley, Powley, gammon and spinach, "Heigh ho," said Anthony Rowley.

5. "Oh, Mr. Frog, please sing a song, Heigh ho," said Rowley,
   "Oh, Mr. Frog, please sing a song, a song that really is not very long,"
   With a Rowley, Powley, gammon and spinach, "Heigh ho," said Anthony Rowley.

6. "I'm very sorry," said the frog, "Heigh ho," said Rowley,
   "I'm very sorry," said the frog, "a cold has made me just as hoarse as a hog,"
   With a Rowley, Powley, gammon and spinach, "Heigh ho," said Anthony Rowley.

This legend has been popular for four centuries. The earliest record of this song is in a play printed in 1549, *The Complaint of Scotland*. John Liston sang a version of it in Covent Garden. It was popularized in American music halls as a nonsense song. *Frog Went Courting* and *Frog He Would A-Wooing Go* display similarities in both words and music which suggest a common origin.

Looby Loo

U. S.

Swinging rhythm

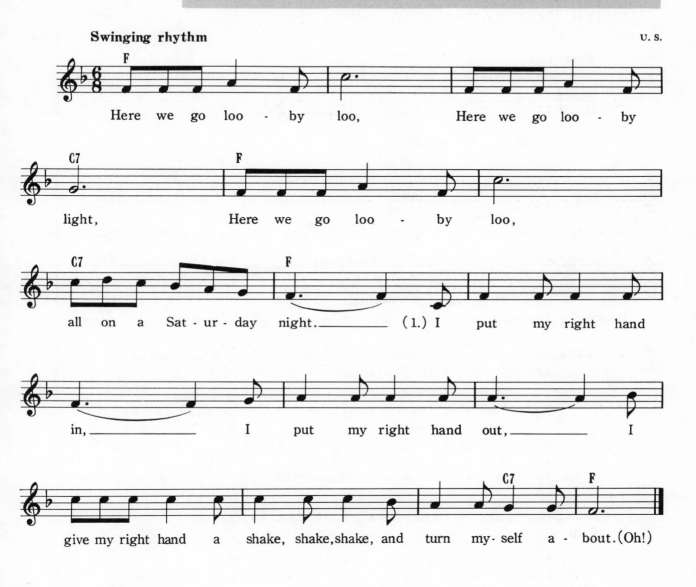

Here we go loo - by loo, Here we go loo - by light, Here we go loo - by loo, all on a Sat - ur - day night. (1.) I put my right hand in, I put my right hand out, I give my right hand a shake, shake, shake, and turn my-self a - bout. (Oh!)

2. I put my left hand in, etc.

3. I put my right foot in, etc.

4. I put my left foot in, etc.

5. I put my head right in, etc.

6. I put my whole self in, etc.

This old singing game originally was played with children at bath time. Now children skip to the music and pantomime the words.

Little Bo-Peep

MOTHER GOOSE RHYME

J. W. ELLIOTT

Simply

1. Lit-tle Bo-Peep has lost her sheep, And can't tell where to find them; Leave them a-lone, and they'll come home, Wag-ging their tails be-hind them.

2. Little Bo-Peep fell fast asleep, and dreamed she heard them bleating;
   When she awoke, 'twas all a joke, for they were still a-fleeting.

3. Then up she took her little crook, determined for to find them,
   But when she looked, they'd all come home, wagging their tails behind them.

Goodby, My Lover, Goodby

With flourish

CHANTEY

1. The ship is sail-ing down the bay, Good-by, my lov-er, good-by.___ We
   My heart will ev-er-more be true, Good-by, my lov-er, good-by.___ Though

may not meet for man-y a day, Good-by, my lov-er, good-by.___
now we sad-ly say___ a-dieu, Good-by, my lov-er, good-by.___

234

Goodby, My Lover, Goodby

By - low, my ba - by, By - low, my ba - by,

By - low, my ba - by, Good - by, my lov-er, good - by. _____

2. Then cheer up till we meet again, goodby, my lover, goodby,
   I'll try to bear my weary pain, goodby, my lover, goodby,
   Though far I roam across the sea, goodby, my lover, goodby,
   My every thought of you shall be, goodby, my lover, goodby.

The origin of this song is unknown. It appears to be a combination of a chantey and a lullaby. It has been a favorite on college campuses for many years.

For the Beauty of the Earth

FOLLIOTT S. PIERPONT

CONRAD KOCHER

Thoughtfully

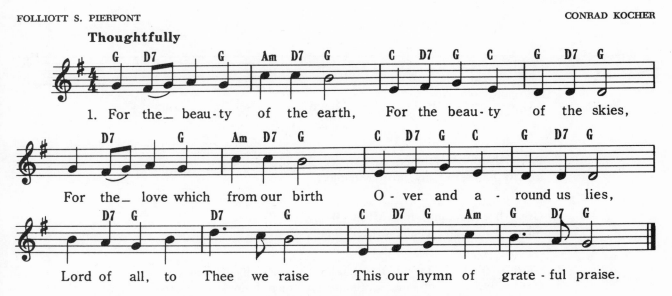

1. For the_ beau-ty of the earth, For the beau-ty of the skies,

For the_ love which from our birth O - ver and a - round us lies,

Lord of all, to Thee we raise This our hymn of grate - ful praise.

2. For the beauty of each hour of the day and of the night,
   Hill and vale and tree and flower, sun and moon and stars of light,
   Lord of all, to Thee we raise this our hymn of grateful praise.
3. For the joy of human love, brother, sister, parent, child,
   Friends on earth and friends above, for all gentle thoughts and mild,
   Lord of all, to Thee we raise this our hymn of grateful praise.

This hymn was written for the communion service by Folliott Sanford Pierpont (1835-1917). A graduate of Queen's College, Cambridge, Pierpont wrote other hymns, but *For the Beauty Of The Earth* (1864) is the only one for which he is remembered. His words are sung most often to a melody written by Conrad Kocher.

Mister Banjo

LOUISIANA CREOLE

Jauntily

Look at the dan - dy there, Mis - ter Ban - jo,

Does - n't he put on airs! (Mis - ter Ban - jo)
omit on D.C.

Verse

1. Hat cocked on one side, Mis - ter Ban - jo,

Walk - ing stick in hand, Mis - ter Ban - jo.

2. Boots that go "crank-crank," Mister Banjo,
   Yellow gloves, O my, Mister Banjo.

3. Great big diamond ring, Mister Banjo,
   Silver watch and chain, Mister Banjo,

1. Gardez milat là, O mu'sieu Banjo, Cummen li insolent.
   Gardez milat là, O mu'sieu Banjo, Cummen li insolent.
   Chapo cote, O mu'sieu Banjo, Cane à so'main, O mu'sieu Banjo,
   Gardez milat là, O mu'sieu Banjo, Cummen li insolent.

This Louisiana folk song reflects the mixed cultural background which remains a part of New Orleans. This colorful old Mississippi River settlement, where *Mr. Banjo* flourished, was founded by the French and occupied by the Spanish. In 1803, it was purchased by the United States, and admitted to the Union in 1812. The large Negro population added still a fourth cultural influence to music in that area.

Old Folks at Home

STEPHEN C. FOSTER   STEPHEN C. FOSTER

With feeling

1. 'Way down up-on the Swa-nee riv-er, Far, far a - way,
   All up and down the whole cre-a-tion, Sad - ly I roam,

There's where my heart is turn-ing ev-er, There's where the old folks ____ stay.
Still long-ing for the old plan-ta-tion, And for the old folks at home.

Chorus

All the world is sad and drear-y, Eve-ry where I roam;

Oh, dear ones, how my heart grows wear-y, Far from the old folks at home.

2. All around the little farm I wandered when I was young,
   There many happy days I've squandered, there many songs I've sung.
   When I was playing with my brother, happy was I,
   Oh, take me to my kind old mother, there let me live and die.

3. One little hut among the bushes, one that I love,
   Still sadly to my memory rushes, no matter where I rove.
   When will I see the bees a-humming all around the comb?
   When will I hear the banjo tumming, down in my good old home?

This song has been translated into every European language as well as into Asian and African tongues. It is rated one of a small group of songs beloved by the entire world and one of the author's greatest. Stephen C. Foster wrote it when he was 25 years old and before he had ever been in the South. It was published in 1851 and at first was credited to E. P. Christy of the Christy Minstrels, as were many of Foster's songs. In a *Musical World* publication of 1852, the report appeared: "The publishers keep two presses running on it, and sometimes three, yet they cannot supply the demand." That year everyone in the country was singing *Old Folks At Home,* and its popularity has continued.

The Muffin Man

Cheerfully

ENGLAND

1. O do you know the muf-fin man, the muf-fin man, the muf-fin man, O do you know the muf-fin man, that lives in Dru-ry Lane?

2. O yes I know the muffin man, etc.
3. O have you seen the muffin man, etc.
4. Where did you see the muffin man, etc.

This old English game song has rhythm suitable for skipping and marching. It often is used as a question and answer song, and offers excellent opportunity for the singers to make up verses about a variety of activities.

O God, Beneath Thy Guiding Hand

LEONARD BACON

JOHN HATTON

Majestically

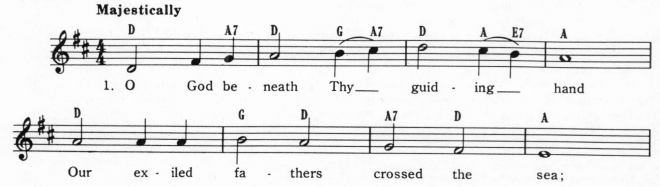

1. O God be-neath Thy guid-ing hand

Our ex-iled fa-thers crossed the sea;

O God, Beneath Thy Guiding Hand

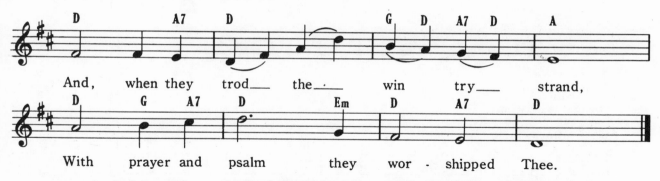

And, when they trod__ the·__ win try__ strand,

With prayer and psalm they wor - shipped Thee.

2. And here Thy name, O God of love, their children's children shall adore,
Till these eternal hills remove, and spring adorns the earth no more.

This patriotic hymn was written by the Rev. Leonard Bacon (1802-1881) in 1833 for the two-hundredth anniversary celebration of the founding of New Haven, Connecticut. Rev. Bacon was a graduate of Yale University and Andover Seminary. While at Andover he compiled the first collection of missionary hymns to be printed in America. At Yale he founded a monthly "Missionary Concert" where he used his hymn collection. After retiring from his pastorate, Rev. Bacon was professor of theology at Yale Divinity School.

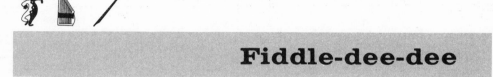

Fiddle-dee-dee

Flippantly

ENGLAND

Fid - dle - dee - dee, Fid - dle - dee - dee, The fly has mar - ried the

bum - ble bee. 1. Says the fly, says he, "Will you

mar - ry me and live with me, sweet bum - ble bee?"

2. Says the bee, says she, "I'll live under your wing,
And you shan't ever feel my sting."

3. When the two were wed they went out to fly,
They sailed away across the sky.

4. All the bees did buzz and the flies did sing,
And bluebells one and all did ring.

5. Then the bumble bee did wink her eye,
To think that she had caught the fly.

Nonsense songs such as this old English folk song were in high favor with children during the sixteenth and seventeenth centuries, and they have remained so to this day.

Now Thank We All Our God

MARTIN RINKART
TR. CATHERINE WINKWORTH

JOHANN CRÜGER

2. O may this bounteous God through all our life be near us,
   With ever joyful hearts and blessed peace to cheer us,
   And keep us in His grace, and guide us when perplexed,
   And free us from all ills in this world and the next.

The Rev. Martin Rinkart (1586-1649) wrote this hymn about 1630. It was translated by Catherine Winkworth in 1858. As a boy, Rev. Rinkart served as a chorister in Leipzig's famous St. Thomas Church. The great composer, Johann Sebastian Bach, later became music director at this church (1736). Of the 66 hymns Rev. Rinkart wrote, this one has received acceptance in Germany and in English speaking countries. Chorales such as *Now Thank We All Our God* have played an important role in German life, and they frequently are heard in homes and streets as well as in churches. This particular hymn is triumphant in tone, and frequently is sung at times of national rejoicing. It also is a favorite hymn of the Thanksgiving season.

Polly Wolly Doodle

U. S.

Speedily

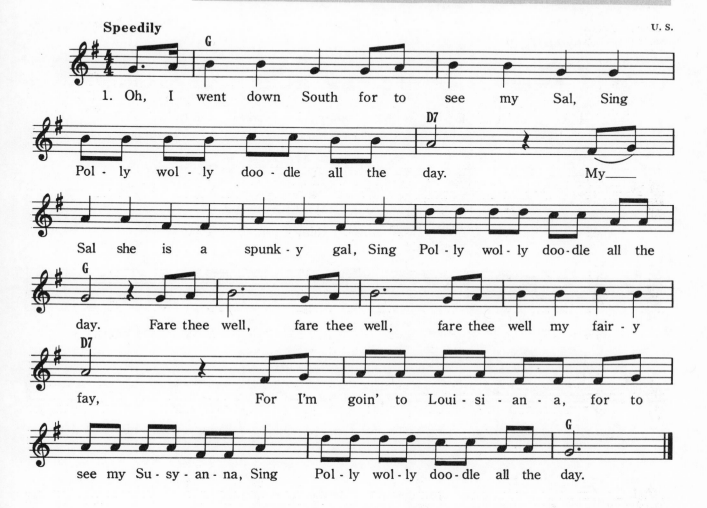

1. Oh, I went down South for to see my Sal, Sing
Pol - ly wol - ly doo - dle all the day. My___
Sal she is a spunk - y gal, Sing Pol - ly wol - ly doo - dle all the
day. Fare thee well, fare thee well, fare thee well my fair - y
fay, For I'm goin' to Loui - si - an - a, for to
see my Su - sy - an - na, Sing Pol - ly wol - ly doo - dle all the day.

2. Oh, my Sal, she is a maiden fair, etc.
   With curly eyes and laughing hair, etc.

3. Oh, a grasshopper sittin' on a railroad track, etc.
   Just pickin' his teeth with a carpet tack, etc.

4. Behind the barn upon my knees, etc.
   I thought I heard a chicken sneeze, etc.

5. He sneezed so hard he couldn't cough, etc.
   He sneezed his head and tail clear off, etc.

This song was popular with the minstrel singers, who performed it frequently on show boats as a "walk-around." The walk-around was the finale of the show. The entire group returned to the stage and formed a semicircle to sing the closing number. Individual performers would step forward to sing a verse, and the end men would interrupt each in turn. The final chorus was sung by the entire company with some stamping, some clapping, and some dancing to the rhythm. *Dixie* was another walk-around song, and these lively numbers brought the delighted audiences to their feet shouting their approval. *Polly Wolly Doodle* also found great favor on college campuses where students made a popular nonsense song of it.

O Come, Little Children

J. P. A. SCHULZ

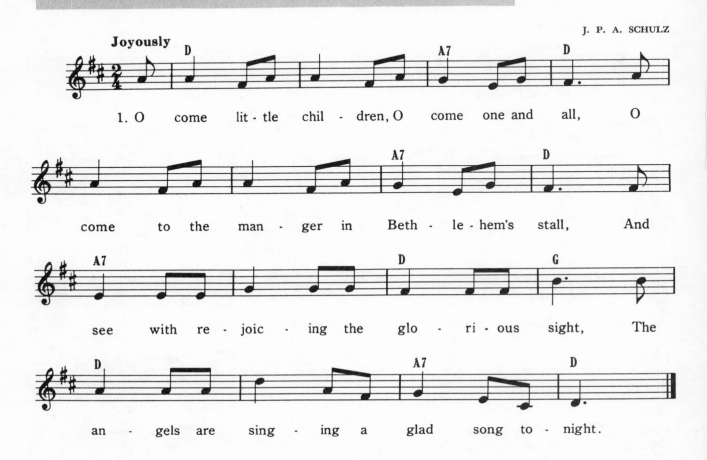

Joyously

1. O come lit-tle chil-dren, O come one and all, O
come to the man-ger in Beth-le-hem's stall, And
see with re-joic-ing the glo-ri-ous sight, The
an-gels are sing-ing a glad song to-night.

2. O come little children, O come near and see
The Babe in the stable, so holy is He,
The star's brilliant gleam lights the stall where he lies,
While angels above Him keep watch in the skies.

Germany is the land of the Christmas Tree, and *Weinachten*, or Holy Night, is Christmas to the German people. Beginning with the eve of December 6, all shops are decorated, and present a festive appearance. Christmas is an affair for the entire family, and the celebration is begun far ahead of the actual day. Advent wreaths and candles begin the fourth Sunday before Christmas. Homemade gifts are hurriedly finished and will be treasured by lucky receivers. Gaily decorated trees of all shapes and sizes appear in shop windows, and many homes in Germany have two trees. These are decorated by the mother in secret, and they are not viewed by the entire family until Christmas Eve when she proudly displays them along with specially baked Christmas cookies. German children believe that their gifts come through the generosity of the *Christkind*, or Christ Child. Their name for Santa Claus is *Kriss Kringle*, and they believe he watches children throughout the year and leaves gifts for good children and switches or rods for naughty children. In some German families presents are wrapped in many layers of paper, called a *Julkapp*, each with a different person's name on it. The package goes to the next name after each unwrapping until it reaches the person for whom it was meant. Churches are left open during the holiday season, and German families go together to services both on Christmas eve and Christmas day. *O Come, Little Children* is an old German Carol.

Green Grow the Lilacs

Unhurried

U. S.

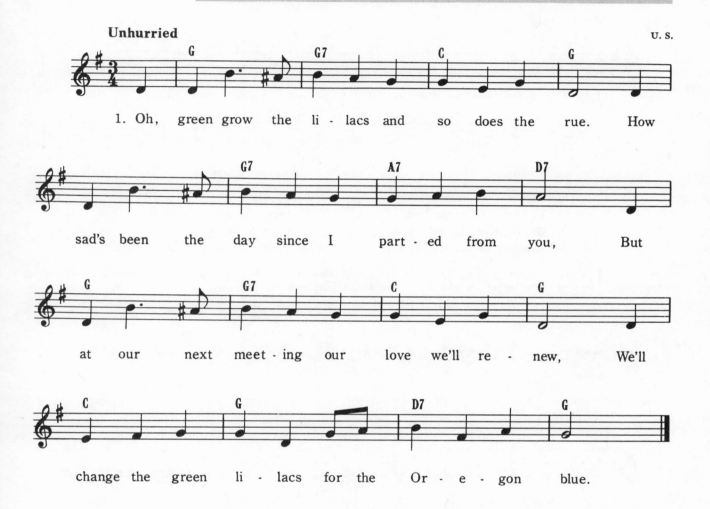

1. Oh, green grow the li - lacs and so does the rue. How sad's been the day since I part - ed from you, But at our next meet - ing our love we'll re - new, We'll change the green li - lacs for the Or - e - gon blue.

2. I once had a sweetheart but now I have none,
   He's gone far and left me to live all alone,
   He's gone far and left me contented to be,
   He must love another better than he loves me.

3. On top of the mountain where green lilacs grow,
   And deep in the valley where still waters flow,
   I met my true love and he proved to be true,
   We changed the green lilacs for the Oregon blue.

This American folk song was extremely popular on the Western plains, and may have originated in Texas. The melody is an old Irish air.

243

The Old Gray Goose
(GO TELL AUNT RHODY)

U. S.

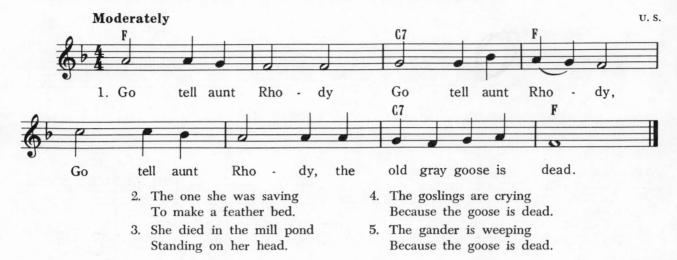

Moderately

F   C7   F

1. Go   tell aunt Rho - dy   Go   tell aunt Rho - dy,

Go   tell aunt Rho - dy, the   old gray goose is   dead.

2. The one she was saving
   To make a feather bed.

3. She died in the mill pond
   Standing on her head.

4. The goslings are crying
   Because the goose is dead.

5. The gander is weeping
   Because the goose is dead.

The names of countless aunts, varying from one section of the country to the other, have been used in this nursery song. It is a variation of an old tune, *The Good Shepherd*.

Now the Day Is Over

SABINE BARING-GOULD   JOSEPH BARNBY

Calmly

1. Now the day is   o - ver,   Night is draw - ing   nigh,

Shad - ows of the   eve - ning   steal   a - cross the   sky.

2. Father, give the weary calm and sweet repose,
   With Thy tenderest blessing may our eyelids close.

3. When the morning wakens, then may I arise
   Pure, and fresh, and sinless in Thy holy eyes.

Sir Joseph Barnby (1838-1896) was an important nineteenth century organist, composer, and conductor. He was a choir boy at seven, a music teacher at eleven, an organist at twelve, and a music master at fifteen. He was knighted in 1892. Among his many compositions are 45 anthems and 246 hymn tunes. A complete collection of the latter was made in 1897. *Now The Day Is Over* is one of his most familiar hymns. The words were written by the Rev. Sabine Baring-Gould.

Old Chisholm Trail

With a swing

COWBOY

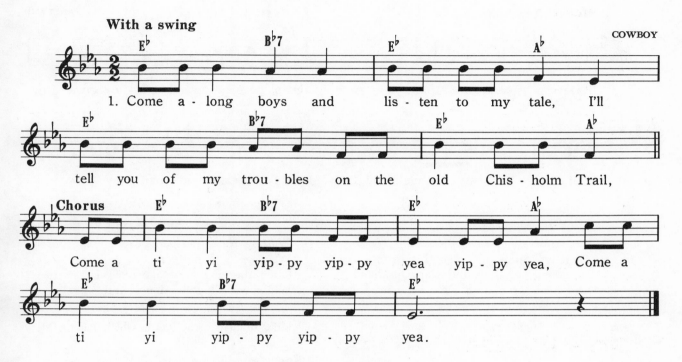

1. Come a-long boys and lis-ten to my tale, I'll
tell you of my trou-bles on the old Chis-holm Trail,

Chorus
Come a ti yi yip-py yip-py yea yip-py yea, Come a
ti yi yip-py yip-py yea.

2. I started up the trail October twenty third,
   I started up the trail with the two U herd, etc.

3. I woke one morning on the Chisholm trail,
   Rope in my hand and a cow by the tail, etc.

4. Cloudy in the west and it looks like rain,
   My darned old slicker's in the wagon again, etc.

5. Went to the boss to draw out my roll,
   He figured me out nine dollars in the hole, etc.

6. Going to sell my outfit just as quick as I can,
   And I won't punch cows for any man, etc.

7. With my knees in the saddle and my seat in the sky,
   I'll quit punching cows in the sweet by and by, etc.

According to legend, this song had a verse for every mile of trail from Texas to Kansas. Armed cowboys brought the first herd of 2,400 longhorn cattle from San Antonio to the newly opened yards of J. G. McCoy in Abilene in 1867. The route followed a trail blazed by Jesse Chisholm, a trader and government interpreter who was half Cherokee Indian. On the long cattle drives, cowboys sang to pass the time and to amuse themselves. During the night watches they sang to quiet the herd, locate other riders, and keep themselves awake. The refrain may have been borrowed from the Indians.

Oats, Peas, Beans

Moderately fast

ENGLAND

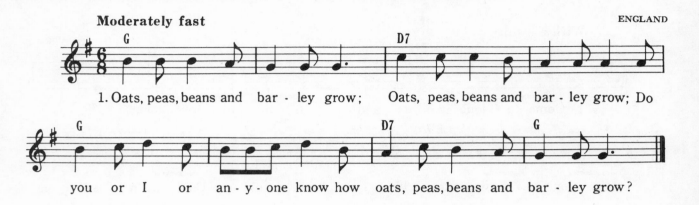

1. Oats, peas, beans and bar-ley grow; Oats, peas, beans and bar-ley grow; Do

you or I or an-y-one know how oats, peas, beans and bar-ley grow?

2. First the farmer sows his seed,
   Then he stands and takes his ease;
   He stamps his foot and claps his hands,
   And turns around to view his lands.

3. Waiting for a partner,
   Waiting for a partner,
   Open the ring and take one in
   While we all gaily dance and sing.

This is an old circle singing game which came from England. Children dramatize the words which tell the story of the farmer, his work, and his successful harvest.

Go Tell It on the Mountain

Resolutely

SPIRITUAL

1. When I was a seek-er, I sought both night and day; I

asked the Lord to help me, And He showed me the way.——

Chorus

Go tell it on the moun-tains, O-ver the hills and eve-ry where;——

Go Tell It on the Mountain

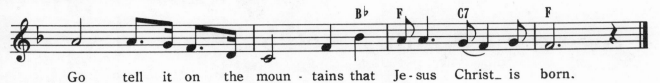

Go tell it on the moun-tains that Je-sus Christ_ is born.

2. He made me a watchman upon the city wall,
   And if I serve Him truly, I am the least of all,

3. In the time of David some said he was a king,
   And if a child is true born, the Lord will hear him sing.

The verses of spirituals such as this one often are sung by a leader or solo voice, and the refrain by the entire group. This call and answer technique also is found in African tribal songs. *Go Tell It On The Mountain* is one of the few spirituals with a Christmas theme.

Lonesome Valley

With melancholy

WHITE SPIRITUAL

1. Je-sus walked_____ this lone-some val-ley,_____ He had to walk_____ it by Him-self,_____ O no-bod-y else could walk it for Him,_____ He had to walk it by_____ Him-self..

2. We must walk this lonesome valley, we have to walk it by ourselves,
   O nobody else can walk it for us, we have to walk it by ourselves.

3. You must go and stand your trial, you have to stand it by yourself,
   O nobody else can stand it for you, you have to stand it by yourself.

White spirituals were the religious songs of the American frontier. Primitivism, fervor, and simplicity were their hallmark. Formal religious services were unknown on the frontier. Meetings and revivals were conducted by circuit-riding preachers. Many of these who had "answered the call" brought more zeal and emotion than training and experience to their ministry. A major portion of these meetings was given over to hymn singing. Old hymns were used, religious words were adapted to well-known secular melodies, and new hymns were composed to meet the spiritual needs of the pioneers. Frequently, the ardor of their singing matched the wild and primitive tenor of their wilderness existence.

Swing the Shining Sickle
(THANKSGIVING SONG)

ALICE RILEY   JANET GAYNOR

Steadily

1. Swing   the shin-ing   sick - le,   cut   the rip-ened grain,

Flash   it   in the sun - light,   swing it once a - gain.

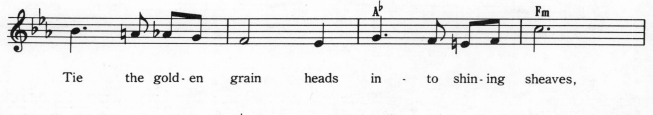

Tie   the gold-en   grain   heads   in - to shin-ing sheaves,

Beau - ti-ful their col - ors   as the au - tumn leaves.

2. Pick the rosy apples, pack away with care,
   Gather in the corn ears, gleaming everywhere.
   Now the fruits are gathered, all the grains are in,
   Nuts are in the attic, corn is in the bin.

3. Loudly blows the north wind through the shivering trees,
   Bare are all the branches, fallen all the leaves.
   Gathered is the harvest for another year,
   Now our day of gladness, Thanksgiving Day is here.

In early America before farm machinery was invented, crops were cut with a sickle and gathered by the field hands. This action song lends itself to dramatization, and the action words indicate appropriate gestures.

O Come, O Come, Immanuel

TR. JOHN M. NEALE

PLAINSONG

With dignity

1. O come, O come Im-man-u-el, And
ran-som cap-tive Is-ra-el, That
mourns in lone-ly ex-ile here Until the Son of God ap-pear.

Chorus
Re-joice! Re-joice! Im-man-u-el Shall
come to thee, O Is-ra-el!

2. O come, Thou Wisdom from on high, and order all things, far and nigh,
   To us the path of knowledge show, and cause us in her ways to go.

3. O come, Desire of Nations, bind all peoples in one heart and mind,
   Bid envy, strife, and quarrels cease, fill the whole world with heaven's peace.

The date of origin of this old hymn is unknown. It most often is used during advent — the four Sundays before Christmas — as a hymn and as a processional. The melody is from an ancient plainsong which probably dates back to the thirteenth century. The term "plainsong" is derived from the Latin *cantus planus,* a thirteenth century name for the Gregorian chant. It is used synonymously with the latter, but also in a wider sense, as a general denomination for the ancient style of monophonic and rhythmically free melody which is the common possession of the various Western liturgies as well as those of the East. It also may be applied to similar bodies of non-Christian liturgical music in order to indicate that this music is neither harmonic nor strictly measured.

A - Roving

CHANTEY

Zestfully

1. In Ply - mouth town there lived a maid, Bless you good

peo - ple! In Ply - mouth town there lived a maid, Mark

well what I___ do say! In Ply - mouth town there

lived a maid, And she was mis - tress___ of her trade, I'll

go no more a - rov - ing with you, fair maid.

Chorus

A - rov - ing___ a - rov - ing,___ Since rov - ing's been my___

ru - i - in, I'll go no more a - rov - ing with you, fair maid.

2. I took this fair maid for a walk, bless you, good people!
I took this fair maid for a walk, mark well what I do say!
I took this fair maid for a walk, and we had such a pleasant talk;
I'll go no more a-roving with you, fair maid.

250

A-Roving

3. I took her hand within my own, bless you, good people!
   I took her hand within my own, mark well what I do say!
   I took her hand within my own, and said, "I'm bound to my old home,"
   I'll go no more a-roving with you, fair maid.

The verse may be sung by a solo voice with the whole group joining on the phrases, "Bless you, good people" and "Mark well what I do say." Sung to an old familiar tune and thought originally to have been a shore song, this became a romantic sea chantey. Sailors sang it stepping in rhythm as they wound the anchor chain around the capstan and prepared to set sail.

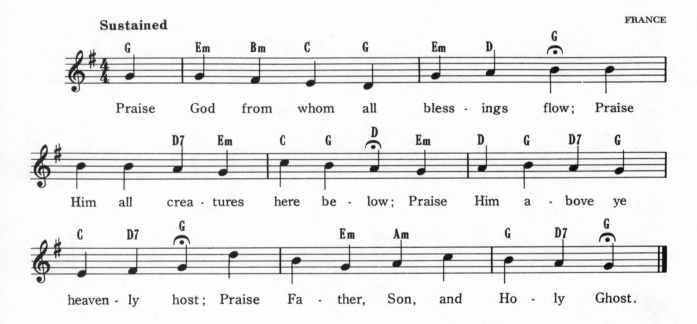

Praise God from Whom All Blessings Flow
(DOXOLOGY) (OLD HUNDREDTH)

FRANCE

Sustained

Praise God from whom all bless - ings flow; Praise Him all crea - tures here be - low; Praise Him a - bove ye heaven - ly host; Praise Fa - ther, Son, and Ho - ly Ghost.

This melody has been famous for at least four centuries. It originated in France where it was a popular love song. In 1551 a version of the One Hundred Thirty-fourth Psalm was adapted to it, and was printed in the *Genevan Psalter* entitled *Or Sus Servitours du Seigneur*. Some authorities attribute this version to Louis Bourgeois. The hymn was sung in the British Isles. Melodies well known and loved often have served for multiple sets of words as this one does. English Pilgrims and French Hugenots brought it to America where it was one of the first hymns of praise to be sung in their new land. Words to it appeared in the *Ainsworth Psalter* in 1612 based on the One-hundredth Psalm from which the title comes. Both words and music were published in 1698 in the *Bay Psalm Book* with these earlier words:

Make ye a joyful sounding noyse
Unto Jehovah, all the earth;
Serve ye Jehovah with gladness;
Before His presence come with mirth.

251

The Ash Grove

WALES

Stately

1. The ash grove, how graceful, how plainly 'tis speaking, The wind through it playing has language for me.
When over its branches the sunlight is breaking, A host of kind faces is gazing at me.

The friends of my childhood again are before me, Each step wakes a mem'ry, as freely I roam. With soft whispers laden, its leaves rustle o'er me; The ash grove, the ash grove that sheltered my home.

2. My laughter is over, my step loses lightness,
Old countryside measures steal soft on my ear;
I only remember the past and its brightness,
The dear ones I mourn for again gather here.
From out of the shadows their loving looks greet me,
And wistfully searching the leafy green dome,
I find other faces fond bending to greet me;
The ash grove, the ash grove alone is my home.

The Ash Grove

1. Yn Mhalas Llwyn On gynt, fe drigai pendefig
   Efe oedd ysgweiar ac arglwydd y wlad;
   Ac iddo un eneth a anwyd yn unig
   A hi' nol yr hanes oedd aeres ei thad.
   Aeth Cariad i'w gweled, yn lân a phur lencyn,
   Ond codai'r ys gweiar yn afar ac erch,
   I saethu'r bachgenyn, ond gwŷrodd ei linyn,
   A'i ergyd yn wyrgam i fynwes ei ferch.

This Welsh song is famous throughout the world. A version of it is included in *The Beggar's Opera* which began a revolution in the musical theatre with its first performance in London in 1728. The "opera" is a spoken play with songs set to popular tunes of the day interspersed. John Gay wrote the dialogue and lyrics, and John Pepusch selected and arranged the music. It is both a parody of Italian opera and a satire on political corruption of the period.

Early One Morning

ENGLAND

Leisurely

1. Oh, ear - ly one morn - ing just as the sun was ris - ing, I heard a maid sing___ in the val - ley be - low.

Chorus

Oh, don't de - ceive___ me, oh, don't de - ceive___ me, How___ could you use_____ a poor___ maid - en so?

2. Remember the promise you made to your loved one,
   Remember the place where you promised to be true.

3. Oh, fresh is the garland, and lovely the roses
   I've picked from the garden to lay at your feet.

4. So sang the sweet maiden, her sadness bewailing,
   Thus sang the poor maid in the valley below.

Sentimental songs which entreat a loved one to be true are common to all countries. This one from England is sung to an old folk melody.

Sleep, Baby, Sleep

Tranquilly

GERMANY

1. Sleep, ba-by, sleep, Thy fa-ther guards the sheep. Thy
moth-er shakes the dream-land tree, and down fall pleas-ant
dreams for thee. Sleep, ba-by, sleep. Sleep, ba-by, sleep.

2. Sleep, baby sleep, the white clouds are the sheep,
The stars like lambs run up and down, the moon, their shepherd, leads them on,
Sleep, baby, sleep, sleep, baby sleep.

3. Sleep, baby sleep, I'll give to you a sheep
Who wears a tinkling bell so bright, and he'll be with you all the night,
Sleep, baby, sleep, sleep, baby sleep.

The melody to which these words are sung is a very old German lullaby.

Go Down Moses

Deliberately

SPIRITUAL

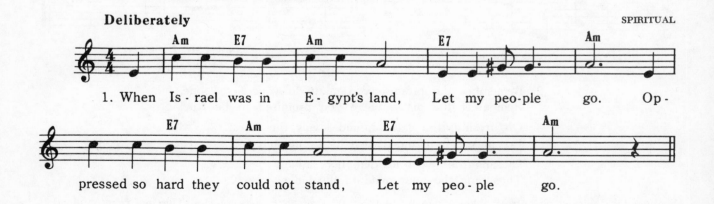

1. When Is-rael was in E-gypt's land, Let my peo-ple go. Oppressed so hard they could not stand, Let my peo-ple go.

254

Go Down Moses

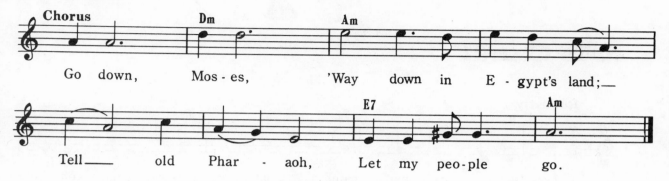

Go down, Mos-es, 'Way down in E-gypt's land;— Tell— old Phar-aoh, Let my peo-ple go.

2. Thus saith the Lord, bold Moses said, Let my people go!
If not, I'll smite your first born dead, Let my people go!

In 1871 Fisk University sent its choir on a fund-raising tour. The group charmed listeners with spirituals its members had sung since childhood, among them *Go Down Moses*. Legend has it that the Moses of the song was the ex-slave and famous abolitionist leader Harriet Tubman. Reverend L. C. Lockwood, a chaplain for refugee slaves, notated the song as he heard it sung by Negro Civil War troops.

Little Wheel A-turning

With animation

U. S.

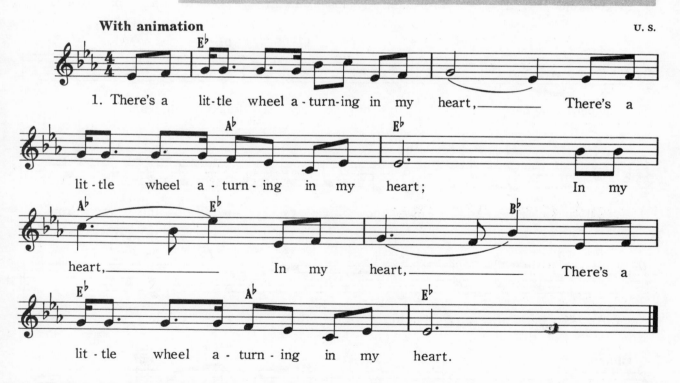

1. There's a lit-tle wheel a-turn-ing in my heart,————— There's a lit-tle wheel a-turn-ing in my heart; In my heart,——————— In my heart,——————— There's a lit-tle wheel a-turn-ing in my heart.

2. There's a little song a-singing in my heart, etc.   3. Oh, I feel so very happy in my heart, etc.

4. Oh, I feel just like a-shouting in my heart, etc.

The simplicity and repetition of the words to this song make it an excellent choice for singers to add verses of their own invention.

Erie Canal

U. S.

Robustly

1. I've got a mule, her name is Sal, Fif-teen miles on the E-rie Ca-nal. She's a good old work-er and a good old pal, Fif-teen miles on the E-rie Ca-nal. We've hauled some barg-es in our day, Filled with lum-ber, coal and hay, And we know eve-ry inch of the way From Al-ba-ny to Buf-fa-lo.

Chorus F

Low bridge, eve-ry-bod-y down,

Erie Canal

Low bridge, 'cause were com-ing to a town; And you'll

al - ways know your neigh-bor, You'll al - ways know your pal, If you've

ev - er nav - i - gat - ed on the E - rie Ca - nal.

2. We'd better get along, old pal, fifteen miles on the Erie Canal,
   You can bet your life I'd never part from Sal, fifteen miles on the Erie Canal;
   Get up there, mule, here comes a lock, we'll make Rome by six o'clock,
   One more trip and back we'll go, back we'll go to Buffalo.

The Erie Canal, authorized in 1817 and completed in 1825, was of immense significance in the development of the United States. Connecting Lake Erie (Buffalo) and the Hudson River (Albany), the 363-mile waterway linked the east to the west. It was by far the most spectacular transportation development of the period. The cheap all-water route carried agricultural produce from the west to the east and manufactured goods from the east to the west. Cities sprang up along the route. With transportation no longer a problem, pioneers by tens of thousands settled vacant western lands. The canal teemed with boats and barges. Songs of the mule skinners who drove the mules along the tow paths as they hauled the flat-bottom carriers echoed across the country day and night. Low bridges were built across the canal at frequent intervals. The skinners shouted a warning to the passengers on the boats when approaching a bridge. The call "low bridge ahead" was a signal for everyone on board to drop flat on the deck until the bridge was cleared.

White Coral Bells
ROUND

ENGLAND

Clearly

1. White cor - al bells up - on a slen - der stalk,
2. Oh, don't you wish that you could hear them ring?

Lil - ies of the val - ley deck my gar - den walk,
That will hap - pen on - ly when the fair - ies sing.

257

The Linden Tree

WILHELM MÜLLER
TR. THEODORE BAKER

FRANZ SCHUBERT

Expressively

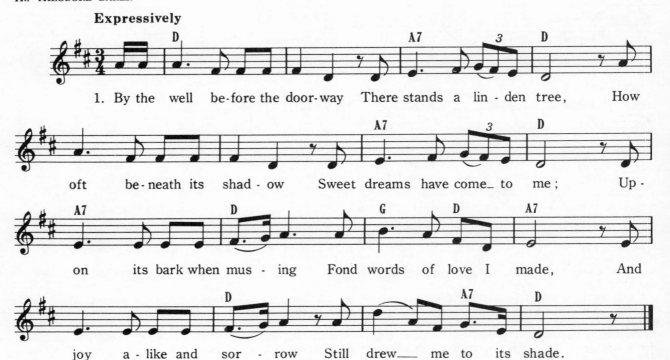

1. By the well be-fore the door-way There stands a lin-den tree, How oft be-neath its shad-ow Sweet dreams have come to me; Up-on its bark when mus-ing Fond words of love I made, And joy a-like and sor-row Still drew me to its shade.

2. Now many leagues I'm far from the dear old linden tree,
   I ever hear it murmur: "Peace thou wouldst find with me."
   Though many leagues I'm far from the dear old linden tree,
   I ever hear it murmur, "Peace thou wouldst find with me."

1. Am Brunnen vor dem Tore, da steht ein Lindenbaum;
   Ich träumt' in seinem Schatten so manchen süssen Traum,
   Ich schnitt in seine Rinde so manches liebe Wort;
   Es zog in Freud' und Leide zu ihm mich immer fort.

2. Nun bin ich manche Stunde entfernt von jenem Ort,
   Und immer hör' ich's rauschen: du fändest Ruhe dort!
   Nun bin ich manche Stunde entfernt von jenem Ort,
   Und immer hör' ich's rauschen: du fändest Ruhe dort!

The Linden Tree is the fifth of the 24 songs in the song cycle *Winter Journey* (*Winterreise*) by Franz Schubert (1797-1828). The text is by the German poet, Wilhelm Müller (1794-1827), whose chief poetical works are lyrical, and are very popular in Germany. Muller taught Latin and Greek at Dessau, and he is the father of the celebrated philologist, Friedrich Max Müller. The linden tree has dense, heart-shaped leaves and fragrant, yellowish flowers. The flowers appear in June, and their strong, sweet scent attracts bees seemingly from all other plants. The inner bark of the tree has long, tough fibers which American Indians used to make ropes. The wood is prized for its white color. Linden trees range in height from 70 to 140 feet, and reach maturity in 90 to 140 years.

The Blue Tail Fly
(JIMMY CRACK CORN)

DAN EMMETT

U. S.

Capriciously

1. When I was young I used to wait on mas-ter and give him his plate, And

pass the bot-tle when he got dry, And brush a-way the blue tail fly.

Chorus

Jim-my crack corn and I don't care, Jim-my crack corn and I don't care,

Jim-my crack corn and I don't care, my mas-ter's gone a - way.

2. When he'd ride in the afternoon
   I'd follow with my hickory broom,
   The pony being rather shy
   When bitten by the blue tail fly.

3. Once when he rode around the farm
   The flies about him thick did swarm,
   The pony which was very shy
   Was bitten by the blue tail fly.

4. The pony run, he jump, he pitch,
   He threw my master in the ditch,
   He died; the jury wondered why;
   The verdict was, "The blue tail fly."

5. They laid him under a 'simmon tree,
   His epitaph is there to see:
   "Beneath this stone I'm forced to lie,
   A victim of the blue tail fly."

This popular show tune of the 1840's was written by the famous minstrel man, Dan Emmett. The melody may have been an older folk tune of Negro origin. Emmett was loved by the South for the many famous songs he wrote about that section of the country. Emmett was honored when he made a southern tour singing his songs when he was more than eighty years old. This is a singing game song which is excellent for skipping and panto-mime.

O Susanna

STEPHEN C. FOSTER   STEPHEN C. FOSTER

With excitement

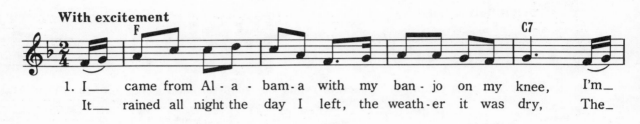

1. I__ came from Al - a - bam - a with my ban - jo on my knee, I'm__
It__ rained all night the day I left, the weath - er it was dry, The__

going to Lou' - si - an - a my_____ true love for to see.
sun so hot I froze to death, Su - san - na don't you cry.

Chorus

O Su - san - na, O don't you cry for me, For I've

come from Al - a - bam - a with my ban - jo on my knee.

2. I had a dream the other night, when everything was still;
   I thought I saw Susanna, acoming down the hill;
   The buckwheat cake was in her mouth, the tear was in her eye,
   Says I, I'm coming from the South, Susanna, don't you cry!

E. P. Christy, one of the most famous of the minstrels, kept a sharp watch out for songs which would be good box office draws. *O Susanna*, introduced by the Christy Minstrels in 1848, was an instant hit and became the theme of the forty-niners as they headed for the western gold fields. Christy claimed the song as his own composition (a frequent practice of his) and the then-unknown young composer, Stephen Foster, was not credited with it until much later.

Tinga Layo

Rhythmically

WEST INDIES

Tin - ga La - yo, come, lit - tle don - key come, Tin - ga La - yo, come, lit - tle don - key, come. My don - key walk, my don - key talk, my don - key cut with a knife and fork. Tin - ga La - yo, come, lit - tle don - key come, Tin - ga La - yo,

1. come, lit - tle don - key come, My don - key
2. come lit - tle don - key come.

Tinga Layo, ay, mi burrito, ven,
Tinga Layo, ay, mi burrito, ven,
Burrito si, burrito no, burrito come con tenedor.
Tinga Layo, ay, mi burrito, ven,
Tinga Layo, ay, mi burrito, ven,
Burrito si, burrito no, burrito come con tenedor.
Tinga Layo, ay, mi burrito, ven,
Tinga Layo, ay, mi burrito.

From *Canciones Para La Juventud de America*, copyright by the Faculty of Music of the Chile University and the Association for Music Education of Chile, published by Pan American Union, Washington, D. C. Used by permission.

Like folk songs of all places, this song from the West Indies reflects the rhythms, familiar things, and activities of the people. The West Indies includes a large group of islands between the United States and South America which are divided into the Bahamas, Greater Antilles, and Lesser Antilles. They were discovered October 12, 1492 by Columbus who mistakenly believed he had reached India. They are identified with high adventure. Their fine climate makes them a desirable vacation spot. Tobacco and sugar cane are their principal products.

The Old Brass Wagon

Square dance rhythm

MIDWESTERN U. S.

1. Cir - cle to the left, the old brass wag - on,
Cir - cle to the left, the old brass wag - on, Cir - cle to the left, the
old brass wag - on, You're the one my dar - ling.

2. Circle to the right, the old brass wagon, etc.
3. Swing, oh swing, the old brass wagon, etc.
4. Promenade around, the old brass wagon, etc.
5. Swing your partner, the old brass wagon, etc.
6. Break and swing, the old brass wagon, etc.
7. Promenade in, the old brass wagon, etc.

This American singing game uses the traditional square dance figures. Verses may be added to accommodate the desired number of dance figures with the words indicating what the dancers are to do. This song flourished in the midwest, and was a great favorite of the pioneers.

The Holly and the Ivy

Warmly

ENGLAND

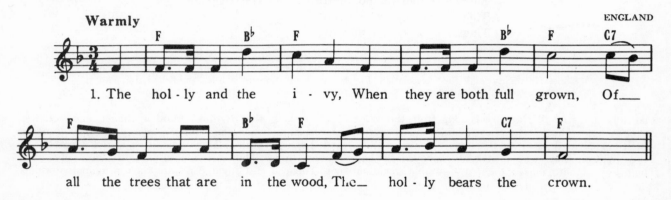

1. The hol - ly and the i - vy, When they are both full grown, Of__
all the trees that are in the wood, The__ hol - ly bears the crown.

The Holly and the Ivy

The ris-ing of the sun,—— And the run-ning of the deer, The——
play-ing of the mer-ry or-gan, The sweet sing-ing of the choir.

2. The holly bears a prickle as sharp as any thorn,
   And Mary bore sweet Jesus Christ, on Christmas day in the morn;

3. The holly bears a berry as red as any blood,
   And Mary bore sweet Jesus Christ to do poor sinners good;

4. The holly bears a blossom as white as any flower,
   And Mary bore sweet Jesus Christ to be the dear Saviour.

This English Christmas carol is a favorite in English-speaking countries. The words tell in symbolic terms the story of the death of Jesus Christ.

The Mulberry Bush

Playfully

ENGLAND

1. Here we go round the mul-ber-ry bush, the
mul-ber-ry bush, the mul-ber-ry bush. Here we go round the
mul-ber-ry bush, so ear-ly in—— the morn-ing.

2. This is the way we wash our clothes, etc.
3. This is the way we dry our clothes, etc.
4. This is the way we iron our clothes, etc.
5. This is the way we fold our clothes, etc.
6. This is the way we mend our clothes, etc.
7. This is the way we scrub the floor, etc.

The melody of this popular game song is an old English country dance tune, *Nancy Dawson*, which dates from the eighteenth century. On the first verse, the group moves around in a circle, hands joined. In subsequent verses, the words are pantomimed in place. Players often make up additional verses about familiar chores. The mulberry once was considered sacred to marriage festivals. The red mulberry is a native of America, and has fruit of a deep red color. The white mulberry was brought here from the Orient where its leaves are used for food for silkworms.

Captain Jinks

Pertly

ENGLAND

1. I'm___ Cap - tain Jinks of the Horse Ma - rines; I feed my horse on corn and beans, And sport young la - dies in their teens, Though a cap - tain in the ar - my. I teach young la - dies how to dance, How to dance, how to dance, I teach young la - dies how to dance, For I'm the pet of the ar - my. I'm___ Cap - tain Jinks of the Horse Ma - rines; I feed my horse on corn and beans, And of - ten live be - yond my means, Though a cap - tain in the ar - my.

264

Captain Jinks

2. I joined my corps when twenty-one,
Of course I thought it capital fun;
When the enemy came, of course I run,
For I'm not cut out for the Army.
When I left home, Mama, she cried,
Mama, she cried, Mama, she cried,
When I left home, Mama, she cried,
"He's not cut out for the Army!"

3. The first day I went out to drill
The bugle sound made me quite ill;
Of battle fields I've had my fill,
And that won't do for the Army.
The officers, they all did shout,
All did shout, all did shout,
The officers, they all cried out,
"Let's put him out of the Army!"

4. My tailor's bills came in so fast,
Forced me one day to leave at last;
And ladies, too, no more did cast
Sheep's eyes at me in the Army.
My creditors at me did shout,
At me did shout, at me did shout,
My creditors at me did shout,
"Why, kick him out of the Army!"

5. When Captain Jinks comes home at night
Pass your partner by the right,
Swing your neighbor so polite,
For that's the style in the Army.
All join hands and circle left,
Circle left, circle left,
All join hands and circle left,
For that's the style in the Army.

In 1868 a musical comedy company from London headed by William Lingard delighted New York theatregoers with *Captain Jinks*. Soon everyone was singing it across the country. Members of the United States Cavalry often referred to themselves as the "horse marines."

This Old Man

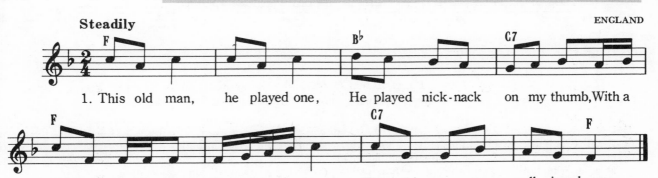

Steadily   ENGLAND

1. This old man, he played one, He played nick-nack on my thumb, With a nick-nack pad-dy whack give the dog a bone! This old man came roll-ing home.

2. This old man, he played two,
He played nick-nack on my shoe.

3. This old man, he played three,
He played nick-nack on my knee.

4. This old man, he played four,
He played nick-nack on my door.

5. This old man, he played five,
He played nick-nack on my hive.

6. This old man, he played six,
He played nick-nack on my sticks.

7. This old man, he played sev'n,
He played nick-nack till elev'n.

8. This old man, he played eight,
He played nick-nack on my gate.

9. This old man, he played nine,
He played nick-nack on my spine.

10. This old man, he played ten,
He played nick-nack over again.

This popular children's song from England serves for a variety of activities. It is a familiar marching rhythm, a favorite counting song, and is excellent for pantomime.

Shoo, Fly, Don't Bother Me

BILLY REEVES   FRANK CAMPBELL

Enthusiastically

Shoo, fly, don't both-er me, Shoo, fly, don't both-er me,

Shoo, fly, don't both-er me, For I be-long to some-bod-y. *Fine*

Verse

1. I feel, I feel, I feel, I feel like a morn-ing star, I

feel, I feel, I feel, I feel like a morn-ing star. *D.C.*

2. I feel, I feel, I feel, I feel, like my mother said,
   Like angels pouring 'lasses down on my little head.

This was the most popular nonsense song of the Civil War. The words were written by Billy Reeves and the music by Frank Campbell. It was published in 1869. Union soldiers sang it often, and it was a great favorite of Negro troops. The words were a conglomerate of old river boat songs in large degree. *Shoo, Fly, Don't Bother Me* be-came a favorite fiddling tune during western expansion, and a popular singing game song.

The Slumber Boat

ALICE RILEY   JANET GAYNOR

Dreamily

1. Ba - by's boat's the sil - ver moon sail - ing in the sky;____

The Slumber Boat

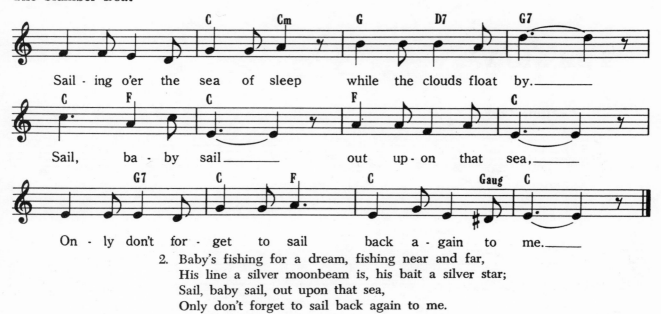

Sail - ing o'er the sea of sleep while the clouds float by.

Sail, ba - by sail out up - on that sea,

On - ly don't for - get to sail back a - gain to me.

2. Baby's fishing for a dream, fishing near and far,
His line a silver moonbeam is, his bait a silver star;
Sail, baby sail, out upon that sea,
Only don't forget to sail back again to me.

This lovely old lullaby is sung with a gentle, rocking rhythm.

Old Texas
(BURY ME NOT ON THE LONE PRAIRIE)

Deliberately   COWBOY

1. I'm going to leave old Tex - as now,
They've plowed and fenced my cat - tle range,

They've got no use for the long - horned cow.
And the peo - ple there are all so strange.

2. I'll take my horse, and I'll take my rope,
I'll hit the trail upon a lope;
Say *adiós* to the Alamo,
And turn my face towards Mexico.

BURY ME NOT ON THE LONE PRAIRIE

1. O bury me not on the lone prairie
Where the coyotes howl and the wind blows free,
Where the buffalo roams o'er a prairie sea,
O bury me not on the lone prairie.

In early America, many different sets of words telling diverse stories and legends were sung to favorite or familiar tunes. *Old Texas* and *Bury Me Not On The Lone Prairie* were sung to the same tune, and shared a common sentiment of deep sadness. Such laments were not uncommon on the plains. *Bury Me Not On The Lone Prairie* struck a responsive chord in lonely cowboys, and the words were sung to a variety of tunes. Many parodies have been sung to this song, and the "lone prair-ee" has become a stereotoype of the early west.

Tell Me Why

COLLEGE SONG

Sentimentally

1. Oh, tell me why the stars do shine, Oh, tell-me why the i - vy twines, Oh, tell me why the o - cean's blue, And I will tell you just why I love you.

2. Because God made the stars to shine,
   Because God made the ivy twine,
   Because God made the ocean blue,
   That is the reason why I love you.

In early England barbershops became musical centers. While customers waited their turn to receive the various services performed there, they played instruments supplied for their amusement and sang together. They sang in four part "close" harmony, and the style came to be known as barbershop quartet. This type of quartet singing became popular in the United States in the 1890's. It found favor in homes, vaudeville acts, at parties, and on college campuses. "The Society for the Preservation and Encouragement of Barber Shop Quartet Singing in America" was founded in 1938, and there are countless numbers of these quartets in America today. *Tell Me Why* is a standard with barbershop quartet singers.

Sing-a-ling-a-ling

U. S.

Cheerfully

O — — — we sing - a - ling - a - ling with
(Sing name)

all our hearts for you; We hope there'll be some

thing - a - ling - a - ling that we can do for you. In

au - tumn, win - ter, spring - a - ling - a - ling and

all the whole year through, We'll ring - a - ling - a - ling and

sing - a - ling - a - ling and ching - a - ling - a - ling for you.

Any name desired may be used in this familiar American greeting song.

Steal Away

SPIRITUAL

Sincerely

Steal a - way,   steal a - way,   steal a - way to Je - sus.

Steal a - way,   steal a - way home,   I don't have long to stay here.

Verse

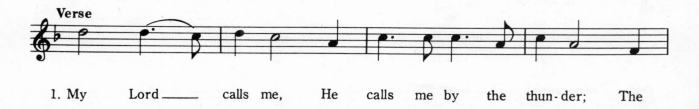

1. My   Lord___ calls me,   He   calls me by   the thun-der;   The

trum-pet sounds with - in___ my soul, I   don't have long to   stay here.

2. Green trees are bending, poor sinners, they stand trembling,
   The trumpet sounds within my soul, I don't have long to stay here.

3. My Lord he calls me, He calls me by the lightning,
   The trumpet sounds within my soul, I don't have long to stay here.

Steal Away is among the best known and most beautiful of the wealth of Negro spirituals in the American song heritage. According to legend, this song was used to signal secret meetings in the surrounding countryside. Some believe the words seem indicative of such secret rendezvous.

Lightly Row

GERMANY

Airily

1. Light - ly row, light - ly row, o'er the shin - ing waves we go;

Smooth - ly glide, smooth - ly glide, on the si - lent tide.

Let the winds and wa - ters be min - gled with our mel - o - dy,

Sing and float, sing and float, in our lit - tle boat.

2. Far away, far away, echo in the rocks at play,
Calling not, calling not, to this lonely spot.
Only with the sea bird's note shall our dying music float,
Lightly row, lightly row, echo's voice is low.

3. Happy we, full of glee, sailing o'er the wavy sea,
Happy we, full of glee, sailing o'er the sea,
Luna sheds her clearest light, stars are sparkling, twinkling bright,
Happy we, full of glee, sailing o'er the sea.

The melody to which these words are sung is an old German folk tune.

Little 'Liza Jane

U. S.

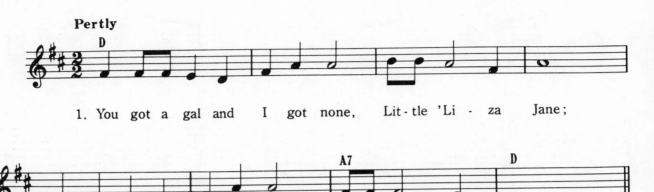

1. You got a gal and I got none, Lit-tle 'Li - za Jane;

Come my love and be my one, Lit-tle 'Li - za Jane.

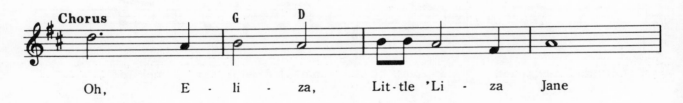

Chorus

Oh, E - li - za, Lit-tle 'Li - za Jane

Oh, E - li - za, Lit-tle 'Li - za Jane.

2. I've got a house in Baltimore, Little 'Liza Jane,
   Street cars run right to my door, Little 'Liza Jane.

3. Brussels carpets on my floor, Little 'Liza Jane,
   Silver knocker on my door, Little 'Liza Jane.

4. Come, my love, and marry me, Little 'Liza Jane,
   You'll be happy, wait and see, Little 'Liza Jane.

This song is used for a wide variety of group and street games, and lends itself to pantomime.

272

Sweet Nightingale

ENGLAND

The nightingale is a small warbler with a russet colored back and buff to white under parts. It lives in shrubs and low trees, and is known for the beauty of its varied and melodious song. The male bird sings both day and night during the mating season.

Hush, Little Baby

U. S.

Serenely

1. Hush, lit - tle ba - by, don't say a word, Dad-dy's gon-na buy you a

mock - ing bird, And if that mock - ing bird won't sing,

Dad - dy's gon - na buy you a dia - mond ring. 2. (And)

2. And if that diamond ring turns to brass,
   Daddy's gonna buy you a looking glass,
   And if that looking glass gets broke,
   Daddy's gonna buy you a billy goat.

3. And if that billy goat won't pull,
   Daddy's gonna buy you a cart and bull,
   And if that cart and bull turn over,
   Daddy's gonna buy you a dog named Rover.

4. And if that dog named Rover won't bark,
   Daddy's gonna buy you a horse and cart,
   And if that horse and cart fall down,
   You'll still be the sweetest little baby in town.

This American folk song was sung to quiet small children, and was a great favorite in the southern mountain area.

Appendix

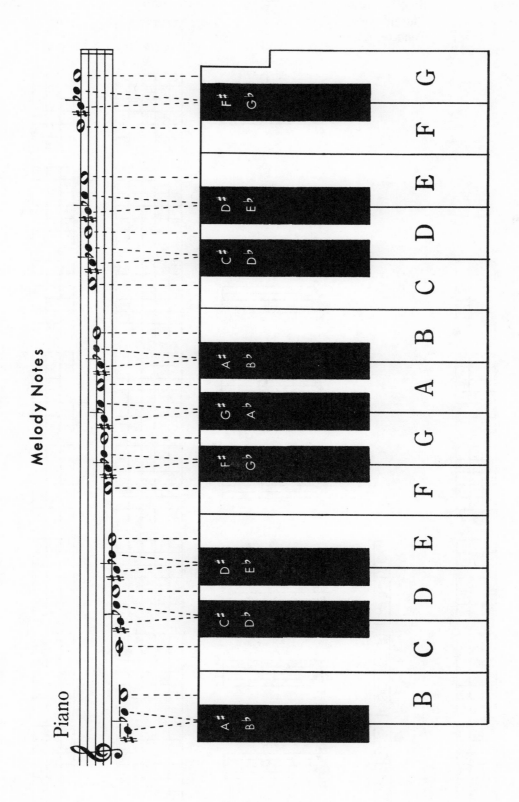

Appendix

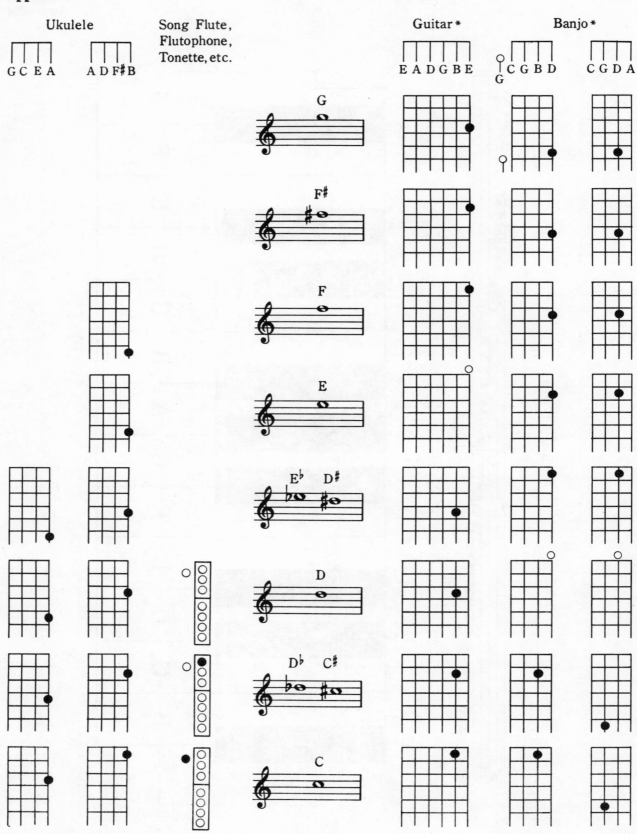

* *Sounds an octave lower.*

276

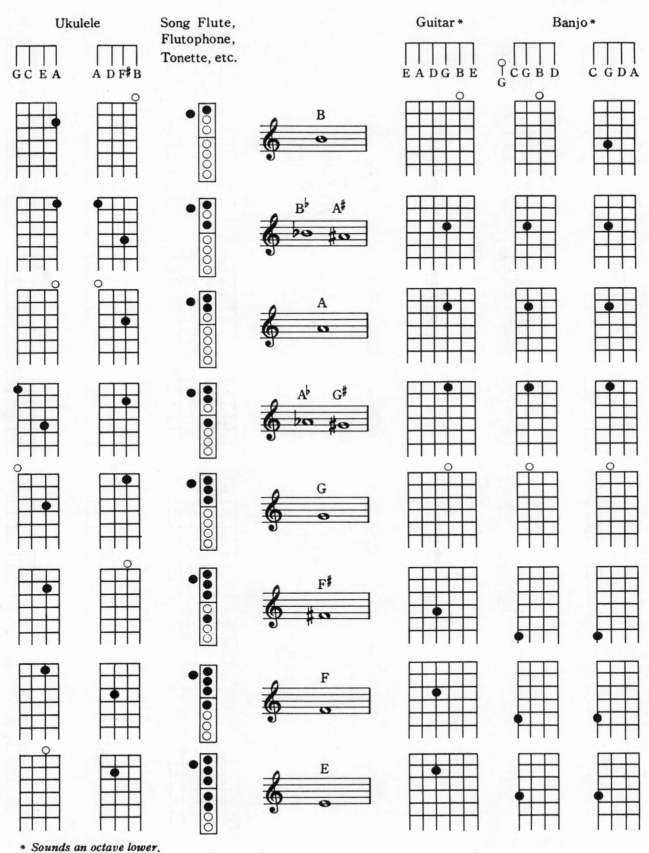

* Sounds an octave lower.

Appendix

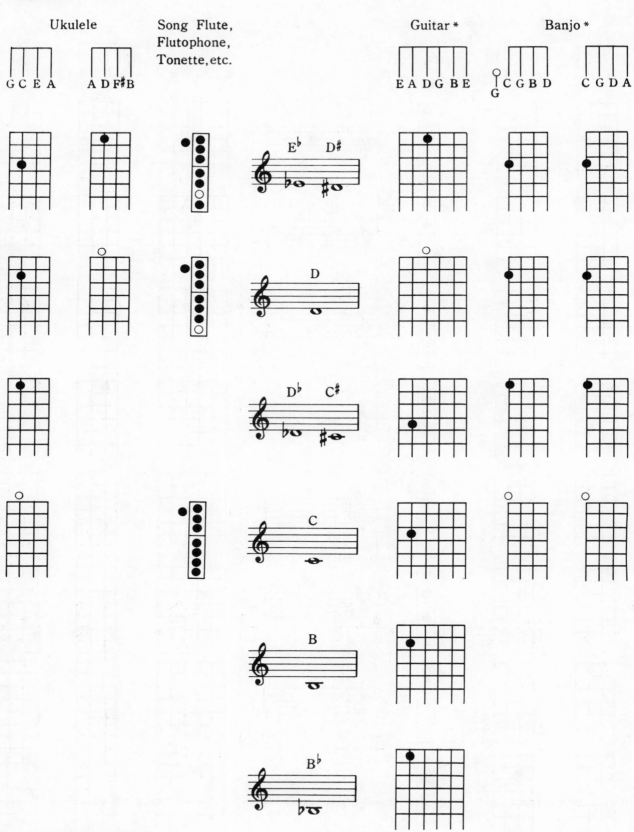

* *Sounds an octave lower.*

Principal Chords

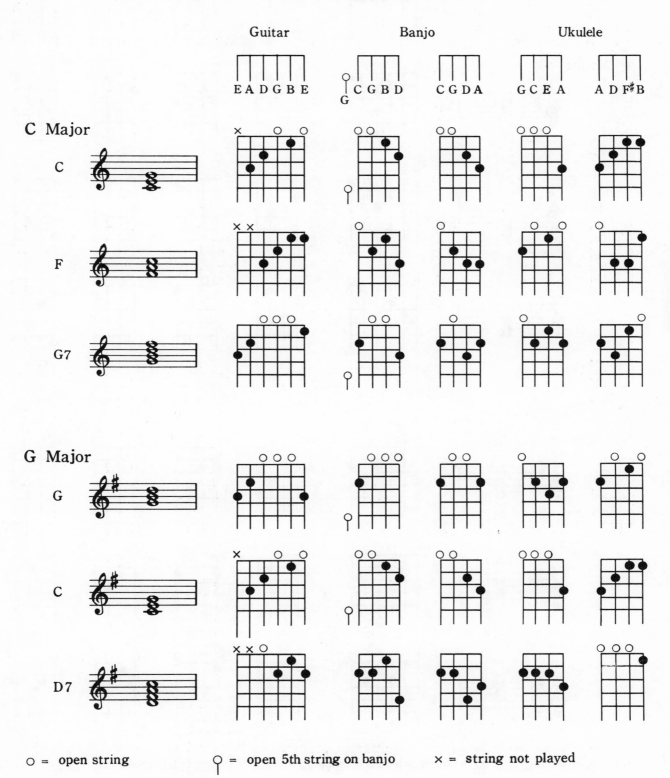

○ = open string   ♀ = open 5th string on banjo   × = string not played

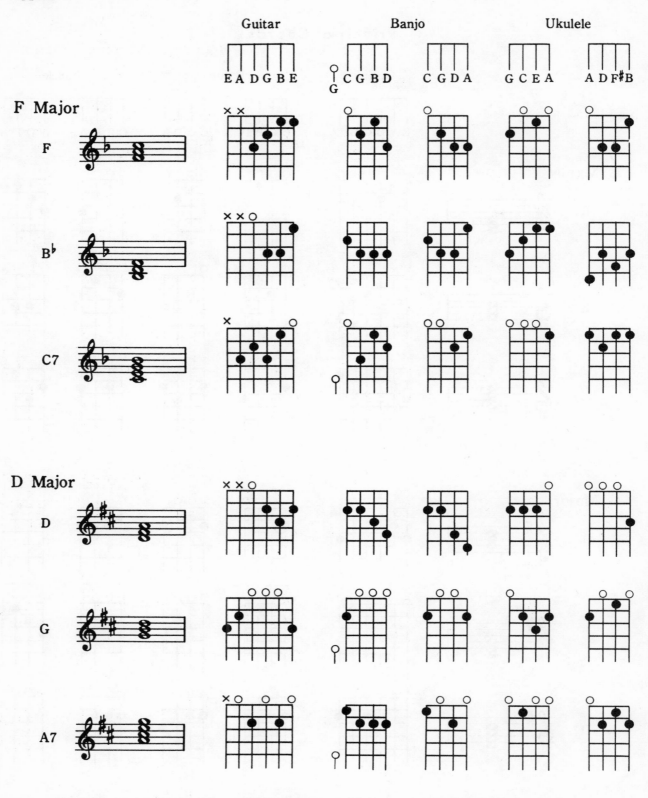

O = open string   Q = open 5th string on banjo   × = string not played

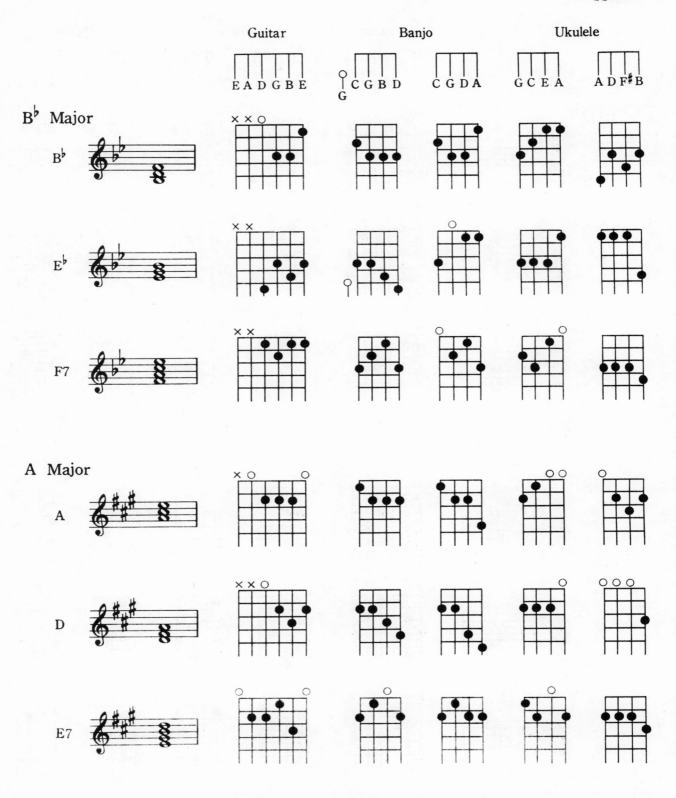

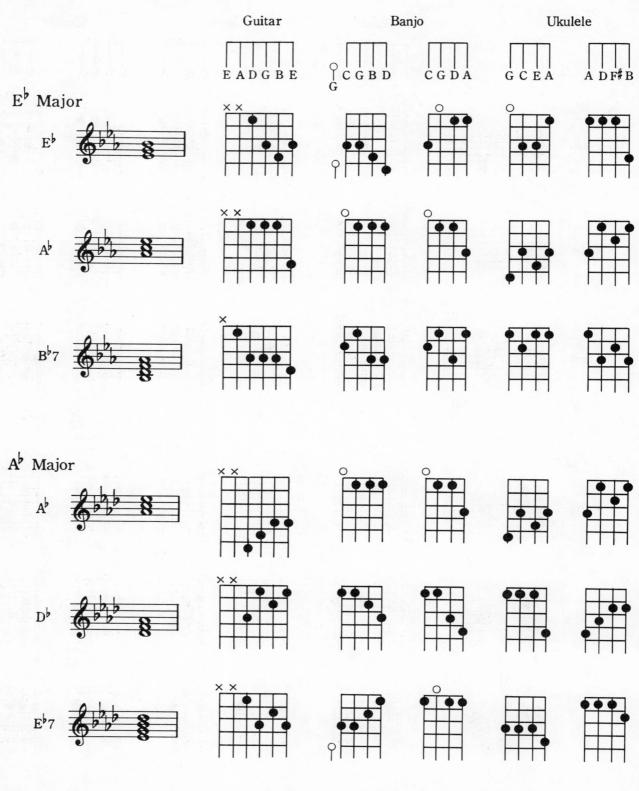

O = open string   ⚲ = open 5th string on banjo   × = string not played

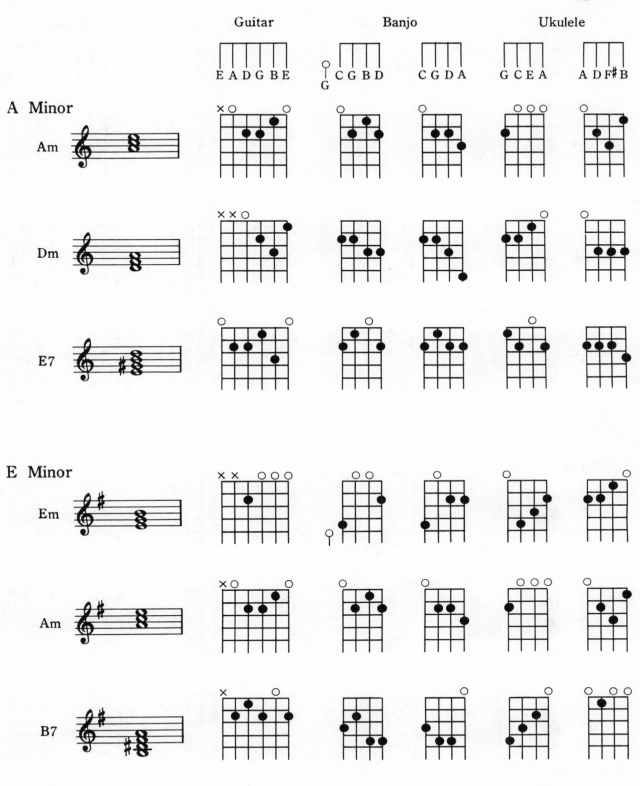

Guitar Banjo Ukulele

E A D G B E   G C G B D   C G D A   G C E A   A D F♯ B

A Minor

Am

Dm

E7

E Minor

Em

Am

B7

○ = open string   ⚲ = open 5th string on banjo   × = string not played

Appendix

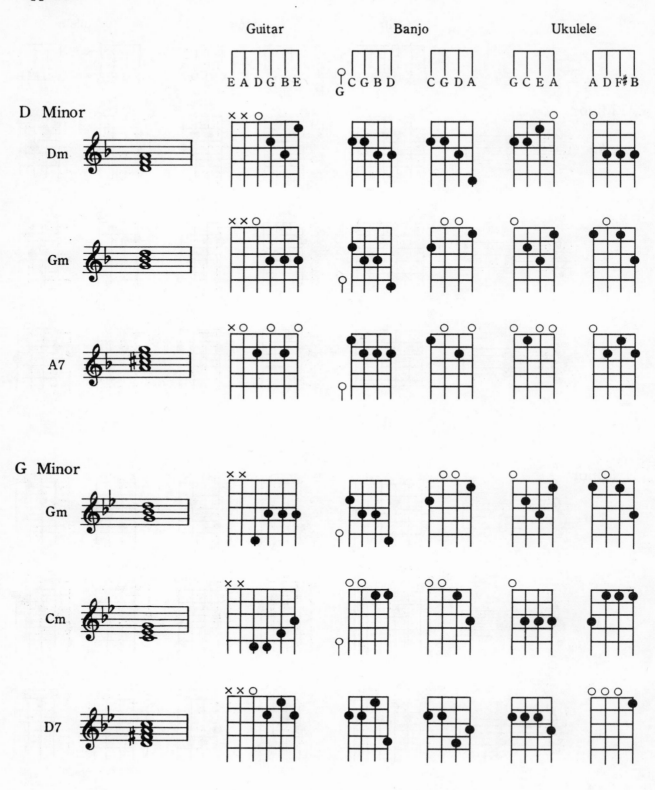

		Guitar	Banjo		Ukulele	
		E A D G B E	G C G B D	C G D A	G C E A	A D F# B

D Minor

Dm

Gm

A7

G Minor

Gm

Cm

D7

○ = open string   ⟟ = open 5th string on banjo   × = string not played

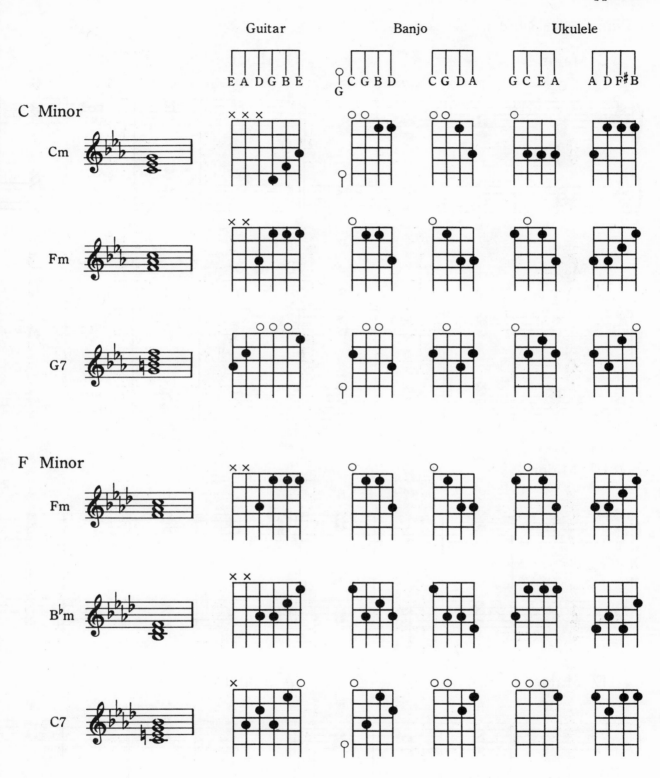

O = open string   🎵 = open 5th string on banjo   × = string not played

Appendix

Piano　(Simplified arrangements)

C Major

G Major

F Major

D Major

B♭ Major

A Major

E♭ Major

A♭ Major

A Minor

E Minor

D Minor

G Minor

C Minor

F Minor

Other Chords Used in This Book

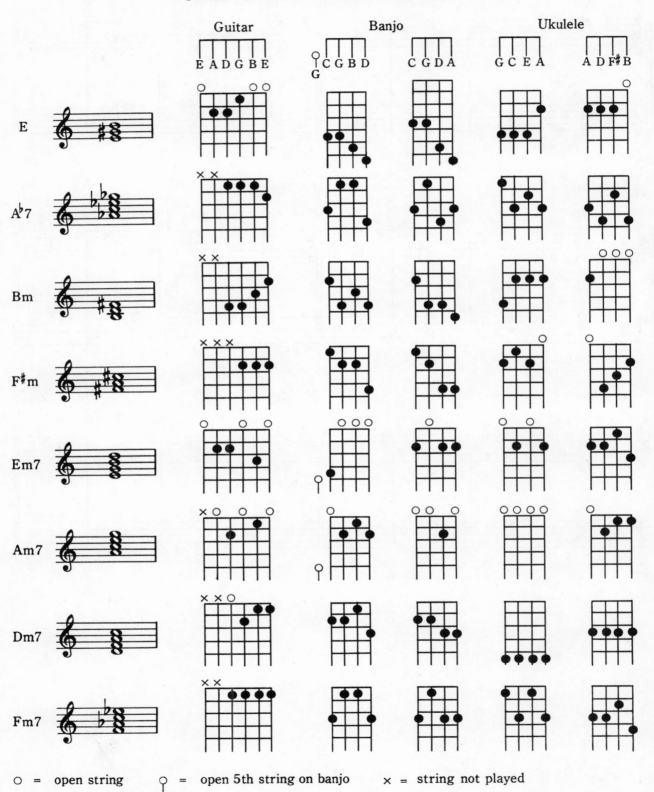

○ = open string   ⚲ = open 5th string on banjo   × = string not played

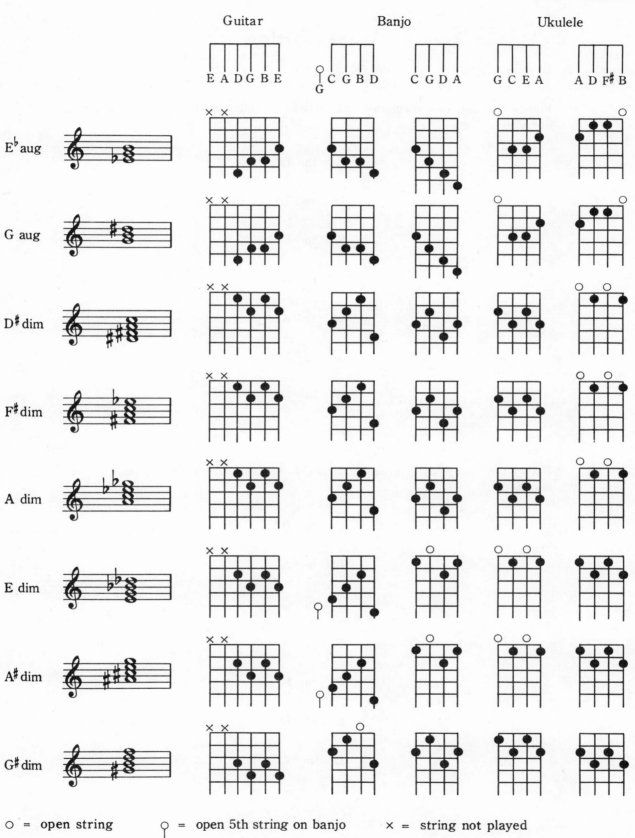

○ = open string   ○⃒ = open 5th string on banjo   × = string not played

Transposition

Ukulele

Follow the G-C-E-A diagrams with A-D-F$^\sharp$-B tuning to transpose a song *up* one step:

C   to   D

D   to   E

E$^\flat$ to   F

F   to   G

G   to   A

A$^\flat$ to   B$^\flat$

B$^\flat$ to   C

Follow the A-D-F$^\sharp$-B diagrams with G-C-E-A tuning to transpose a song *down* one step:

C   to   B$^\flat$

B$^\flat$ to   A$^\flat$

A   to   G

G   to   F

F   to   E$^\flat$

E   to   D

D   to   C

Guitar

Use a capo to transpose as follows:

Location of capo	Transposition	For example
On first fret	up ½ step or down 5½ steps	C to D$\flat$
On second fret	up 1 step or down 5 steps	C to D
On third fret	up 1½ steps or down 4½ steps	C to E$\flat$
On fourth fret	up 2 steps or down 4 steps	C to E
On fifth fret	up 2½ steps or down 3½ steps	C to F
On sixth fret	up 3 steps or down 3 steps	C to F$\sharp$ or G$\flat$
On seventh fret	up 3½ steps or down 2½ steps	C to G

Classified Song Index

An (A) after a song title indicates that the song can be accompanied on the Autoharp. An (M) after a song title indicates the song is within the range of the wind melody instruments (Song Flute, Tonette, Flutophone, etc.) and has no more than one sharp or flat in the key signature.

 Autoharp

 Wind Melody Instrument

BIRTHDAY

Happy Birthday (A, M), 210
Las Mañanitas (A, M), 182

CHRISTMAS

Adeste Fideles (M), 154
Angels We Have Heard on High (A), 47
Away in a Manger (A, M), 32
Birthday of a King, 124
Bring a Torch, Jeannette, Isabella (A, M), 70
Deck the Halls (A), 127
First Noel, The (M), 86
Friendly Beasts, The (A, M), 194
Fum, Fum, Fum (A, M), 64
God Rest You Merry, Gentlemen, 174
Good King Wenceslas (M), 180
Hark! The Herald Angels Sing (A, M), 23
Holly and the Ivy, The (A, M), 262
I Saw Three Ships (A, M), 50
It Came Upon the Midnight Clear (A), 20
Jingle Bells, 149
Jolly Old Saint Nicholas, 88
Joy to the World (A, M), 51
Mary's Lullaby, 57
O Christmas Tree (A, M), 77
O Come, All Ye Faithful (M), 154
O Come, Little Children, 242
O Little Town of Bethlehem (M), 227
O Tannenbaum (A, M), 77
Pat-a-pan (M), 45
Rise Up, Shepherd, and Follow, 137
Silent Night (A), 223
Twelve Days of Christmas, The (A, M), 9
Up on the Housetop, 198
We Three Kings of Orient Are (M), 92
We Wish You a Merry Christmas (M), 95
What Child Is This, 10

COWBOY, HERDING, AND PLAIN

Bury Me Not on the Lone Prairie (A, M), 267
Cowboy's Lament (A, M), 83
Dogie Song (A, M), 2

Get Along, Little Dogies (A, M), 2
Goodby, Old Paint (A, M), 185
Green Grow the Lilacs (A, M), 243
Home on the Range (A, M), 84
Lone Star Trail (A, M), 82
Night Herding Song (A, M), 203
Old Brass Wagon, The (A, M), 262
Old Chisholm Trail, 245
Old Texas (A, M), 267
Red River Valley (A, M), 111
Streets of Laredo (A, M), 83
Sweet Betsy from Pike (A, M), 152
Whoopee Ti-yi-yo (A, M), 2

HANUKKAH

O Hanukkah (M), 172
Rock of Ages, 122

LOVE, SENTIMENT, AND NOSTALGIA

Aloha Oe (A, M), 14
Annie Laurie (A), 58
Ash Grove, The (A), 252
Auld Lang Syne (A, M), 60
Aura Lee (A, M), 3
Ay, Ay, Ay, 33
Barbara Allen, 31
Beautiful Heaven, 12
Bendemeer's Stream, 24
Bobby Shafto (A), 73
Cielito Lindo, 12
Cindy (A), 46
Clementine (A, M), 176
Cockles and Mussels (A, M), 102
Cuckoo, The (A, M), 151
Down in the Valley (A, M), 8
Early One Morning, 253
Farewell To Thee (A, M), 14
Girl I Left Behind Me, The, 59
Green Grow the Lilacs (A, M), 243
Greensleeves, 10
Home (A), 202

Classified Song Index

LULLABY AND SLEEP

MOTHER GOOSE AND NURSERY

NONSENSE, NOVELTY, AND FUN

Classified Song Index

Mister Banjo (A, M), 236
Sur le Pont d'Avignon (A, M), 93

German

Ach du Lieber Augustin (A, M), 159
Cradle Song (Schubert) (A, M), 147
Did You Ever See a Lassie (A, M), 159
Home (A), 202
Johnny Schmoker, 218
Linden Tree, The, 258
Lullaby (Brahms) (A. M), 222
Mein Hut (A, M), 187
Music Alone Shall Live (M), 216
My Hat (A, M), 187
O Christmas Tree, 77
O Tannenbaum, 77
Silent Night (A), 223

Hawaiian

Aloha Oe (A, M), 14
Farewell to Thee (A, M), 14

Hebrew

Rock of Ages, 122
Zum Gali Gali, 191

Italian

Santa Lucia, 108

Latin

Adeste Fideles (M), 154
Dona Nobis Pacem (M), 186
O Come, All Ye Faithful (M), 154

Middle English

Sumer Is Icumen In, 65

Scotch Dialect

Auld Lang Syne, (A, M), 60

Spanish

A la Puerto del Cielo (A, M), 76
At the Gate of Heaven (A, M), 76
Ay, Ay, Ay, 33
Beautiful Heaven, 12
Cielito Lindo, 12
Fum, Fum, Fum (A, M), 64
Las Mañanitas (A, M), 182
Tinga Layo (A, M), 261

Welch

All Through the Night (A, M), 40
Ash Grove, The (A), 252

Alphabetical Song Index

Alphabetical Song Index

Alphabetical Song Index